You've got this.

This is the final stretch of your CPA Exam preparation – the Final Review. You've diligently studied these topics, and now it's crunch time. This Final Review has completely new content from the Becker CPA Exam Review and focuses on the key concepts on the CPA Exam. Remember, fortune favors the brave, but the CPA Exam favors the prepared.

Access Becker's Final Review

You will need to download the Final Review assets. To get started, log in to your account at **online.becker.com**, click the download icon and follow the download instructions.

What's inside

Your Final Review is designed to mimic the actual CPA Exam, and has all-new task-based simulations and multiple-choice questions. If you need help at any point, remember that you still have access to the features of the CPA Exam Review, including:

- SkillMaster videos that coach you through task-based simulations
- Access to 1-on-1 academic support from our experienced CPA instructors
- Unlimited practice tests to work on your weaknesses

You're not in it alone!

For tips, stories and advice, visit our blog at **becker.com/theplusside**. You can also collaborate with other Becker students studying FAR on our Facebook study group at **facebook.com/groups/BeckerFARStudyGroup/**.

Exam day tips

We want you to be prepared and confident when exam day rolls around. Here are some tips to keep in mind:

+ Arrive at least 30 minutes early on exam day.

+ Bring your NTS and two forms of identification.

+ Your cell phone is NOT allowed in the testing center, even during scheduled breaks.

+ No outside calculators are allowed. The testing software will have a built-in calculator for you to use.

+ Breathe. Relax. Ground yourself. You've got this.

Becker.

Join the community!

Becker.

ACADEMIC HELP
Click on Customer and Academic Support under Student Resources at
becker.com/cpa-review

CUSTOMER SERVICE AND TECHNICAL SUPPORT
Call 1-877-CPA-EXAM (outside the U.S. +1-630-472-2213)
or contact us at becker.com/cpa-review/cpa-contact.

This textbook contains information that was current at the time of printing. Your course software will be updated on a regular basis as the content that is tested on the CPA Exam evolves and as we improve our materials. Note the version reference below and select your replacement textbook under Replacement Products at **becker.com/cpa-replacement-products** to learn if a newer version of this book is available to be ordered.

CPA Exam Review

Financial Final Review

For Exams Scheduled
After December 31, 2019

V 3.5

COURSE DEVELOPMENT TEAM

Timothy F. Gearty, CPA, MBA, JD, CGMA . . . . Editor in Chief, Financial/Regulation (Tax) National Editor

Angeline S. Brown, CPA, CGMA. . . . . Sr. Director, Product Management

Mike Brown, CPA, CMA, CGMA . . . . Director, Product Management

Valerie Funk Anderson, CPA . . . . Sr. Manager, Curriculum

Stephen Bergens, CPA. . . . . Manager, Accounting Curriculum

Cheryl Costello, CPA, CGMA . . . . Sr. Specialist, Curriculum

Tom Cox, CPA, CMA . . . . Financial (GASB & NFP) National Editor

Steven J. Levin, JD . . . . Regulation (Law) National Editor

Danita De Jane . . . . Director, Course Development

Joe Antonio . . . . Manager, Course Development

Shelly McCubbins, MBA. . . . . Project Manager, Course Development

CONTRIBUTING EDITORS

Teresa C. Anderson, CPA, CMA, MPA	Michelle Moshe, CPA, DipIFR
Katie Barnette, CPA	Peter Olinto, JD, CPA
Jim DeSimpelare, CPA, MBA	Sandra Owen, JD, MBA, CPA
Tara Z. Fisher, CPA	Michelle M. Pace, CPA
Melisa F. Galasso, CPA	Michael Potenza, CPA, JD
R. Thomas Godwin, CPA, CGMA	Jennifer J. Rivers, CPA
Holly Hawk, CPA, CGMA	Josh Rosenberg, MBA, CPA, CFA, CFP
Patrice W. Johnson, CPA	Jonathan R. Rubin, CPA, MBA
Julie D. McGinty, CPA	Michael Rybak, CPA, CFA
Sandra McGuire, CPA, MBA	Denise M. Stefano, CPA, CGMA, MBA
Stephanie Morris, CPA, MAcc	Elizabeth Lester Walsh, CPA, CITP

Permissions

Material from *Uniform CPA Examination Selected Questions and Unofficial Answers*, 1989–2019, copyright © by American Institute of Certified Public Accountants, Inc., is reprinted and/or adapted with permission.

Any knowing solicitation or disclosure of any questions or answers included on any CPA Examination is prohibited.

Financial

Final Review Sections

Financial Section I | *Conceptual Framework, Standard-Setting, and Financial Reporting*

A   General Purpose Financial Statements

B   Cash Flows

C   Public Company Reporting: SEC

D   Public Company Reporting: Earnings per Share

E   Public Company Reporting: Segment Reporting

Financial Section II | *Selected Financial Statement Accounts*

A   Trade Receivables

B   Inventory

C   Property, Plant, and Equipment (PP&E)

D   PP&E: Nonmonetary Exchanges

E   Investments

F   Intangible Assets

G   Impairment of Intangible Assets and PP&E

H   Payables and Accrued Liabilities

I   Long-Term Debt

J   Equity

K   Revenue Recognition

L   Compensation and Benefits

M   Income Taxes

Financial Section III | *Select Transactions*

A   Accounting Changes and Error Corrections

B   Business Combinations

C   Contingencies

D   Derivatives and Hedge Accounting

E   Foreign Currency Transactions and Translation

F   Leases

G   Research and Development

H   Software Costs

I   Subsequent Events

J   Fair Value Measurements

K   Partnerships

(continued on next page)

(continued)

Financial Section IV | *State and Local Governments*

A   State and Local Government Concepts

B   Form and Content of CAFR

C   Financial Reporting Entity

D   Typical Items and Specific Types of Transactions

Financial Section V | *Not-for-Profit Accounting and Reporting*

A   General Purpose Financial Statements

B   Revenue Recognition

Introduction

Final Review is a condensed review that reinforces your understanding of the most heavily tested concepts on the CPA Exam. It is designed to help focus your study time during those final days between your Becker CPA Exam Review course and your exam date.

This Book

Becker's Final Review is arranged based on the AICPA's blueprints. The blueprints outline the technical content to be tested on each of the four parts of the CPA Exam. The blueprints can be found in the back sections of Becker's main CPA textbooks.

The Software

The Final Review software uses an interactive eBook (IEB) format. Watch the introduction video in the Final Review software for a tour of the IEB features.

We recommend progressing through this course in the following order:

- Review the IEB content, including the video introduction to each topic and the lecture audio associated with each page of the IEB.
- Work the embedded multiple-choice questions for each topic as you progress through the content.
- Work the related multiple-choice questions in the question bank for each topic. There are links from the IEB to the question bank.
- Once you have completed all of the IEB sections, topics, and multiple-choice questions, do the practice Simulations in the software.

Becker Customer and Academic Support

You can access Becker's Customer and Academic Support under Student Resources at:

> http://www.becker.com/cpa-review.html

You can also access Academic Support by clicking on the Academic Support button in the Becker software. You can access customer service and technical support from Customer and Academic Support or by calling 1-877-CPA-EXAM (outside the U.S. +1-630-472-2213).

I Conceptual Framework, Standard-Setting, and Financial Reporting

Notes

Financial Final Review

© Becker Professional Education Corporation. All rights reserved.

General Purpose Financial Statements

1 Income Statement and Statement of Retained Earnings

1.1 Reported on Income Statement

1.1.1 Income (or Loss) From Continuing Operations (Gross and Net of Tax)

Income from continuing operations includes operating activities (i.e., revenues, costs of goods sold, selling expenses, and administrative expenses), nonoperating activities (e.g., other revenues and gains and other expenses and losses), and income taxes.

1.1.2 Income (or Loss) From Discontinued Operations (Net of Tax)

The (normal) loss from discontinued operations can consist of three elements: (1) an impairment loss; (2) income/loss from actual operations; and (3) a gain/loss on disposal. All of these amounts are included in discontinued operations in the period in which they occur.

1.2 Reported on Statement of Retained Earnings

1.2.1 Change in Accounting Principle (Net of Tax)

The cumulative effect of a change in accounting principle is presented net of tax. It is the cumulative effect (calculated as of the beginning of the first period presented) of a change from one acceptable method of accounting to another ("GAAP to GAAP" or "IFRS to IFRS") because the new method presents the financial information more fairly than the old method.

Question 1   MCQ-09319

Allison Corporation's current year income from continuing operations before taxes was $1,000,000 before taking the following items into consideration:

- Depreciation was understated by $100,000.
- A strike by the employees of a supplier resulted in a loss of $200,000. This strike was the first such strike that Allison had encountered.
- The inventory at December 31 of the prior year was overstated by $300,000. The inventory at December 31 of the current year was correct.
- A flood in Allison's Houston facility destroyed equipment worth $500,000. The facility had just been rebuilt from damages that occurred in a flood in the prior year.

What was Allison's adjusted income from continuing operations before taxes?

1. $1,000,000
2. $900,000
3. $700,000
4. $500,000

2 Comprehensive Income

Comprehensive income includes all changes in equity during a period, except those resulting from investments by owners and distributions to owners. Comprehensive income is net income plus other comprehensive income.

Other comprehensive income includes:

- Pension adjustments
- Unrealized gains and losses on available-for-sale debt securities
- Foreign currency items
- Instrument-specific credit risk
- Effective portion of cash flow hedges
- Revaluation surplus (IFRS only)

Question 2	MCQ-09289

Szuba Corporation reported the following transactions for the current year:

Sales	$500,000
Cost of goods sold	300,000
Operating expenses	100,000
Cash dividend	50,000
Unrealized gain on available-for-sale debt security	10,000
Unrealized gain on trading debt security	20,000

Ignoring income taxes, Szuba should report other comprehensive income of:

1. $80,000
2. $10,000
3. $60,000
4. $30,000

3 Notes to Financial Statements

Notes are an integral part of the financial statements. The first note is the summary of significant accounting policies, which includes methods, policies, and criteria (e.g., methods: LIFO, FIFO, straight-line). The other notes provide the details of the financial statements.

IFRS requires an explicit and unreserved statement of compliance with IFRS in the notes to the financial statements.

Question 3   MCQ-09754

A major research university receives over half of its grant funding from a single federal government agency. The university's rationale for disclosing this in the notes to the financial statements is most likely to:

1. Show the vulnerability if that particular funding source were to disappear.
2. Show the need for additional funding sources to augment current grant inflows.
3. Highlight the strength of the relationship between the government and the university.
4. Quantify what would happen to future grant revenues if that funding source went away.

Task-Based Simulations

Task-Based Simulation 1: Calculations

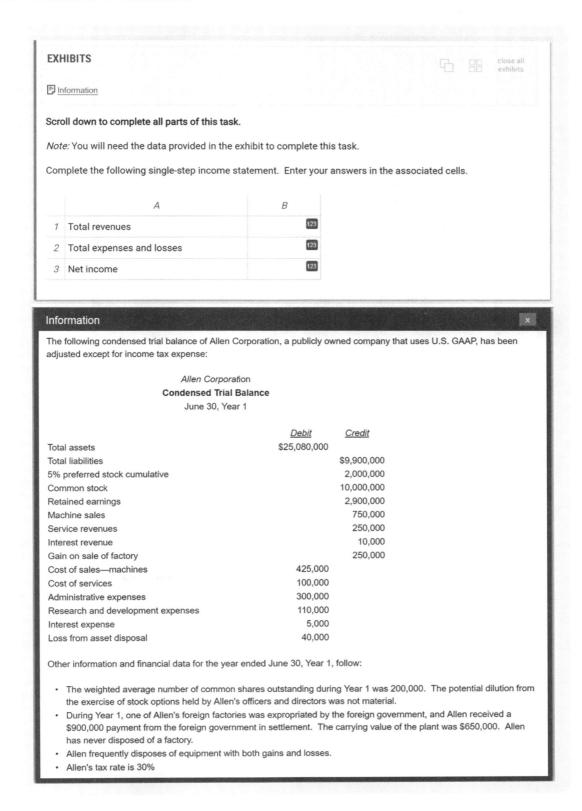

EXHIBITS

close all exhibits

📄 Information

Scroll down to complete all parts of this task.

Note: You will need the data provided in the exhibit to complete this task.

Complete the following single-step income statement. Enter your answers in the associated cells.

	A	B
1	Total revenues	123
2	Total expenses and losses	123
3	Net income	123

Information   x

The following condensed trial balance of Allen Corporation, a publicly owned company that uses U.S. GAAP, has been adjusted except for income tax expense:

Allen Corporation
Condensed Trial Balance
June 30, Year 1

	Debit	*Credit*
Total assets	$25,080,000	
Total liabilities		$9,900,000
5% preferred stock cumulative		2,000,000
Common stock		10,000,000
Retained earnings		2,900,000
Machine sales		750,000
Service revenues		250,000
Interest revenue		10,000
Gain on sale of factory		250,000
Cost of sales—machines	425,000	
Cost of services	100,000	
Administrative expenses	300,000	
Research and development expenses	110,000	
Interest expense	5,000	
Loss from asset disposal	40,000	

Other information and financial data for the year ended June 30, Year 1, follow:

• The weighted average number of common shares outstanding during Year 1 was 200,000. The potential dilution from the exercise of stock options held by Allen's officers and directors was not material.
• During Year 1, one of Allen's foreign factories was expropriated by the foreign government, and Allen received a $900,000 payment from the foreign government in settlement. The carrying value of the plant was $650,000. Allen has never disposed of a factory.
• Allen frequently disposes of equipment with both gains and losses.
• Allen's tax rate is 30%

A General Purpose Financial Statements

	A	B
1	Total revenues	$1,260,000
2	Total expenses and losses	$1,064,000
3	Net income	$196,000

Row 1: Total revenues

Revenues:	
Machine sales	$750,000
Service revenues	250,000
Interest revenues	10,000
Gain on sale of factory	250,000
Total revenues	$1,260,000

Row 2: Total expenses and losses

Expenses:	
Cost of sales -- machines	$425,000
Cost of services	100,000
Administrative expenses	300,000
Research and development expenses	110,000
Interest expense	5,000
Loss from asset disposal	40,000
Income tax expense	84,000[1]
Total expenses and losses	1,064,000

Row 3: Net income

Net income	$196,000

[1] Total revenues = $1,260,000
Total expenses other than taxes = $980,000
Difference (pretax income) = $280,000
$84,000 = 30% x $280,000

Task-Based Simulation 2: Comprehensive Income

Scroll down to complete all parts of this task.

The following information pertains to the current year annual report to the shareholders of Texas Corporation.

Net income	$460,000
Effective portion of unrealized losses on cash flow hedge derivatives	(120,000)
Unrealized losses on marketable debt securities classified as AFS	(26,000)
Foreign currency translation gain	40,000
Pension funded status adjustment	(4,000)

Assuming a tax rate of 30%, calculate the following by entering the appropriate values in the associated cells.

	A	B
1	Other comprehensive income	123
2	Comprehensive income	123

Explanation

	A	B
1	Other comprehensive income	($77,000) 123
2	Comprehensive income	$383,000 123

Row 1: ($77,000) (see below for calculation)

Row 2: $383,000

Net income		$460,000
	(120,000)	
	(26,000)	
	(4,000)	
	40,000	
	(110,000) × 30% tax	
	- 33,000	
		(77,000)
Comprehensive income		$383,000

Notes

1 Methods of Presentation

The direct method and the indirect method are the two methods of presentation for the statement of cash flows. The two methods are identical except for the cash flows from operating activities and for some disclosures. A presentation of cash flow per share is prohibited. Both U.S. GAAP and IFRS encourage the use of the direct method. Regardless of the method of presentation, the sections of the statement of cash flows are:

- Operating activities (CFO)
- Investing activities (CFI)
- Financing activities (CFF)
- Supplemental disclosures

Investing and financing activities are the same presentation for the direct and indirect methods. There are two approaches to presenting the operating activities but the results are the same. Under U.S. GAAP, operating activities require a reconciliation of "net income to net cash" for both methods. In addition, the direct method requires a cash basis income statement.

2 Operating Activities (Indirect Method)

The indirect method (reconciliation of net income to net cash) begins with accrual net income and reconciles it to cash flow from operating activities by adding noncash amounts, such as depreciation, amortization and losses on dispositions of assets and subtracting gains on dispositions of assets. Other adjustments to next income include changes in current assets and current liabilities, such as A/R, A/P, inventory, etc.

Indirect Method

Letterman Inc.
Statement of Cash Flows
For the Year Ended 12/31/Year X

Cash flows from operating activities:		
Net income		$ 50,000
Adjustments		
Decrease in accounts receivable	$ 25,000	
Increase in inventory	(10,000)	
Increase in accounts payable	20,000	
Increase in income taxes payable	6,000	
Total adjustments		41,000
Net cash provided by operating activities		91,000
Cash flows from investing activities:		
Cash paid to purchase equity securities	(3,000)	
Net cash used in investing activities		(3,000)
Cash flows from financing activities:		
Cash dividends paid	(2,000)	
Net cash used in financing activities		(2,000)
Net increase in cash and cash equivalents		86,000
Cash and cash equivalents at the beginning of the year		99,000
Cash and cash equivalents at the end of the year		$185,000

Question 1   MCQ-09277

Sykes Corporation's comparative balance sheets at December 31, Year 2 and Year 1, reported accumulated depreciation balances of $800,000 and $600,000 respectively. Property with a cost of $50,000 and a carrying amount of $40,000 was the only property sold in Year 2. Depreciation charged to operations in Year 2 was:

1. $190,000
2. $200,000
3. $210,000
4. $220,000

3 Operating Activities (Direct Method)

The direct method is a cash basis income statement. The statement is prepared by adjusting the accrual amounts reported in the income statement to the cash basis. A "reconciliation of net income to net cash" is required under U.S. GAAP. The totals for the "reconciliation" and "cash basis income statement" are the same. Operating activities include:

- Cash received from customers
- Cash paid to suppliers and employees
- Operating expenses paid in cash
- Interest received and paid
- DIvidends received (but not dividends paid)
- Taxes paid
- Purchase and sale of trading securities classified as current assets

Question 2   MCQ-09322

In its year-end income statement, Black Knights Company reported cost of goods sold of $450,000. Changes occurred in several balance sheet accounts during the year as follows:

Inventory	$160,000	decrease
Accounts payable-suppliers	40,000	decrease

What amount should the Black Knights Company report as cash paid to suppliers in its cash flow statement, prepared under the direct method?

1. $250,000
2. $330,000
3. $570,000
4. $650,000

Direct Method
(preferred presentation)

Letterman Inc.
Statement of Cash Flows
For the Year Ended 12/31/Year X

Cash flows from operating activities:

Cash received from customers	$125,000	
Cash paid to suppliers and employees	(30,000)	
Income taxes paid	(4,000)	
Net cash provided by operating activities		$ 91,000

Cash flows from investing activities:

Cash paid to purchase equity securities	(3,000)	
Net cash used in investing activities		(3,000)

Cash flows from financing activities:

Cash dividends paid		(2,000)
Net cash used in financing activities		(2,000)
Net increase in cash and cash equivalents		86,000
Cash and cash equivalents at the beginning of the year		99,000
Cash and cash equivalents at the end of the year		$185,000

Same

Reconciliation of net income to net cash provided by operating activities:

Net income		$ 50,000

Adjustments to reconcile net income to net cash provided:

Decrease in accounts receivable	$ 25,000	
Increase in inventory	(10,000)	
Increase in accounts payable	20,000	
Increase in income taxes payable	6,000	
Total adjustments		41,000
Net cash provided by operations		$ 91,000

See
Indirect
Method

4 Investing Activities

Investing activities generally involve changes in non-current assets, inclusive of the purchase or sale of property, plant, investments, equipment and marketable securities (excluding trading securities classified as current assets). Depreciation expense and/or the accumulated depreciation on assets disposed of, and gains/losses on assets disposed of, are a few key accounts that must be considered in determining the balance of the cash used or provided by the investing activities.

Question 3   MCQ-09395

The Year 11 balance sheet of Cool Tools Inc. reported the following fixed asset balances:

	Year 11	Year 10
Fixed assets	$160,000	$128,000
Accumulated depreciation	(53,000)	(41,000)
Fixed assets, net	$107,000	$ 87,000

On January 1, Year 11, Cool Tools purchased fixed assets for $50,000 and sold fixed assets with an original cost of $18,000 and a book value of $6,000 for $10,000. Cool Tools made no other long-term asset purchases or sales during Year 11. What is Cool Tools' net cash used in investing activities and the amount of the depreciation adjustment to the operating section of Cool Tools' statement of cash flows prepared using the indirect method?

	Net Cash Used in Investing Activities	Depreciation Adjustment in Operating Section
1.	$32,000	$12,000
2.	$32,000	$24,000
3.	$40,000	$12,000
4.	$40,000	$24,000

5 Financing Activities

Financing activities generally involve changes in non-current liabilities and stockholders' equity, including payment or retirement of long-term notes, long-term bonds, the issuance or re-acquisition of company stock, and dividends paid.

Question 4	MCQ-09262

During Year 1, Brianna Company had the following transactions related to its financial operations:

Payment for the retirement of long-term bonds payable (carrying value $740,000)	$750,000
Distribution in Year 1 of cash dividend declared in Year 0 to preferred shareholders	62,000
Carrying value of convertible preferred stock of Brianna converted into common shares	120,000
Proceeds from sale of treasury stock (carrying value at cost $86,000)	95,000

On its Year 1 statement of cash flows, net cash used in financing activities should be:

1. $717,000
2. $716,000
3. $597,000
4. $535,000

6 Noncash Investing and Financing Activities

Certain transactions do not affect cash: purchasing assets with a note, entering into a capital lease, or exchanging bonds for stock. Look for a transaction that is, in effect, a barter transaction. These transactions are not included on the body of the statement of cash flows but are included in supplemental disclosures.

7 Cash Equivalents

Cash equivalents are short-term, highly liquid investments (maturing 90 days or less from the date of purchase) that are readily convertible into cash or so near their maturity that the risk of a change in value is insignificant. Cash equivalents are included with cash in the statement of cash flows.

Question 5	MCQ-09337

Kong Co. purchased a three-month U.S. Treasury bill. Kong's policy is to treat as cash equivalents all highly liquid investments with an original maturity of three months or less when purchased. How should this purchase be reported in Kong's statement of cash flows?

1. As an outflow from operating activities.
2. As an inflow from investing activities.
3. As an outflow from financing activities.
4. Not reported.

8 IFRS vs. U.S. GAAP

IFRS allows more flexibility than U.S. GAAP in classifying cash flows related to interest, dividends, and income taxes. The following table summarizes the classification differences between U.S. GAAP and IFRS:

Transaction	U.S. GAAP	IFRS
Interest received	CFO	CFO or CFI
Interest paid	CFO	CFO or CFF
Dividends received	CFO	CFO or CFI
Dividends paid	CFF	CFO or CFF
Taxes paid	CFO	CFO, CFI, CFF

IFRS classifies taxes paid as CFO, but allows allocation to CFI or CFF for portions specifically identified with investing and financing activities.

9 Additional Supplemental Disclosures

Interest paid and income taxes paid must be disclosed.

Question 6   MCQ-09417

Which of the following supplemental disclosures to the statement of cash flows is not required when the indirect method is used?

1. Income taxes paid.
2. Reconciliation of net income to net cash provided by operating activities.
3. Interest paid.
4. Noncash investing and financing activities.

Task-Based Simulations

Task-Based Simulation 1: Cash Flows

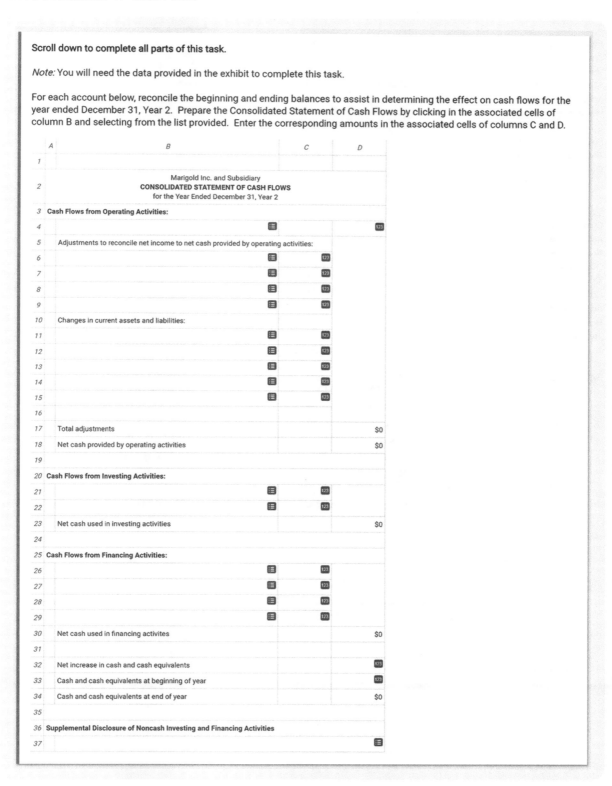

Scroll down to complete all parts of this task.

Note: You will need the data provided in the exhibit to complete this task.

For each account below, reconcile the beginning and ending balances to assist in determining the effect on cash flows for the year ended December 31, Year 2. Prepare the Consolidated Statement of Cash Flows by clicking in the associated cells of column B and selecting from the list provided. Enter the corresponding amounts in the associated cells of columns C and D.

	A	B	C	D
1				
2		Marigold Inc. and Subsidiary **CONSOLIDATED STATEMENT OF CASH FLOWS** for the Year Ended December 31, Year 2		
3		**Cash Flows from Operating Activities:**		
4				123
5		Adjustments to reconcile net income to net cash provided by operating activities:		
6			123	
7			123	
8			123	
9			123	
10		Changes in current assets and liabilities:		
11			123	
12			123	
13			123	
14			123	
15			123	
16				
17		Total adjustments		$0
18		Net cash provided by operating activities		$0
19				
20		**Cash Flows from Investing Activities:**		
21			123	
22			123	
23		Net cash used in investing activities		$0
24				
25		**Cash Flows from Financing Activities:**		
26			123	
27			123	
28			123	
29			123	
30		Net cash used in financing activites		$0
31				
32		Net increase in cash and cash equivalents		123
33		Cash and cash equivalents at beginning of year		123
34		Cash and cash equivalents at end of year		$0
35				
36		**Supplemental Disclosure of Noncash Investing and Financing Activities**		
37				

B   Cash Flows

Information

Below are the consolidated workpaper balances of Marigold Inc. and its subsidiary, Rose Corporation, as of December 31, Year 1 and Year 2:

Assets	Year 2	Year 1	Net change increase (decrease)
Cash	$313,000	$195,000	$118,000
Marketable debt securities for trading, at cost	175,000	175,000	0
Allowance to reduce marketable debt securities to market	(13,000)	(24,000)	11,000
Accounts receivable (net)	418,000	440,000	(22,000)
Inventories	595,000	525,000	70,000
Land	385,000	170,000	215,000
Plant and equipment	755,000	690,000	65,000
Accumulated depreciation	(199,000)	(145,000)	(54,000)
Goodwill	57,000	60,000	(3,000)
Total assets	$2,486,000	$2,086,000	

Liabilities and Stockholders' Equity			
Current portion of long-term note	$150,000	$150,000	$0
Accounts payable and accrued liabilities	595,000	474,000	121,000
Note payable, long term	300,000	450,000	(150,000)
Deferred income taxes	44,000	32,000	12,000
Minority interest in net assets of subsidiary	179,000	161,000	18,000
Common stock par $10	580,000	480,000	100,000
Additional paid-in capital	303,000	180,000	123,000
Retained earnings	335,000	195,000	140,000
Treasury stock at cost		(36,000)	36,000
Total liabilities and stockholders' equity	$2,486,000	$2,086,000	

Additional information:

1. On January 20, Year 2, Marigold Inc. issued 10,000 shares of its common stock for land having a fair value of $215,000.

2. On February 5, Year 2, Marigold Inc. reissued all of its Treasury stock for $44,000.

3. On May 15, Year 2, Marigold Inc. paid a cash dividend of $58,000 on its common stock.

4. On August 8, Year 2, equipment was purchased for $127,000.

5. On September 30, Year 2, equipment was sold for $40,000. The equipment cost $62,000 and had a carrying amount of $34,000 on the date of sale.

6. On December 15, Year 2, Rose Corporation paid a cash dividend of $50,000 on its common stock.

7. Deferred income taxes represent temporary differences relating to the use of certain methods for income tax reporting that differ from methods used for financial reporting.

8. Net income for Year 2 was as follows:

   Consolidated net income: $198,000
   Rose Corporation: $110,000

9. Marigold Inc. owns 70% of its subsidiary, Rose Corporation. There was no change in the ownership interest in Rose Corporation during Year 1 and Year 2. There were no intercompany transactions other than the dividend paid to Marigold Inc. by its subsidiary.

10. Sales were $2,200,000.

11. Purchases were $1,500,000.

12. Goodwill was determined to be impaired by $3,000.

Select an option below

- ○ Capital expenditures for equipment
- ○ Cash dividend paid to minority shareholder of subsidiary
- ○ Cash dividend paid by parent company
- ○ Cash paid to suppliers
- ○ Cash received from customers
- ○ Decrease in accounts receivable
- ○ Decrease in allowance to reduce marketable debt securities to market
- ○ Depreciation
- ○ Gain on sale of equipment
- ○ Impairment of goodwill
- ○ Increase in A/P and accrued liabilities
- ○ Increase in deferred income taxes
- ○ Increase in inventories
- ○ Interest paid
- ○ Interest received
- ○ Issuance of common stock to purchase land for $215,000
- ○ Minority interest in net income of subsidiary
- ○ Net income
- ○ Principal payment on note payable
- ○ Proceeds from sale of equipment
- ○ Proceeds from sale of treasury stock

RESET   CANCEL   ACCEPT

B Cash Flows

Marigold Inc. and Subsidiary
CONSOLIDATED STATEMENT OF CASH FLOWS
for the Year Ended December 31, Year 2

Cash Flows from Operating Activities:

Net income		$198,000
Adjustments to reconcile net income to net cash provided by operating activities:		
Minority interest in net income of subsidiary	$33,000	
Depreciation	82,000	
Impairment of goodwill	3,000	
Gain on sale of equipment	(6,000)	
Change in current assets and liabilities:		
Decrease in accounts receivable	22,000	
Increase in inventories	(70,000)	
Increase in A/P and accrued liabilities	121,000	
Increase in deferred income taxes	12,000	
Decrease in allowance to reduce marketable debt securities to market	(11,000)	
Total adjustments		186,000
Net cash provided by operating activities		$384,000

Cash Flows from Investing Activities:

Proceeds from sale of equipment	40,000	
Capital expenditures for equipment	(127,000)	
Net cash used by investing activities		(87,000)

Cash Flows from Financing Activities:

Proceeds from sale of treasury stock	44,000	
Cash dividend paid by parent company	(58,000)	
Cash dividend paid to minority shareholder of subsidiary	(15,000)	
Principal payment on note payable	(150,000)	
Net cash used in financing activities		(179,000)

Net increase in cash and cash equivalents		118,000
Cash and cash equivalents at beginning of year		195,000
Cash and cash equivalents at end of year		$313,000

Supplemental disclosure of Noncash Investing and Financing Activities
    Issuance of common stock to purchase land for $215,000

Task-Based Simulation 2: Research

An entity presenting a statement of cash flows should disclose its policy for determining which items are cash equivalents. Find the citation that provides guidance on this disclosure.

Enter your response in the answer fields below. Guidance on correctly structuring your response appears above and below the answer fields.

> Type the topic here.
>
> *Correctly formatted FASB ASC topics are 3 digits.*
>
> FASB ASC [ ] - [ ] - [ ] - [ ]
>
> ⓘ Some examples of correctly formatted FASB ASC responses are 205-10-05-1, 323-740-S25-1, 260-10-60-1A, 715-30-35-95, 820-10-35-16BB and 810-10-55-205AE

Explanation

Source of answer for this question:

FASB ASC 230-10-50-1

Keywords: Cash equivalents policy

Notes

1 Securities Offering Registration Statements

When a company issues new securities, it is required to submit a registration statement to the SEC that includes disclosures about the securities being offered for sale, information similar to that filed in the annual filing, and audited financial statements.

2 Form 10-K

Form 10-K must be filed annually by U.S. registered companies (issuers). The filing deadline for Form 10-K is 60 days after the end of the fiscal year for large accelerated filers, 75 days after the end of the fiscal year for accelerated filers, and 90 days after the end of the fiscal year for all other registrants. These forms contain financial disclosures, including a summary of financial data, management's discussion and analysis (MD&A), and audited financial statements prepared using U.S. GAAP.

3 Form 10-Q

Form 10-Q must be filed quarterly by U.S. registered companies (issuers). The filing deadline for Form 10-Q is 40 days after the end of the fiscal quarter for large accelerated filers and accelerated filers, and 45 days after the end of the fiscal quarter for all other registrants. This form contains unaudited financial statements prepared using U.S. GAAP, interim period MD&A, and certain disclosures.

Question 1	MCQ-09750

The common stock price for Brevard Co. (a registered U.S. company) is $40 per share. The company has 6 million common shares outstanding. In order to meet the filing deadlines required by the SEC, Brevard must (after the fiscal period ends) file the following reports within:

	10-K	10-Q
1.	75 days	40 days
2.	75 days	45 days
3.	60 days	40 days
4.	60 days	45 days

4 Form 8-K

This form is filed to report major corporate events such as corporate asset acquisitions or disposals, changes in securities and trading markets, changes to accountants or financial statements, and changes in corporate governance or management.

5 Forms 3, 4, and 5

These forms are required to be filed by directors, officers, or beneficial owners of more than 10 percent of a class of equity securities of a registered company.

6 Regulation S-X

Regulation S-X outlines the form and content of financial statements to be included in SEC filings. Under Regulation S-X, annual financial statements filed with the SEC must be audited and must include balance sheets for the two most recent fiscal years and statements of income, changes in owners' equity, and cash flows for each of the three fiscal years preceding the date of the most recent audited balance sheet.

Question 2   MCQ-09678

Under Regulation S-X, an entity's annual financial statements filed with the SEC should include at least three of each of the following, *except the*:

1. Statement of changes in owners' equity.
2. Statement of cash flows.
3. Income statement.
4. Balance sheet.

---

1 Reporting Requirement

All public entities must present earnings per share on the face of the income statement.

- **Simple Capital Structure:** Has only common stock, or no other securities that can become common stock. An entity with a simple capital structure is required to present basic earnings per share (EPS).

- **Complex Capital Structure:** If securities that can be converted into common stock, inclusive of convertible preferred stock, convertible bonds, options, and warrants. All entities with complex capital structures must present basic and diluted per share amounts (assuming that there is dilution).

2 Basic EPS

$$\text{Basic EPS} = \frac{\text{Income available to common shareholders}}{\text{Weighted average number of common shares outstanding}}$$

The income available to common shareholders must be reduced by the dividends declared on noncumulative preferred stock, or by the dividends accumulated in the current period on any cumulative preferred stock whether or not those dividends have actually been declared.

To determine the weighted average number of shares outstanding, weight each total of shares outstanding by the amount of time that the total was outstanding. Stock dividends and stock splits are treated as if they had occurred at the beginning of the earliest period presented.

Question 1 MCQ-09397

The Burken Co. has one class of common stock outstanding and no other securities that are potentially convertible into common stock. During Year 10, 100,000 shares of common stock were outstanding. In Year 11, two distributions of additional common shares occurred: On April 1, 20,000 shares of treasury stock were sold, and on July 1, a 2-for-1 stock split was issued. Net income was $410,000 in Year 11 and $350,000 in Year 10. What amounts should Burken report as earnings per share in its Year 11 and Year 10 comparative income statements?

	Year 11	Year 10
1.	$1.78	$3.50
2.	$1.78	$1.75
3.	$2.34	$1.75
4.	$2.34	$3.50

3 Diluted EPS

3.1 Convertible Securities

Diluted EPS is calculated taking into consideration any security (convertible preferred stock, convertible bonds, stock option or warrant, or contingent issuance of stock) that can be converted into common stock. Any conversion, exercise, or contingent issuance that has an antidilutive effect (increases EPS or decreases loss per share) is not included in the calculation. No antidilution is presented.

$$\text{Diluted EPS} = \frac{\text{Income available to common shareholders} + \text{Interest on conversion of bonds (net of tax)}}{\text{Weighted average number of common shares, assuming all dilutive securities are converted to common stock}}$$

3.2 Options and Warrants

Options and warrants are accounted for using the treasury stock method. An assumption is made that "in the money" (average market price > exercise price) options and/or warrants are exercised and that the proceeds from the exercise are used to buy back shares for the treasury. The incremental shares (difference between the shares "sold" and the shares "reacquired") are added to the denominator.

Example

A company has 1,000 stock options outstanding (for one share each), which are exercisable at $30 each. If the average market price is $50 per share, then the options are "in the money" and therefore dilutive. When the options are assumed to be exercised for the purposes of computing diluted EPS, it is assumed that the company will receive $30,000, which can be used to purchase 600 shares of stock ($30,000 / $50 share = 600 shares). The company will need to issue 400 new shares (1000 shares - 600 repurchased). The 400 newly issued shares will be added to the weighted average number of common shares outstanding when computing diluted EPS.

$$1{,}000 \text{ shares} - \left(\frac{1{,}000 \times 30 \text{ option price}}{50 \text{ average price}} \right) = \text{Shares added to denominator}$$

$$1{,}000 - 600 = \underline{400 \text{ shares}}$$

Question 2
MCQ-09370

Hutchins Company had 200,000 shares of common stock, 50,000 shares of convertible preferred stock, and $2,000,000 of 10% convertible bonds outstanding during the current year. The preferred stock was convertible into 40,000 shares of common stock.

During the current year, Hutchins paid dividends of $1.00 per share on the common stock and $2.00 per share on the preferred stock. Each $1,000 bond was convertible into 50 shares of common stock. The net income for the year was $1,000,000 and the income tax rate was 30%.

Diluted earnings per share for the current year was (rounded to the nearest penny):

  1. $5.00
  2. $3.35
  3. $3.53
  4. $3.06

D   Public Company Reporting: Earnings per Share

Task-Based Simulations

Task-Based Simulation 1: Research

The CEO of Logan Corporation wants to disclose EPS in the notes to the financials only. Find the proper citation that defines the location of EPS presentation in the financial statements.

Enter your response in the answer fields below. Guidance on correctly structuring your response appears above and below the answer fields.

Type the topic here.
Correctly formatted FASB ASC topics are 3 digits.

FASB ASC [   ] - [   ] - [   ] - [   ]

ⓘ Some examples of correctly formatted FASB ASC responses are 205-10-05-1, 323-740-S25-1, 260-10-60-1A, 715-30-35-95, 820-10-35-16BB and 810-10-55-205AE

Explanation

Source of answer for this question:

FASB ASC 260-10-45-2

Keywords: EPS presentation

Task-Based Simulation 2: Research

What is the treatment of purchased put options in the computation of diluted earnings per share? Find the proper citation that provides guidance to answer this question.

Enter your response in the answer fields below. Guidance on correctly structuring your response appears above and below the answer fields.

> Type the topic here.
>
> *Correctly formatted FASB ASC topics are 3 digits.*
>
> FASB ASC [   ] - [   ] - [   ] - [   ]
>
> ⓘ Some examples of correctly formatted FASB ASC responses are 205-10-05-1, 323-740-S25-1, 260-10-60-1A, 715-30-35-95, 820-10-35-16BB and 810-10-55-205AE

Explanation

Source of answer for this question:

FASB ASC 260-10-45-37

Keywords: Purchased put options

1 Operating Segments

An operating segment is a part of an enterprise:

- that engages in business activities.
- whose operating results are regularly reviewed by the enterprise's chief operating decision maker.
- for which discrete financial information is available.

2 Reporting Segments

An operating segment is a reportable segment if it has at least 10 percent of the combined amounts of:

- revenue from sales to unaffiliated customers and intersegment transfers for all of the entities reported; or
- profit or loss; or
- assets.

If the segment does not meet the 10 percent limit, it is not separately disclosed unless all the reportable combined sales to unaffiliated customers is less than 75 percent of the total company sales revenue made to outsiders. If this limit is not achieved, additional segments must be disclosed despite their failure to satisfy one of the thresholds.

Question 1 MCQ-09272

The Houston Fellowship Corporation has three operating segments for which the following information was available:

	Beer	Wine	Pretzels
Sales to outsiders	$18,000	$24,000	$36,000
Intersegment sales	3,600	2,200	4,200
Total	$21,600	$26,200	$40,200

In addition, revenues generated at corporate headquarters were $4,000. What is the minimum amount of revenue that each of these operating segments must have to be considered a reportable segment?

1. $7,800
2. $9,200
3. $8,000
4. $8,800

Question 2 MCQ-09391

Selected financial results from Water Works Inc.'s five operating segments were as follows:

Segment	Total revenues	Total profit	Total assets
Rain	$ 100,000	$ 70,000	$ 300,000
Snow	130,000	30,000	350,000
Ice	600,000	300,000	700,000
Hail	95,000	15,000	190,000
Steam	400,000	220,000	550,000
	$1,325,000	$635,000	$2,090,000

The company had no intersegment sales. Which operating segment(s) is (are) deemed to be reportable segments?

1. Ice only.
2. Ice and Steam.
3. Ice, Steam, and Snow.
4. Ice, Steam, Snow, and Rain.

II | Selected Financial Statement Accounts

Notes

1 Accounts Receivable

Accounts receivable are reported at their net realizable value (AR—allowance for doubtful accounts).

There are two GAAP methods to compute bad debt expense using the allowance method. The direct write-off method is not GAAP.

1.1 Income Statement Approach

Bad debts are estimated as a percentage of net credit sales, resulting in bad debt expense for the period.

Allowance for DA	
Write-offs	Beginning balance
	Recoveries
	Bad debt expense (% of credit sales)
	Ending balance

1.2 Balance Sheet Approach

Bad debts are estimated as a percentage of ending accounts receivable or based on an aging of accounts receivable; emphasis is on the valuation of the receivables. This results in the ending balance for allowances for doubtful accounts and the bad debt expense is the "plug."

Allowance for DA	
Write-offs	Beginning balance
	Recoveries
	Bad debt expense (plug)
	Ending balance (based on A/R not expected to be collected)

A   Trade Receivables

Question 1   MCQ-09316

Fernandez Company had an accounts receivable balance of $150,000 on December 31, Year 2 and $175,000 on December 31, Year 3. The company wrote off $40,000 of accounts receivable during Year 3. Sales for Year 3 totaled $600,000, and all sales were on account.

The amount collected from customers on accounts receivable during Year 3 was:

1. $575,000
2. $531,000
3. $535,000
4. $600,000

Question 2   MCQ-09402

On its December 31, Year 2 balance sheet, Red Rock Candle Company reported accounts receivable of $855,000, net of an allowance for doubtful accounts of $45,000. On December 31, Year 3, Red Rock's balance sheet showed gross accounts receivable of $922,000 and Red Rock's income statement reported sales of $3,000,000. During the year, accounts receivable of $35,000 were written off and $18,000 were recovered. Based on past experience, 5% of Red Rock's ending accounts receivable are uncollectible. How much should Red Rock report as bad debt expense on its Year 3 income statement?

1. $18,100
2. $35,000
3. $46,100
4. $150,000

2 Pledging

A company may use its accounts receivable as collateral for loans. The company retains title to the receivables but pledges that it will use the proceeds to pay off the loans. Pledging requires note disclosure only.

3 Factoring

A company may sell its receivables to a factor either with or without recourse. "With recourse" means the seller retains the risk of any losses on collection. "Without recourse" means that the buyer assumes the risk of any losses on collection.

Question 3   MCQ-09331

Stanberry Company sold $500,000 of net accounts receivable to Cork Company for $450,000. The receivables were sold outright on a without recourse basis, and Stanberry Company retained no control over the receivables.

The Journal Entries to record the sale would be which of the following?

1.

DR	Cash	$500,000	
CR	Accounts receivable (net)		$500,000

2.

DR	Cash	$450,000	
DR	Loss on sale of accounts receivable	50,000	
CR	Accounts receivable (net)		$500,000

3.

DR	Cash	$450,000	
DR	Unrealized loss on sale of accounts receivable	50,000	
CR	Accounts receivable (net)		$500,000

4.

DR	Cash	$450,000	
DR	Due from Cork Company	50,000	
CR	Accounts receivable (net)		$500,000

Notes

1 Perpetual and Periodic Concepts

Inventory is property held for resale, property held in production (work-in-process), or raw materials consumed in the process of production. Just like the cost of any other asset, the cost of inventory includes all costs incurred in getting the inventory onto the premises and ready for sale or use.

Inventory is accounted for under either a *periodic method* or a *perpetual method*. With the perpetual method, a running total of the inventory is maintained as goods are purchased and sold and the cost of goods sold is updated as sales occur. With the periodic method, a running total is not maintained, and the cost of goods sold cannot be determined until the end of the period when the ending inventory is counted.

1.1 Periodic Inventory—Cost of Goods Sold

Beginning inventory	$XXX
Plus: Purchases	XXX
Equal: Cost of goods available for sale	XXX
Less: Ending inventory	(XXX)
Cost of goods sold	XXX

1.2 Goods in Transit

1.2.1 FOB Shipping Point

Title passes to the buyer when goods are shipped and in transit. Hence title passed when shipped, but no possession.

1.2.2 FOB Destination

Title passes to the buyer when goods are received. Hence, no title and no possession until received

B Inventory

Question 1   MCQ-09282

Mixon Corporation, a manufacturer of small tools, provided the following information from its accounting records for the year ended December 31, Year 1:

Inventory at December 31, Year 1 (based on a physical count of goods in Mixon's plant at cost on December 31, Year 1)	$1,750,000
Accounts payable at December 31, Year 1	1,200,000
Net sales (sales less sales returns)	8,500,000

Additional information is as follows:

1. Included in the physical count were tools billed to a customer FOB shipping point on December 31, Year 1. These tools had a cost of $28,000 and were billed at $35,000. The shipment was on Mixon's loading dock at 5:00 PM on December 31, Year 1 waiting to be picked up by the common carrier.
2. Goods were in transit from a vendor to Mixon on December 31, Year 1. The invoice cost was $50,000, and the goods were shipped FOB shipping point on December 29, Year 1.

What would be the adjusted inventory at December 31, Year 1?

   1. $1,750,000
   2. $1,715,000
   3. $1,700,000
   4. $1,800,000

2 Inventory Valuation Methods

Under both IFRS and U.S. GAAP, the appropriate inventory valuation method can be applied to a single item, a category, or total inventory, provided that the method most clearly reflects periodic income.

2.1   U.S. GAAP

Under U.S. GAAP, inventory is valued at the lower-of-cost-or-market when using LIFO or the retail inventory method. Cost is determined using an appropriate inventory cost flow assumption. Market generally means current replacement cost, provided the current replacement cost does not exceed net realizable value (the "market ceiling") or fall below net realizable value reduced by normal profit margin (the "market floor"). In all other cases (not LIFO or retail), U.S. GAAP requires the lower of cost or net realizable value, the same as IFRS.

2.2   International Financial Reporting Standards (IFRS)

Under IFRS, inventory is valued at the lower-of-cost or net realizable value. Cost is determined using an appropriate inventory cost flow assumption. Net realizable value is net selling price less costs to complete and sell the inventory.

Question 2	MCQ-09327

Simmons, Inc. uses lower-of-cost-or-market to value its inventory. Data regarding an item in its inventory is as follows:

Cost	$26
Replacement cost	20
Selling price	30
Cost of completion	2
Normal profit margin	7

What is the lower-of-cost-or-market for this item?

1. $21
2. $20
3. $28
4. $26

3 Inventory Costing Methods

The common inventory cost flow methods are specific identification, FIFO, LIFO, and weighted average. LIFO is not permitted under IFRS.

3.1   FIFO

FIFO inventory consists of the most recent costs and the cost of goods sold consists of the older costs.

3.2   LIFO

LIFO inventory consists of the older costs and the cost of goods sold consists of the most recent costs.

In periods of rising prices, FIFO and LIFO will have opposite effects on inventory, cost of goods sold and net income. FIFO results in the highest inventory, and reports the lowest cost of goods sold and hence the highest net income. LIFO reports the lowest inventory, and reports the highest prices in cost of goods sold and hence the lowest net income. In periods of decreasing prices, the effects are of course the opposite.

On the CPA Exam, prices are generally rising, therefore:

> LIFO = Lowest ending inventory / Lowest net income
>
> FIFO = Highest ending inventory / Highest net income

Questions related to the effect of overstatement and understatement errors are common on the exam. Note that if ending inventory is overstated, then cost of goods is understated, and net income is overstated; if ending inventory is understated, the opposite is true. Errors in ending inventory have the same effect on net income (move in the same direction); errors in beginning inventory move in the opposite direction.

3.3   Weighted Average—Used With Periodic Inventory

$$\text{Weighted average cost per unit} = \frac{\text{Cost of goods available for sale}}{\text{Number of units available for sale}}$$

The weighted average cost per unit is used to determine both cost of goods sold and ending inventory.

3.4 Moving Average—Used With Perpetual Inventory

The unit cost changes each time there is a new purchase.

	Units	Units Cost	Total Costs	Total Units	Moving Average
Beginning inventory	100	$5	$500	100	$5.00
Purchases	200	$6	$1,700	300	$5.67

3.5 Dollar-Value LIFO

■ Inventory under dollar-value LIFO is measured in dollars and is adjusted for changing price levels. When converting from FIFO to dollar-value LIFO, a price index is used.

■ The company groups similar inventory items into "pools."

■ Each pool is assigned a conversion index. It can be computed internally or obtained from external sources.

3.5.1 Calculation

■ Internally computed price index formula:

$$\text{Price index} = \frac{\text{Ending inventory at current year dollar}}{\text{Ending inventory at base year dollar}}$$

■ The LIFO layer added in the current year is multiplied by the price index and added to the dollar-value LIFO computation.

Date	At Base Year Cost	At Current Year Cost	At Dollar Value LIFO
1/1/Year 1	$50,000	$50,000	$50,000
Year 1 layer	10,000	40,000	?? [a]
12/31/Year 1	$60,000	$90,000	?? [b]

Step 1: $90,000/$60,000 = 3/2

Step 2: $10,000 × 3/2 = $15,000 [a]

Step 3: $50,000 + $15,000 = $65,000 [b]

3.6 Gross Profit Method

The gross profit method can be used to prepare interim financial statements. The gross profit percentage is known and is used to calculate cost of goods sold.

Sales	100%
CGS	80% (Plug)
Gross profit	20%

3.7 Conventional Retail Method

Converts inventory at retail to inventory at cost. This is accomplished via a cost/retail ratio. Markups are included in the ratio, whereas, markdowns are excluded, resulting in lower of cost or market.

	At Cost	At Retail	
Beginning inventory	$15,000	$ 35,000	
Purchases	$ 5,000	$ 12,000	
Markups	–	3,000	
Available for sale	$20,000	$ 50,000	= 40% Cost/retail ratio
Sales		$(30,000)	
Markdowns		(5,000)	
Ending inventory at retail		$ 15,000	
Ending inventory at LCM (15,000 × 40)	$ 6,000		

Question 3 — MCQ-09386

The Loyd Company had 150 units of product Omega on hand at December 1, Year 1, costing $400 each. Purchases of product Omega during December were as follows:

Date	Units	Unit Cost
December 7	100	$440
December 14	200	$460
December 29	300	$500

Sales during December were 500 units. The cost of inventory at December 31, Year 1 under the FIFO method would be closest to:

1. $100,000
2. $104,000
3. $115,000
4. $125,000

Question 4   MCQ-09312

The Loyd Company had 150 units of product Omega on hand at December 1, Year 1 costing $400 each. Purchases of product Omega during December were as follows:

Date	Units	Unit Cost
December 7	100	$440
December 14	200	$460
December 29	300	$500

Sales during December were 500 units. The cost of inventory at December 31, Year 1 under the LIFO method would be:

1. $100,000
2. $104,000
3. $75,000
4. $125,000

Question 5   MCQ-09398

The Loyd Company had 150 units of product Omega on hand at December 1, Year 1 costing $400 each. Purchases of product Omega during December were as follows:

Date	Units	Unit Cost
December 7	100	$440
December 14	200	$460
December 29	300	$500

Sales during December were 500 units. The cost of inventory at December 31, Year 1 under the weighted average method would be closest to:

1. $100,000
2. $104,000
3. $115,000
4. $125,000

Notes

1 General Concepts

The cost of a fixed asset (or any other asset) is the cost to acquire the asset and place it in condition for its intended use. As an example, purchased equipment would include purchase price, freight in, installation, sale taxes, etc.

- *Ordinary repairs* are expensed, not capitalized.
- *Extraordinary repairs* should be capitalized if they increase the usefulness of the asset and should be recorded by decreasing accumulated depreciation if they increase the life of the asset.
- Land is not a depreciable asset; land improvements are.
- Sometimes, fixed assets are acquired in a "basket" purchase. The amount paid must be allocated to the various assets acquired, generally on a relative fair value or appraisal value basis.

2 Reporting Fixed Assets

2.1 U.S. GAAP

Under U.S. GAAP, the carrying value of a fixed asset is calculated as follows:

$$\text{Carrying value} = \text{Historical cost} - \text{Accumulated depreciation} - \text{Impairment}$$

2.2 IFRS

Under IFRS, fixed asset carrying value can be calculated using the cost model or the revaluation model. The cost model is the method used under U.S. GAAP. Under the revaluation model, fixed assets are revaluated to fair value by asset class at a specific point in time and then reported as follows:

$$\begin{array}{c}\text{Carrying value} \\ \text{(revaluation model)}\end{array} = \begin{array}{c}\text{Fair value on} \\ \text{revaluation date}\end{array} - \begin{array}{c}\text{Subsequent accumulated} \\ \text{depreciation}\end{array} - \begin{array}{c}\text{Subsequent} \\ \text{impairment}\end{array}$$

When fixed assets are revalued under IFRS, revaluation losses are reported on the income statement and revaluation gains are reported in other comprehensive income as revaluation surplus. When the fair value of a revalued asset differs materially from its carrying amount, a further revaluation is required.

Question 1   MCQ-09360

On June 30, Year 1, Bluebird Inc. purchased a $750,000 tract of land for a new regional office. Costs related to purchasing the property and preparing the land for construction included:

Legal fees	$32,000
Title guarantee insurance	15,000
Cost to clear timber from land	18,000
Proceeds from sale of timber	7,000
Excavation costs for office building	20,000

In its December 30, Year 1 balance sheet, Boyd should report a balance in the land account of:

1. $797,000
2. $808,000
3. $815,000
4. $828,000

3 Interest on Self-Constructed Assets

Interest on self-constructed assets is capitalized based on the weighted average of the accumulated expenditures multiplied by an appropriate interest rate and cannot exceed actual interest costs. Interest on inventory routinely manufactured is not capitalized.

Question 2   MCQ-09375

On January 1, Year 1, Bluebird Inc. borrowed $10 million at a rate of 9% for 5 years and began construction of its new regional office building. Bluebird has no other debt. During Year 1, Bluebird's weighted average accumulated construction expenditures totaled $3,750,000. What should Bluebird report as interest expense on its income statement for Year 1?

1. $337,500
2. $500,000
3. $562,500
4. $900,000

4 Depreciation

Generally, the depreciation methods on the CPA Exam include *straight-line*, *sum-of-the-years-digits*, and *declining balance methods*. Depreciation is a rational and systematic cost allocation process closely tied to properly matching revenue and expenses. Under IFRS, the depreciation method used must match the expected pattern of fixed asset consumption. This is not required under U.S. GAAP.

4.1 Component Depreciation

Component depreciation is required under IFRS. Separate significant components of a fixed asset with different lives should be recorded and depreciated separately. The carrying amount of parts or components that are replaced should be derecognized.

4.2 Depreciation Methods

Depreciation is caused by physical factors such as wear, tear, and use.

4.2.1 Straight-Line

$$\frac{\text{Cost} - \text{Salvage value}}{\text{Estimated useful life}} = \text{Depreciation expense}$$

4.2.2 Units-of-Production (Productive Output)

$$\frac{\text{Cost} - \text{Salvage value}}{\text{Total estimated units or hours}} = \frac{\text{Depreciation}}{\text{rate}} \times \frac{\text{Units produced or}}{\text{hours used in a period}} = \frac{\text{Depreciation}}{\text{expense}}$$

4.2.3 Sum-of-Years'-Digits

$$\text{Depreciation rate} = \frac{\text{Remaining life}}{\text{SYD}}$$

The *numerator* is the remaining life of the asset at the beginning of the current year.

The *denominator* is the sum of the digits for the number of years of asset life (3-year life = 1 + 2 + 3 = 6):

$$(\text{Cost} - \text{Salvage value}) \times \frac{\text{Remaining life}}{\text{SYD}} = \text{Depreciation expense}$$

4.2.4   Declining Balance

The salvage value is not considered upfront; it is considered at the end.

The asset should never be depreciated below the estimated salvage value.

$$BV \times Rate = \text{Depreciation for the period}$$

$$Rate = \frac{100\%}{N} = R \quad \begin{array}{c} \text{If double} = 2R \\ \hline \text{If } 150\% = 1.5R \end{array}$$

$N = Useful\ life$

Question 3   MCQ-09330

McDonnell Company purchased a machine on January 1, Year 1 for $250,000. The machine was estimated to have a useful life of 10 years, with a salvage value of $50,000. During Year 3, it became apparent that the machine would not be usable past December 31, Year 5 and that the salvage value at that point would be $0.

What would be the accumulated depreciation at December 31, Year 3? Assume the company uses the straight-line method.

1. $100,000
2. $60,000
3. $110,000
4. $70,000

1 Exchanges Having Commercial Substance (U.S. GAAP)

An exchange has commercial substance if the future risk, timing or amount of cash flows change as a result of the transaction. A fair value approach is used.

- Gains/Losses are always recognized on exchanges having commercial substance.
- Gains/Losses are the difference between the FV and BV of the old asset.
- The fair value of assets given up is assumed to be equal to the fair value of assets received, including any cash given or received in the transaction.

New asset (FV of old asset plus cash given, if any)	$XXX	
Accumulated depreciation of asset given up	XXX	
Cash received (if any)	XXX	
Loss (if any)	XXX	
Old asset at historical cost		$XXX
Cash given (if any)		XXX
Gain (if any)		XXX

Question 1   MCQ-09345

Pate paid $50,000 and gave a plot of undeveloped land with a carrying amount of $320,000 and a fair value of $450,000 to Bizzell Co. in exchange for a plot of undeveloped land with a fair value of $500,000. The land was carried on Bizzell's books at $350,000. The exchange is one that has commercial substance under U.S. GAAP.

At what amount is the land received from Pate recorded on Bizzell's books?

1. $370,000
2. $320,000
3. $500,000
4. $450,000

2 Exchanges Lacking Commercial Substance (U.S. GAAP)

If projected cash flows after the exchange are not expected to change significantly, then the exchange lacks commercial substance and a book value approach is used.

- All losses are recognized on exchanges lacking commercial substance.
- Gains are recognized based on the nature of the transaction:
  - No boot received = No gain
  - Boot given = No gain
  - Boot received < 25% = Recognize gain in proportion to boot received
  - Boot ≥ 25% of total consideration = Monetary exchange (Both parties to exchange recognize all gains and losses)

Question 2   MCQ-09412

Which of the following statements regarding nonmonetary exchanges is/are correct under U.S. GAAP?

I. A fair value approach is used to record an exchange that lacks commercial substance.

II. An exchange is considered to have commercial substance if the future risk, timing, or amount of cash flows changes as a result of the transaction.

III. In all nonmonetary exchanges, it is assumed that the fair value given up is equal to the fair value received.

IV. In exchanges having commercial substance, the gain or loss on the exchange is calculated by comparing the book value of the asset given to the fair value of the asset received.

    1. I only.
    2. II only.
    3. II and III.
    4. II, III, and IV.

---

3 Exchanges of Similar Assets and Dissimilar Assets (IFRS)

Under IFRS, nonmonetary exchanges are characterized as exchanges of similar assets and exchanges of dissimilar assets. Exchanges of dissimilar assets are regarded as exchanges that generate revenue and are accounted for in the same manner as exchanges having commercial substance under U.S. GAAP. Exchanges of similar assets are not regarded as exchanges that generate revenue and no gains are recognized.

1 Debt Securities

1.1 Investments in Debt Securities

Under U.S. GAAP, there are three debt securities portfolio classifications: trading, available-for-sale, and held-to-maturity.

1.1.1 Trading Securities

Trading debt securities are intended for active trading. The portfolio itself is carried at cost and is reported at fair value in the financial statements through the use of a valuation account. Unrealized gains or losses are reported on the income statement.

DR	Unrealized loss	$XXX
CR	Trading debt securities	$XXX
	OR	
DR	Trading debt securities	$XXX
CR	Unrealized gain	$XXX

1.1.2 Available-for-Sale (AFS) Securities

AFS debt securities are carried at cost and are reported at fair value in the financial statements through the use of a valuation account. Unrealized gains or losses are reported in other comprehensive income (the "U" in **PUFIER**).

DR	Unrealized loss	$XXX
CR	Available-for-sale debt securities	$XXX
	OR	
DR	Available-for-sale debt securities	$XXX
CR	Unrealized gain	$XXX

1.1.3 Held-to-Maturity (HTM) Securities

The HTM classification is appropriate when the investor has the ability and intent to hold the debt securities to maturity. The portfolio itself is reported in the financial statements at amortized cost.

1.2   Debt Impairment

Under the current expected credit losses (CECL) model, available-for-sale debt securities and held-to-maturity debt securities should be reported at the net amount expected to be collected using an allowance for expected credit losses. Expected credit losses are determined based on current conditions, past experience, and future expectations. A credit loss is recognized as a current period expense on the income statement and as an offsetting allowance on the balance sheet. Increases and decreases in expected credit losses are reflected on the income statement in the period incurred when the estimate of expected credit losses changes.

1.2.1   Held-to-Maturity Debt Securities

If it is probable that all amounts due (principal and interest) will not be collected on a debt investment reported at amortized cost, the investment should be reported at the present value of the principal and interest that is expected to be collected. The credit loss is the difference between the amortized cost and the present value.

1.2.2   Available-for-Sale Debt Securities

Impairment on available-for-sale securities is accounted for differently from impairment on held-to-maturity securities because the investor has the option to sell an available-for-sale security if the loss on the sale will be less than the expected credit loss. As a result, the credit loss reported in net income on an available-for-sale security is limited to the amount by which fair value is below amortized cost. Any additional loss is reported as an unrealized loss in other comprehensive income.

1.3   Realized Gains/Losses

Realized gains/losses are recognized in net income when a debt security is sold or impaired.

Trading Debt Securities		
DR Cash	$XXX	
CR Trading debt securities		$XXX
CR Realized gain		XXX
OR		
DR Cash	XXX	
DR Realized loss	XXX	
CR Trading debt securities		XXX

Available-for-Sale Debt Securities

Facts:

Cost	$100
FV 1/01/Year 1	120
Sold 9/15/Year 1	150

DR	Cash	$150	
DR	Unrealized gain (PUFIER)	20	
CR	Available-for-sale debt securities		$120
CR	Realized gain		50

1.4   Summary of Investments in Debt Securities

Summary of Investments in Debt Securities

Classification	Balance Sheet	Reported	Unrealized Gain/Loss	Realized Gain/Loss
Trading stocks and bonds	Current or non-current	Fair value at balance sheet date	Income statement	Income statement
Available-for-sale stocks and bonds	Current or non-current	Fair value at balance sheet date	Other comprehensive income PUFIER	Realized gain/loss in income statement. Unrealized gain/loss is reversed
Held-to-maturity bonds	Current or non-current	Amortized cost	None	Not applicable

Question 1   MCQ-09293

The following data pertain to Tyne Co.'s investments in marketable debt securities:

		Market Value	
	Cost	12/31/Y2	12/31/Y1
Trading	$150,000	$155,000	$100,000
Available-for-sale	150,000	130,000	120,000

There are no expected credit losses. What amount should Tyne report as unrealized gain (loss) in its Year 2 income statement?

1. $55,000
2. $50,000
3. $60,000
4. $65,000

E   Investments

Question 2 MCQ-09353

Money for Nothing Enterprises ("MNE") held the following available-for-sale debt securities during Year 2:

	Cost	Market Value 12/31/Y1	Sales Price	Market Value 12/31/Y2
Alpha Corp.	$50,000	$53,000	$57,000	--
Beta Corp.	35,000	30,000		$38,000
Omega Corp.	21,000	27,000		24,000

There are no expected credit losses. What will MNE report as unrealized gain on available-for-sale securities on its Year 2 statement of comprehensive income (ignore taxes)?

1. $2,000
2. $3,000
3. $6,000
4. $8,000

Question 3 MCQ-09368

Money for Nothing Enterprises ("MNE") held the following available-for-sale debt securities during Year 2:

	Cost	Market Value 12/31/Y1	Sales Price	Market Value 12/31/Y2
Alpha Corp.	$50,000	$53,000	$57,000	--
Beta Corp.	35,000	30,000		$38,000
Omega Corp.	21,000	27,000		24,000

There are no expected credit losses. What will MNE report as accumulated other comprehensive income on its 12/31/Y2 balance sheet (ignore taxes)?

1. $2,000
2. $3,000
3. $6,000
4. $8,000

Question 4

Tyler Co. paid $150,000 on January 1, Year 1, to purchase a $150,000, five-year bond at par value. Tyler classified the investment as held-to-maturity. On December 31, Year 1, Tyler determined that the present value of the interest and principal to be paid by the issuer over the life of the bond is $142,000. The fair value of the bond on December 31, Year 1, was $144,000. What amount should Tyler report as a credit loss in its Year 2 income statement?

1. $0
2. $2,000
3. $6,000
4. $8,000

Question 5

Diamond Inc. purchased the following available-for-sale debt securities at par during Year 1:

	Values as of 12/31/Year 1	
	Purchase price	Fair value
ABC Corp.	$50,000	$55,000
XYZ Corp.	$35,000	$30,000

On December 31, Year 1, Diamond determined that the present value of the principal and interest expected to be received on the investment in XYZ Corp. is $33,000. What will Diamond report as unrealized gain or loss on available-for-sale securities on its Year 1 statement of comprehensive income?

1. $2,000 gain
2. $5,000 gain
3. $0
4. $3,000 loss

2 Investments in Equity Securities

2.1 Investments in Equity Securities

Equity investments are typically carried at fair value through net income (FVTNI), with unrealized gains/losses included in earnings as they occur. For equity investments that do not have a readily determinable fair value, the practicability exception allows an entity to measure an investment at cost plus/minus observable price changes of identical or similar investments, less impairment.

2.2 Equity Impairment

When a qualitative assessment indicates that equity investments measured using the practicability exception are impaired, the cost basis of the security is written down to fair value and the amount of the write-down is accounted for as a realized loss and included in earnings.

2.3 Realized Gains/Losses

Realized gains/losses equal to the sale price relative to the adjusted cost are booked on the income statement.

3 Equity Method

The equity method must be used if the investor has significant influence over the investee. Even if the investor owns less than 20 percent of the stock of an investee company, but exercises significant influence, the equity method must be used.

With the equity method, income/loss from the investee is the pro rata share of the investee's income/loss. The carrying amount of the investment is reduced by the pro rata share of the dividends paid by the investee.

FV adjustment is the difference between the FV and BV of the assets and/or liabilities of the investee. FV adjustments for non-current assets other than land are subject to depreciation (e.g., equipment).

Investment		Income	
Cost	% of cash dividends	FV adjustment	% of net income
% of net income	FV adjustment	Depreciation	
	Depreciation		

Under both U.S. GAAP and IFRS, joint ventures are accounted for using the equity method.

Question 6   MCQ-09392

On January 1, Year 1, Red Crown, Inc., purchased 25 percent of Red Hand Co.'s outstanding common shares and 40 percent of Red Leaf Co.'s nonvoting preferred stock. Red Crown plans to hold the investments on a long-term basis. Red Hand reported net income of $300,000 for Year 1 and paid common stock dividends of $100,000. Red Leaf reported net income of $450,000 and paid preferred dividends of $200,000. On its December 31, Year 1, income statement, what amount of income from these investments should Red Crown report?

1. $105,000
2. $155,000
3. $205,000
4. $255,000

E Investments

Task-Based Simulations

Task-Based Simulation 1: Definition

Scroll down to complete all parts of this task.

Select the proper classification or accounting treatment for the marketable debt securities transactions (or situations) below by clicking in the associated cell and selecting from the list provided.

	A	B
1	**Marketable Security Description/Accounting Treatment**	**Classification**
2	Investments in bonds issued by a corporation which the investing company will not liquidate prior to collection of principal and interest due.	
3	Debt securities purchased by an entity that has no immediate plans to sell them.	
4	Cash activity associated with the purchase and sale of debt securities displayed in the cash flows from operating activities in the statement of cash flows	
5	Debt securities purchased by a corporation with idle/ excess cash and the corporation routinely buys and sells these securities as ongoing cash requirements.	
6	Unrealized gains and losses resulting from changes in the value of debt securities when there is no deemed impairment receive no accounting treatment.	
7	Unrealized gains and losses resulting from changes in the value of debt securities when there is no deemed impairment are accounted for through other comprehensive income.	

Select an option below

- Trading debt securities
- Available-for-sale debt securities
- Held-to-maturity securities

RESET   CANCEL   ACCEPT

Explanation

Row 2: Held-to-maturity securities
Investments in debt securities shall be classified as held-to-maturity if the reporting enterprise has the positive intent and ability to hold those securities to maturity.

Row 3: Available-for-sale debt securities
Investments that do not meet the qualifications of trading securities or held-to-maturity securities are classified as available-for-sale securities.

Row 4: Trading debt securities
Cash activity from trading securities is displayed in cash flows from operating activities while cash flows from available-for-sale and held-to-maturity securities are displayed in the investing activities section of the statement of cash flows.

Row 5: Trading debt securities
Securities that are bought and held principally for the purpose of selling them in the near term (thus held for only a short period of time) shall be classified as trading securities.

Row 6: Held-to-maturity securities
Held-to-maturity securities are valued at amortized cost. Non-permanent changes in the fair value of held-to-maturity securities do not result in any adjustment to the displayed value of the investment.

Row 7: Available-for-sale debt securities
Unrealized gains and losses resulting from changes in the fair market value of available-for-sale securities are accounted for as a component of other comprehensive income.

E   Investments

Task-Based Simulation 2: Marketable Securities

Scroll down to complete all parts of this task.
Note: You will need the data provided in the exhibit to complete this task.
For each of the securities listed below, enter the amount requested in the associated cell.

PART I
Compute the carrying amount of each security at December 31, Year 2.

	A	B
1	*Held-to-maturity securities*	
2	Arbor Corporation	`123`
3	*Trading debt securities*	
4	Delphi Corporation	`123`
5	*Available-for-sale debt securities*	
6	Gorman Corporation	`123`
7	Jubilee Creations	`123`

PART II
Compute the amount of recognized gain or loss on the income statement as a result of the debt securities transactions.

	A	B
1	*Available-for-sale debt securities*	
2	Gorman Corporation	`123`

PART III
Compute the amount of unrealized gain or loss on the income statement as a result of the debt securities transactions.

	A	B
1	*Trading debt securities*	
2	Delphi Corporation	`123`

PART IV
Compute the amount of unrealized gain or loss in other comprehensive income as a result of the debt securities transactions for Year 1.

	A	B
1	*Available-for-sale debt securities*	
2	Gorman Corporation	`123`
3	Jubilee Creations	`123`

PART V
Compute the ending balance for accumulated other comprehensive income for Year 2.

	A	B
1	*Other comprehensive income* ending balance for Year 2	`123`

Information

The following data has been provided relative to the debt investment portfolio of the Zarbo Corporation. Use this information as the data for your marketable securities task solution.

	Cost	Fair Value 12/31/Y1	Activity in Year 2 Purchases	Sales	Fair Value 12/31/Y2
Held-to-maturity securities					
Arbor Corporation	–	–	55,000	–	45,000
Trading debt securities					
Delphi Corporation	100,000	120,000	–	–	105,000
Available-for-sale debt securities					
Gorman Corporation	125,000	75,000	–	65,000	–
Jubilee Creations	125,000	140,000	–	–	130,000

Additional notes:
- Securities of the Arbor Corporation were purchased at par and there are no current expected credit losses
- Delphi, Gorman, and Jubilee debt securities were purchased during Year 1

Explanation

PART I

Held-to-maturity securities

Arbor Corporation   55,000

Held-to-maturity securities are valued and displayed at their amortized cost. The securities of the Arbor Corporation are displayed at their original purchase price ($55,000). The security was purchased at par so there was no premium or discount to amortize by year end.

Trading debt securities

Delphi Corporation   105,000

Trading securities are displayed at their fair value as shown above.

Available-for-sale debt securities

Gorman Corporation   0
Jubilee Creations   130,000

Available-for-sale debt securities are displayed at their fair value. Gorman Corporation debt was sold and therefore would not be displayed. Jubilee Creations securities are displayed at fair value as shown.

PART II

Available-for-sale debt securities

Gorman Corporation   (60,000)

Inception to date realized gains or losses would be displayed in the year in which available-for-sale debt securities are sold.

Selling price	65,000
Original cost	(125,000)
Recognized loss	(60,000)

PART III

Trading debt securities

Delphi Corporation   (15,000)

Available-for-sale debt securities

Gorman Corporation   0
Jubilee Creations   0

Unrealized gains and losses associated with the change in value of trading debt securities are reported in the income statement, whereas changes in the value of available-for-sale debt securities are reported in other comprehensive income.

Delphi Corp. FMV at Year 1	120,000
Delphi Corp. FMV at Year 2	105,000
Unrealized loss in income statement	15,000

PART IV

Available-for-sale debt securities

Gorman Corporation—Unrealized loss   (50,000)
Jubilee Creations—Unrealized gain   15,000

The amount of unrealized gains and losses on available-for-sale debt securities displayed in other comprehensive income include the changes in value from year to year for securities owned at the end of the year.

PART V

Jubilee Creations

Cost	$125,000	
Fair value Year 1	140,000	
Unrecognized gain Year 1		$15,000
Fair value Year 1	$140,000	
Fair value Year 2	130,000	
Unrecognized loss Year 2		(10,000)
Ending Balance Year 2—Unrecognized gain		$5,000

The $50,000 unrealized loss on the Gorman securities has been reversed upon the sale of securities in Year 2.

Notes

1 Intangible Assets

1.1 Types of Intangible Assets

Patents, copyrights, franchises, trademarks, and goodwill are common intangible assets.

- Purchased intangibles are recorded at cost.

- Under U.S. GAAP, internally developed intangibles are expensed when incurred because research and development costs cannot be capitalized.

- Under IFRS, research costs related to internally developed intangibles must be expensed, but development costs can be capitalized if certain criteria are met.

- Costs of developing, maintaining, or restoring intangible assets that are not specifically identifiable, or have indeterminate lives, such as goodwill, are expensed when incurred.

1.2 Amortization

Under U.S. GAAP, intangible assets are reported at cost less amortization (finite life intangibles only) and impairment.

1.2.1 Finite Life Intangibles

For intangible assets with finite lives, the cost of the asset less its residual value, is amortized over its useful life, generally using the straight-line method. Goodwill cannot be amortized, but is subject to the impairment test.

1.2.2 Indefinite Life Intangibles

Intangible assets that have no legal or economic lives are considered to have indefinite useful lives. These intangible assets are not amortized but are reviewed for impairment periodically.

1.3 IFRS

Under IFRS, intangible assets are reported using the cost model (same as U.S. GAAP) or the revaluation model.

1.3.1 Revaluation Model

Under the revaluation model, revalued intangible assets are reported at fair value on the revaluation date less subsequent amortization and impairment. Revaluation losses are reported on the income statement and revaluation gains are generally reported in other comprehensive income.

F Intangible Assets

Question 1

During Year 1, Innovative Technologies Corp. spent $900,000 developing a product which was granted a patent on June 30, Year 1. The company paid $20,000 in legal and other fees related to the patent registration process. On January 1, Year 2, the company paid $76,000 in legal fees related to the successful defense of the patent in a patent-infringement lawsuit brought by the company's main competitor. The patent's legal life is 17 years and its estimated economic life is 10 years. What will Innovative Technologies report as amortization expense related to the patent on its December 31, Year 2, income statement if the company uses U.S. GAAP?

1. $1,000
2. $2,000
3. $9,500
4. $10,000

Question 2

In a business combination consummated on January 1, Year 1, Wright acquired an intangible asset with an acquisition cost of $5,000,000, a fair value at December 31, Year 1 of $6,000,000, and a finite life of 50 years and also another intangible asset with an acquisition cost of $3,000,000 and a fair value of $2,500,000 at December 31, Year 1, for which a life cannot be determined.

What amount of intangible amortization should Wright recognize for the year ended December 31, Year 1?

1. $0
2. $100,000
3. $150,000
4. $500,000

1 Requirement

The carrying amounts of intangibles (including goodwill) and fixed assets held for use and to be disposed of need to be reviewed at least annually or whenever events or changes in circumstances indicate that the carrying amount may not be recoverable. The process used to determine impairment depends on the type of asset (i.e., intangible or fixed).

2 Impairment of Intangible Assets Other Than Goodwill

The impairment of an intangible asset is recorded by reducing the cost basis of the intangible asset (credit intangible asset) and recording an impairment loss. If the intangible asset is not totally impaired and the intangible asset has a finite life, then the new cost basis is amortized over the remaining life.

2.1 Impairment Test (U.S. GAAP)

2.1.1 Intangible Assets With Finite Lives

When testing an intangible asset with a finite life for impairment, the future cash flows expected to result from the use of the asset and its eventual disposition need to be estimated when testing for impairment. Under U.S. GAAP, if the sum of *undiscounted* expected (future) cash flows is less than the carrying amount, an impairment loss needs to be recognized.

2.1.2 Intangible Assets With Indefinite Lives

When testing an intangible asset with an indefinite life for impairment, the test for recoverability is performed by comparing the fair value of the asset to its carrying value because it is difficult, if not impossible, to estimate future cash flows. If the fair value is less than the carrying amount, an impairment loss needs to be recognized.

2.1.3 Impairment Loss Calculation

The impairment loss is calculated as the amount by which the carrying amount exceeds the fair value of the asset. U.S. GAAP does not permit the reversal of impairment losses unless the asset is held for disposal.

2.2 Impairment Test (IFRS)

Under IFRS, an impairment loss for a long-lived asset other than goodwill is calculated by comparing the carrying value of the asset to the asset's recoverable amount. IFRS define the recoverable amount as the greater of the asset's fair value less costs to sell and the asset's value in use. Value in use is the present value of the future cash flows expected from the intangible asset. IFRS allow the reversal of impairment losses.

Question 1   MCQ-09672

On December 31, an entity analyzed a finite life trademark with a net carrying value of $750,000 for impairment. The entity determined the following:

Fair value	$700,000
Undiscounted future cash flows	$740,000

What is the impairment loss that will be reported on the December 31 income statement under U.S. GAAP?

1. $0
2. $10,000
3. $40,000
4. $50,000

Question 2   MCQ-09673

On December 31, an entity analyzed a finite life trademark with a net carrying value of $750,000 for impairment. The entity determined the following:

Fair value (less costs to sell)	$700,000
Present value of future cash flows	$710,000

What is the impairment loss that will be reported on the December 31 income statement under IFRS?

1. $0
2. $10,000
3. $40,000
4. $50,000

3 Impairment of Goodwill

3.1 Goodwill Impairment (U.S. GAAP)

Under U.S. GAAP, goodwill impairment is calculated on the reporting unit level. A reporting unit is an operating segment, or one level below an operating segment. The goodwill of one reporting unit may be impaired, while the goodwill for other reporting units may or may not be impaired. The evaluation of goodwill impairment is a one-step process.

3.1.1 Quantitative Evaluation of Goodwill

The evaluation of goodwill impairment involves comparing the carrying value of the reporting unit, including goodwill, to the fair value of the reporting unit, including goodwill. If the fair value exceeds the carrying value, there is no impairment. If the fair value is less than the carrying value, there will be an impairment charge equal to the difference between the fair and carrying values. The charge cannot exceed the value of the goodwill that is allocated to that reporting unit.

3.1.2 Assessing Qualitative Factors

Under U.S. GAAP, the goodwill and indefinite life intangible asset impairment tests have been simplified by allowing companies to test qualitative factors to determine whether it is necessary to perform the relevant quantitative impairment tests.

The quantitative impairment tests are not necessary if, after assessing the relevant qualitative factors, an entity determines that *it is not more likely than not* that the fair value of the reporting unit or indefinite life intangible asset is less than its carrying amount. If the qualitative assessment indicates that there is a greater than fifty percent chance that the fair value of the reporting unit or indefinite life intangible asset is less than its carrying amount, then the entity must perform the quantitative impairment test.

3.2 Goodwill Impairment (IFRS)

Under IFRS, goodwill impairment testing is done at the cash-generating unit (CGU) level. A cash-generating unit is defined as the smallest identifiable group of assets that generates cash inflows that are largely independent of the cash inflows from other assets or groups of assets. The goodwill impairment test is a one-step test in which the carrying value of the CGU is compared to the CGU's recoverable amount, which is the greater of the CGU's fair value less costs to sell and its value in use. Value in use is the present value of the future cash flows expected from the CGU. An impairment loss is recognized to the extent that the carrying value exceeds the recoverable amount. The impairment loss is first allocated to goodwill and then allocated on a pro rata basis to the other assets of the CGU.

Question 3   MCQ-09674

On December 31, Star Corp. had a reporting unit that had a book value of $950,000, including goodwill of $130,000. As part of the company's annual review of goodwill impairment, Star determined that the fair value of the reporting unit was $890,000. Star assigned $840,000 of the reporting units fair value to its assets and liabilities other than goodwill. What is the goodwill impairment loss to be reported on December 31 under U.S. GAAP?

1. $50,000
2. $60,000
3. $80,000
4. $110,000

---

4 Impairment of Fixed Assets

When a fixed asset is totally impaired, the obsolete asset and related accumulated depreciation are removed from the accounts, and a loss is recognized for the difference. When a fixed asset is partially impaired, the asset should be written down to a new cost basis. The cost is then depreciated over the remaining life.

4.1 Impairment Test (U.S. GAAP)

Fixed assets are reviewed for impairment at least annually. Under U.S. GAAP, the impairment test is a two-step test that is similar in concept to the two-step impairment test for goodwill. The details of the accounting treatment are actually slightly different for long-term assets to be held and used than for long-term assets to be disposed of.

4.1.1 Step 1

The first step of the impairment test is a screening test to determine if the asset is impaired. In the first step, the total future undiscounted cash flows expected from the use of the asset is compared to the carrying amount of the asset; if the total undiscounted cash flows is less than the carrying amount, there is an impairment loss. If not, there is no impairment loss and the second step of the impairment test is not needed.

4.1.2 Step 2

The second step of the impairment test measures the amount of the impairment loss by the difference between the fair value of the asset and the carrying amount of the asset. The asset is written down to its fair value, and an impairment loss is recognized in income from continuing operations.

4.1.3 Income Statement Presentation

Income statement presentation depends on whether the assets are to be held and used or are to be disposed of.

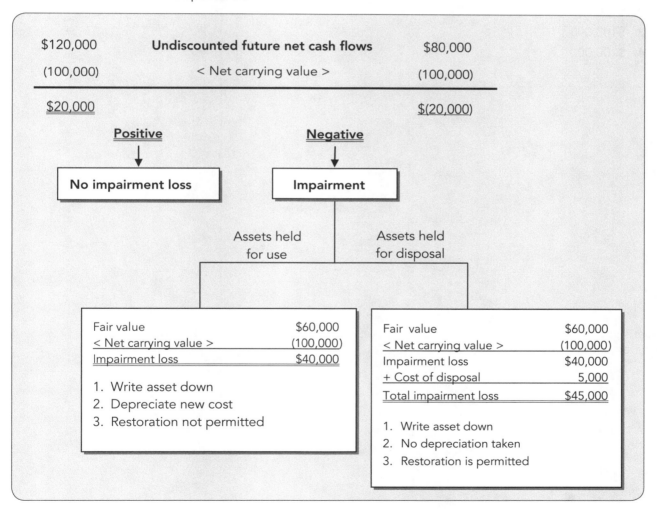

4.2 Impairment Test (IFRS)

Under IFRS, impairment exists if the carrying value of the fixed asset exceeds the higher of 1) fair value less costs to sell; and 2) value in use (present value of expected future cash flows). Restoration is permitted under IFRS for both fixed assets held for sale and fixed assets held for use.

Question 4	MCQ-09285

Sumrall Corporation owns machinery that was purchased 20 years ago. The machinery, which originally cost $2,000,000, has been depreciated using the straight-line method using a 40-year useful life and no salvage value and has a current carrying amount of $1,000,000 and a current fair value of $800,000. Sumrall estimates that the machinery has a remaining useful life of 20 years and will provide net cash inflow of $45,000 per year.

Sumrall should record an impairment loss associated with the machinery of:

1. $0 since there is no impairment.
2. $150,000
3. $100,000
4. $200,000

1 Asset Retirement Obligation

1.1 Definition

An asset retirement obligation (ARO) is a legal obligation associated with the retirement of a tangible long-lived asset that results from the acquisition, construction, development and/or normal operation of a long-lived asset.

- An ARO qualifies for recognition when it meets the definition of a liability.
- Uncertainty about whether performance will be required is factored into the measurement of the liability.

1.2 Measurement of Amounts

- An entity records an asset (asset retirement cost—ARC) and a liability (asset retirement obligation—ARO) equal to the fair value of the asset retirement obligation.
- Accretion expense is the increase in the ARO liability due to the passage of time.
- Depreciation expense decreases the ARC asset reported on the balance sheet.

Question 1   MCQ-09742

Dig Inc. has several natural gas containment systems that must be disposed of in four years at an estimated cost of $200,000. The company plans to book an asset retirement obligation using straight-line depreciation and a 7 percent accretion rate.

After four years, the combination of cumulative accretion and accumulated depreciation will be closest to:

	Accretion	Depreciation
1.	$47,421	$200,000
2.	$47,421	$152,579
3.	$152,579	$47,421
4.	$200,000	$47,421

---

2 Other Liabilities and Debt Covenants

2.1 Current Liabilities

Current liabilities are obligations that mature within one year or the operating cycle, whichever is longer. Current liabilities are valued at their settlement values. The most common current liabilities are:

- Trade accounts payable
- Refundable deposits
- Sales, use and property taxes payable
- Accrued salaries, wages and bonuses
- Unpaid payroll deductions and employer's share of payroll taxes

2.2 Notes Payable

- Notes payable must be recorded at present value at the date of issuance.
- When a note contains either no interest or an unreasonable rate of interest, the present value of the obligation is shown at the appropriate market interest rate. The difference between the face value of the note and its present value is a discount or premium to be amortized over the life of the note using the effective interest method.
  - The market rate of interest should approximate the rate that would have been if negotiated by an independent lender.

2.3 Debt Covenants

Debt covenants prohibit certain actions by debtors that might negatively affect the position of the creditor. When covenants are violated, the loan is in technical default. The creditor and borrower generally work out concessions that may include a higher interest rate to be paid by the borrower.

Question 2 MCQ-09745

An employee earns $5,000 in gross pay per month. In additional to benefits and health care deductions, the employee also has 15 percent withheld for federal and state income taxes, as well as 7.65 percent for Social Security/Medicare taxes. His employer also pays 7.65 percent for its portion of Social Security/Medicare.

Assuming the employer in a given month has not remitted payments to the taxing authority yet, which of the following statements is most accurate?

1. $382.50 will be booked as a payable for the employee portion.
2. $382.50 will be booked as an expense for the employee portion.
3. $1,132.50 will be booked as a payable for the employee portion.
4. $1,132.50 will be booked as an expense for the employer portion.

---

1 Bonds Payable

1.1 Bond Terminology

A bond indenture is a contract that specifies the terms between the bond issuer and the bondholders.

Among the elements of the contract:

■ **Face Value:** The total dollar amount of the bond. Bonds are generally sold in denominations of $1,000 and are quoted in 100s.

■ **Stated/Nominal/Coupon Rate:** The interest to be paid to the bondholders.

■ **Life of the Bond:** The number of periods from the bond date to the maturity date.

■ Frequency of interest payments (annual, semiannual).

1.2 Issuance of Bonds

The selling price of a bond is equal to the *present value* of the future cash payments related to the bond, including both the principal and interest payments using the *effective rate* of interest. The effective/market rate is the rate of interest for bonds of similar risk and maturity on the date the bonds are sold. The effective market rate of interest on a bond is also referred to as the yield.

1.2.1 Bonds Issued at a Discount

A discount results when the market/effective rate exceeds the stated/ coupon rate because investors will pay less than the bond's face value (e.g., 97, 98, 99). Under U.S. GAAP, the discount is amortized over the contractual life of the bonds. Under IFRS, the discount is amortized over the expected life of the bonds.

1.2.2 Bonds Issued at a Premium

A premium results when the market/effective rate is lower than the stated/ coupon rate because investors are willing to pay more than the bond's face value (e.g., 101, 102, 103). Under U.S. GAAP, the premium is amortized over the contractual life of the bonds. Under IFRS, the premium is amortized over the expected life of the bonds.

1.2.3 Bonds Issued at Par

If bonds are issued at par, the stated rate of interest equals the effective rate of interest.

1.2.4 Bond Issuance Costs

Under both IFRS and U.S. GAAP, bond issuance costs are presented on the balance sheet as a direct reduction of the carrying amount of the bond, similar to bond discounts. When bonds are issued, the bond proceeds are recorded net of the bond issuance costs. Bond issuance costs are amortized as interest expense over the life of the bond using the effective interest method.

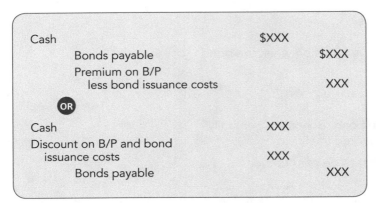

1.3 Issuance of Bonds Between Interest Dates

When bonds are issued between interest dates, the amount of interest that has accrued since the last interest payment is added to the price of the bonds and is reimbursed at the next interest payment date to the purchaser. (The purchaser gets the full interest payment regardless of how long he/she has held the bond.)

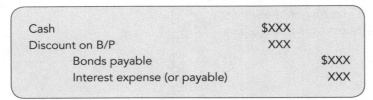

1.4 Amortization of Premiums and Discounts

The carrying amount of a bond is the bond's face value plus the unamortized premium or minus the unamortized discount (and minus any bond issuance costs, as discussed above). At the maturity of a bond, the carrying amount of the bond is equal to the face.

There are two methods to amortize bond discounts, bond issuance costs, or bond premium:

1. **Straight-Line Method:** Tolerated under U.S. GAAP when the difference between this method and the effective interest amortization method is immaterial; prohibited under IFRS.

2. **Effective Interest Amortization Method:** U.S. GAAP/IFRS.

1.4.1 Straight-Line Method

The straight-line method amortizes the premium or discount equally over the life of the bonds.

1.4.2 Effective Interest Method

With the effective interest method, each interest payment is divided into an interest and principal component. The interest component is equal to the carrying amount of the bond at the beginning of the period times the effective interest rate. The difference between the interest component and the interest payment is the amortization of the premium or discount (including any bond issuance costs), and is used to adjust the carrying amount of the bond by decreasing the unamortized premium or discount.

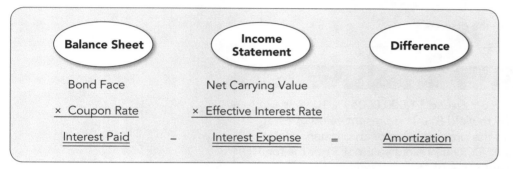

Date	Cash Interest 4%*	Interest Expense 5%**	Amortized Discount	Unamortized Discount	Carrying Amount
1/1/Year 1				50,000	950,000
6/30/Year 1	40,000	47,500	7,500	42,500	957,500
12/31/Year 1	40,000	47,875	7,875	34,625	965,375

*(1,000,000 × 0.04)

**(950,000 × 0.05)

Interest expense	$47,500	
Discount on B/P		$7,500
Cash		40,000
OR		
Interest expense	XXX	
Premium on B/P	XXX	
Cash		XXX

1.5 Retirement of Bonds

Corporations can call or retire bonds prior to maturity. Bonds are retired as a percentage of face value (e.g., 98, 101).

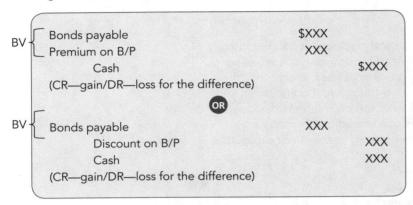

BV ⎰ Bonds payable $XXX
    ⎱ Premium on B/P   XXX
          Cash $XXX
    (CR—gain/DR—loss for the difference)

OR

BV ⎰ Bonds payable   XXX
          Discount on B/P   XXX
          Cash   XXX
    (CR—gain/DR—loss for the difference)

Question 1   MCQ-09381

On January 1, Year 1, Congo.com issued $1,000,000, 9% 10-year bonds (interest paid annually) to yield 8%. The present value of $1 at 9% for 10 years is 0.4224 and the present value of an ordinary annuity of $1 at 9% for 10 years is 6.4177. The present value of $1 at 8% for 10 years is 0.4632 and the present value of an ordinary annuity of $1 at 8% for 10 years is 6.7101. Which of the following is closest to the selling price of the bond?

1. $920,000
2. $1,000,000
3. $1,040,800
4. $1,067,100

Question 2   MCQ-09261

On July 1, Year 1, Cobb Company issued 9% bonds in the face amount of $1,000,000 which mature in ten years. The bonds were issued for $939,000 to yield 10%, resulting in a bond discount of $61,000. Cobb uses the effective interest method of amortizing bond discount. Interest is payable annually on June 30.

At June 30, Year 3, Cobb's unamortized bond discount should be:

1. $52,810
2. $57,100
3. $48,800
4. $43,000

2 Imputing Interest

Notes receivable and notes payable contain an interest element. Money is not loaned for free or for a below-market interest rate. Notes are recorded at present value when the interest rate is not stated or when the stated interest rate is unreasonably low. The difference between the face amount of the note and the present value of the note is recorded as a discount and amortized over the life of the note.

3 Troubled Debt Restructuring

A troubled debt restructuring is one in which the creditor allows the debtor certain concessions such as reduced interest rates, extension of maturity dates, reduction of the face amount of the debt, and reduction of the amount of accrued interest as a result of the debtor's financial difficulty.

3.1 Accounting by the Debtor

3.1.1 Transfer of Assets

■ Recognize gain/loss on:

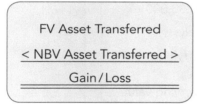

FV Asset Transferred
< NBV Asset Transferred >
Gain / Loss

■ Recognize gain on:

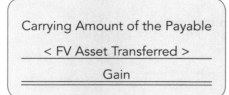

Carrying Amount of the Payable
< FV Asset Transferred >
Gain

3.1.2 Transfer of Equity

■ Recognize gain on:

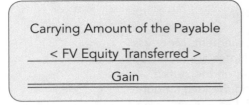

3.1.3 Modification of Terms

In a modification, the debtor accounts for the effects prospectively and does not change the carrying amount or show a gain unless the carrying amount exceeds the total future cash payments specified by the new terms.

3.2 Accounting by the Creditor

A loan restructured in a troubled debt restructuring is accounted for by the creditor as an impaired loan. Bad debt expense is recognized for the difference between the loan amount and the fair value of whatever has been received and/or the present value of expected cash to be received, discounted at the loan's historical effective interest rate.

Question 3   MCQ-09746

Ansley Inc. (which uses IFRS) has debt on its books with a current value of $425,000. For the first time in its history, the company receives debt modifications that will result in future cash flows totaling $280,000.

As a result of the modifications, the company will most likely:

1. Handle the change prospectively, and keep the carrying value the same.

2. Handle the change prospectively, and lower the carrying value over time.

3. Book a gain in current operations and reduce the carrying value of the liability.

4. Book a reduction in interest expense and reduce the carrying value of the liability.

---

1 Capital Stock

1.1 Common Stock

Common stock (CS) normally has a par (or stated) value, for instance, CS $1 par value issued at $5 per share.

DR Cash	$5	
CR Common stock		$1
CR APIC—CS		4

1.2 Preferred Stock

Preferred stock (PS) may be cumulative, noncumulative, or participating as to the payment of dividends and generally has a preferred claim to assets on liquidation of the business. PS $10 par value is issued at $30.

DR Cash	$30	
CR Preferred stock		$10
CR APIC—PS		20

1.2.1 Cumulative

Cumulative preferred stockholders receive current dividends and all dividends in arrears (unpaid from prior years) before dividends are paid to common stockholders.

1.2.2 Participating

Any amounts available for dividend distribution after both preferred and common stockholders receive a specified payment based on the same percentage is divided between preferred and common stockholders on a pro rata basis.

1.2.3 Mandatorily Redeemable

Mandatorily redeemable preferred stock is classified as a liability because it has a maturity date, similar to debt instruments.

1.3   Shares Authorized, Issued, and Outstanding

- **Authorized:** Legal number of shares available for sale (maximum).

- **Issued:** Number of shares sold.

- **Outstanding:** Shares issued less treasury shares. Only outstanding shares are entitled to dividends.

Question 1   MCQ-09325

On September 1, Year 1, Royal Corp., a newly formed company, had the following stock issued and outstanding:

- Common stock, no par, $1 stated value, 5,000 shares originally issued for $15 per share.
- Preferred stock, $10 par value, 1,500 shares originally issued for $25 per share.

Royal's September 1, Year 1, statement of stockholders' equity should report:

	Common Stock	Preferred Stock	Additional Paid-In Capital
1.	$5,000	$15,000	$92,500
2.	5,000	37,500	70,000
3.	75,000	37,500	0
4.	75,000	15,000	22,500

---

2 Treasury Stock

Treasury stock (TS) is stock that has been issued and then repurchased by the issuer. Treasury stock is reported as a contra account to equity. There are two methods used to account for treasury stock under U.S. GAAP: the cost method and the par value method.

2.1 Cost Method

Under the cost method, treasury stock is recorded at cost. The total cost of a treasury share is deducted from the total of the stockholders' equity on the balance sheet. When the TS is reissued for less than its acquisition price the loss is recognized by debiting APIC—treasury stock. Retained earnings is debited if there is not a sufficient balance in the APIC—TS account. When TS is reissued for more than its acquisition price the gain is recognized by crediting APIC—treasury stock.

2.2 Par Value Method

Under the par value method, treasury stock is recorded at par value, and APIC is reduced for the amount of additional paid-in capital that was initially recognized on issuance. The total cost of the TS (par value) is deducted from the common stock account on the balance sheet. When treasury stock is reacquired for less than the original issue price (gain), APIC—treasury stock is recognized. When TS is reacquired for more than the original issue price (loss), any APIC—treasury stock is eliminated and then retained earnings is reduced.

2.3 Gains and Losses

Gains and losses on treasury stock transactions are not reported on the income statement. A company cannot report income dealing in its own stock. Treasury stock is not an asset. Treasury stock does not vote and does not receive dividends.

J Equity

2.4 Summary Chart

Summary Chart of Journal Entries

1. Original Issue

10,000 shares of $10 par value, CS are sold for $15 per share	Cash	150,000	
	Common stock		100,000
Income taxes paid	APIC—CS		50,000

	Cost Method			Par Value Method		
2. Buy Back Below						
200 shares repurchased for $12 per share	Treasury stock	2,400		Treasury stock	2,000	
	Cash		2,400	APIC—CS	1,000	
				Cash		2,400
				APIC—TS		600
3. Reissue Above Cost						
100 shares repurchased for $12 are resold for $15	Cash	1,500		Cash	1,500	
	Treasury stock		1,200	Treasury stock		1,000
	APIC—TS		300	APIC—CS		500
4. Reissue Below Cost						
100 shares repurchased for $12 are resold for $3	Cash	300		Cash	300	
	APIC—TS	300		APIC—TS	600	
	Retained earnings	600		Retained earnings	100	
	Treasury stock		1,200	Treasury stock		1,000

Note: Retained earnings may be debited, but never credited in treasury stock transactions.

Question 2 — MCQ-09426

On January 1, Year 1, Black Dog Corp. began operations and issued 30,000 shares of $5 par common stock for $9/share. On June 30, the company bought back 10,000 shares for $8/share. Then, on September 15, the company resold 5,000 shares for $12/share. What amount of total additional paid-in capital should Black Dog report on its December 31, Year 1 balance sheet if Black Dog uses the cost method to account for its treasury stock?

1. $20,000
2. $120,000
3. $140,000
4. $165,000

3 Dividends and Stock Splits

3.1 Cash Dividends

Cash dividends may be declared on common and/or preferred stock.

Relevant dates for cash dividends are:

■ **Declaration Date:**

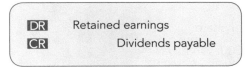

DR   Retained earnings
CR   Dividends payable

■ **Record Date:** The date the stockholders must own the stock in order to receive the dividend declared.

No entry

■ **Payment Date:** The date the dividends are actually disbursed.

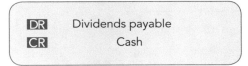

DR   Dividends payable
CR   Cash

3.2 Property Dividends

Property dividends are distributions of noncash assets, such as inventories and investment securities. Property dividends are recorded at *fair value*.

3.3 Stock Dividends

A stock dividend of less than 20–25 percent of the outstanding capital stock is recorded at fair value (small dividend). A stock dividend of greater than 20–25 percent of the capital stock is recorded at par value (large dividend).

3.4 Liquidating Dividends

A liquidating dividend is a dividend in excess of retained earnings.

3.5 Stock Splits

In a stock split, the number of shares outstanding is increased, and the par value is decreased. (In a reverse split, the opposite is true.) There is no change in the total book value of shares outstanding and a memo entry is used to acknowledge a stock split.

Note

Recipient of stock dividends and stock splits recognizes no income. The basis of each share of stock is adjusted accordingly.

3.6 Stock Rights/Warrants

Stock rights/warrants give the holder the right to acquire shares of stock on the payment of a defined amount. A memo entry is made when the rights are issued.

Question 3	MCQ-09265

Boone Corporation's outstanding capital stock at December 15 consisted of the following:

- 30,000 shares of 5% cumulative preferred stock, par value $10 per share, fully participating as to dividends. No dividends were in arrears.
- 200,000 shares of common stock, par value $1 per share.

On December 15, Boone declared dividends of $100,000. What was the amount of dividends payable to Boone's common stockholders?

1. $10,000
2. $34,000
3. $40,000
4. $47,500

4 Retained Earnings

Retained earnings (or deficits) are cumulative earnings (or losses) during the life of the corporation that have not been paid as dividends. A portion of retained earnings may be appropriated (restricted) for legal reasons or as a discretionary action of management. The appropriated retained earnings is distinguished from the unappropriated retained earnings account in the balance sheet.

Retained Earnings
Beginning retained earnings
+ Net income/loss
− Dividends (cash, property, and stock) declared
± Prior period adjustments
± Accounting changes (cumulative effect)
− Treasury stock (when necessary)
+ Adjustment from quasi-reorganization
Ending retained earnings

J Equity

Task-Based Simulations

Task-Based Simulation 1: Retained Earnings

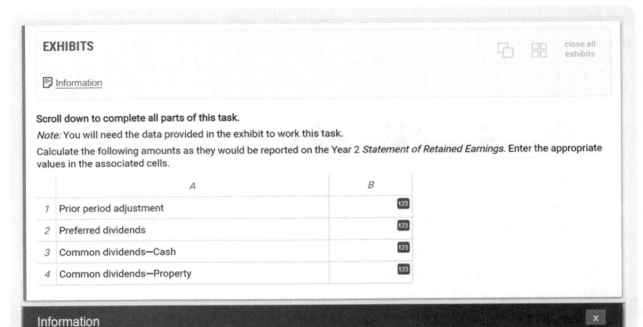

EXHIBITS   close all
                                                                        exhibits

📄 Information

Scroll down to complete all parts of this task.

Note: You will need the data provided in the exhibit to work this task.

Calculate the following amounts as they would be reported on the Year 2 *Statement of Retained Earnings*. Enter the appropriate values in the associated cells.

	A	B
1	Prior period adjustment	123
2	Preferred dividends	123
3	Common dividends—Cash	123
4	Common dividends—Property	123

Information

Kansas Inc. is a publicly held company whose shares are traded in the over-the-counter market. The stockholders' equity accounts at December 31, Year 1, of the prior year had the following balances:

Preferred stock, $100 par value, 6% cumulative; 5,000 shares authorized; 2,000 issued and outstanding	$200,000
Common stock, $1 par value, 150,000 shares authorized; 100,000 issued and outstanding	100,000
Additional paid-in capital	800,000
Retained earnings	1,586,000
Total stockholders' equity	$2,686,000

Transactions during Year 2 and other information relating to the stockholders' equity accounts were as follows:

- February 1, Year 2: Issued 13,000 shares of common stock to Ram Co. in exchange for land. On the date issued, the stock had a market price of $11 per share. The land had a carrying value on Ram's books of $135,000, and an assessed value for property taxes of $90,000.
- March 1, Year 2: Purchased 5,000 shares of its own common stock to be held as treasury stock for $14 per share. Kansas uses the cost method to account for treasury stock. Transactions in treasury stock are legal in the state of incorporation.
- May 10, Year 2: Declared a property dividend of marketable securities held by Kansas to common shareholders. The securities had a carrying value of $600,000; fair value on relevant dates were:

Date of declaration (May 10, Year 2)	$720,000
Date of record (May 25, Year 2)	758,000
Date of distribution (June 1, Year 2)	736,000

- October 1, Year 2: Reissued 2,000 shares of treasury stock for $16 per share.
- November 4, Year 2: Declared a cash dividend of $1.50 per share to all common shareholders of record November 15. The dividend was paid on November 25.
- December 20, Year 2: Declared the required annual cash dividend on preferred stock for Year 2. The dividend was paid on January 5, Year 3.
- January 16, Year 3: Before closing the accounting records for Year 2, Kansas became aware that no amortization had been recorded for the prior year for a patent purchased on July 1, Year 1. The patent was properly capitalized at $320,000 and had an estimated useful life of eight years when purchased. The company's income tax rate is 30%. The appropriate correcting entry was recorded on the same day.
- Adjusted net income for Year 2 was $838,000.

Explanation

	A	B
1	Prior period adjustment	$14,000
2	Preferred dividends	$12,000
3	Common dividends—Cash	$165,000
4	Common dividends—Property	$720,000

Row 1: $14,000

Prior period adjustment which reduces beginning retained earnings balance for prior year error; patent amortization not recorded:

Patent cost $320,000 / Useful life 8 years = $40,000/year × 1/2 year =	$20,000
Less 30% income tax	(6,000)
Prior period adjustment (net of tax)	$14,000

Row 2: $12,000

Preferred dividends ($100 par value at 6% × 2,000 outstanding shares)

Row 3: $165,000

Common dividends - Cash (110,000 common shares outstanding on Nov. 4 = $1.50)

Row 4: $720,000

Common dividends - Property (fair market value of marketable securities on date of declaration)

J   Equity

Task-Based Simulation 2: Stockholders' Equity

EXHIBITS   close all exhibits

📄 Information

Scroll down to complete all parts of this task.

Note: You will need the data provided in the exhibit to work this task.

Calculate the following amounts as they would be reported on the Year 2 *Statement of Stockholders' Equity*. Enter the appropriate values in the associated cells.

	A	B
1	Number of common shares issued at December 31, Year 2	123
2	Amount of common stock issued	123
3	Additional paid-in capital, including treasury stock transactions	123
4	Treasury stock	123

Information   ☒

Kansas Inc. is a publicly held company whose shares are traded in the over-the-counter market. The stockholders' equity accounts at December 31, Year 1, of the prior year had the following balances:

Preferred stock, $100 par value, 6% cumulative; 5,000 shares authorized; 2,000 issued and outstanding	$200,000
Common stock, $1 par value, 150,000 shares authorized; 100,000 issued and outstanding	100,000
Additional paid-in capital	800,000
Retained earnings	1,586,000
Total stockholders' equity	$2,686,000

Transactions during Year 2 and other information relating to the stockholders' equity accounts were as follows:

- February 1, Year 2: Issued 13,000 shares of common stock to Ram Co. in exchange for land. On the date issued, the stock had a market price of $11 per share. The land had a carrying value on Ram's books of $135,000, and an assessed value for property taxes of $90,000.
- March 1, Year 2: Purchased 5,000 shares of its own common stock to be held as treasury stock for $14 per share. Kansas uses the cost method to account for treasury stock. Transactions in treasury stock are legal in the state of incorporation.
- May 10, Year 2: Declared a property dividend of marketable securities held by Kansas to common shareholders. The securities had a carrying value of $600,000; fair value on relevant dates were:

Date of declaration (May 10, Year 2)	$720,000
Date of record (May 25, Year 2)	758,000
Date of distribution (June 1, Year 2)	736,000

- October 1, Year 2: Reissued 2,000 shares of treasury stock for $16 per share.
- November 4, Year 2: Declared a cash dividend of $1.50 per share to all common shareholders of record November 15. The dividend was paid on November 25.
- December 20, Year 2: Declared the required annual cash dividend on preferred stock for Year 2. The dividend was paid on January 5, Year 3.
- January 16, Year 3: Before closing the accounting records for Year 2, Kansas became aware that no amortization had been recorded for the prior year for a patent purchased on July 1, Year 1. The patent was properly capitalized at $320,000 and had an estimated useful life of eight years when purchased. The company's income tax rate is 30%. The appropriate correcting entry was recorded on the same day.
- Adjusted net income for Year 2 was $838,000.

Explanation

	A	B
1	Number of common shares issued at December 31, Year 2	113,000
2	Amount of common stock issued	$113,000
3	Additional paid-in capital, including treasury stock transactions	$934,000
4	Treasury stock	$42,000

Row 1: 113,000

Beginning balance 12/31/Year 1	100,000
Shares issued for land 2/1/Year 2	13,000
Total shares 12/31/Year 2	113,000

Other share transactions during Year 2 do not change number of shares issued, only the number of shares outstanding.

Row 2: $113,000

Balance (100,000 shares × $1 par)	$100,000
Land for shares (13,000 shares × $1)	13,000
	$113,000

Row 3: $934,000

Balance (100,000 shares × $1 par)		$800,000
Land for shares (13,000 shares × $10)		130,000
2,000 shares treasury stock sold × $16	$32,000	
Less cost of treasury stock (2,000 × $14)	(28,000)	
Excess ($2,000 × $2)		4,000
		$934,000

Row 4: $42,000

5,000 treasury shares × $14 cost	$70,000
(2,000) treasury shares × $14 cost	(28,000)
3,000 treasury shares × $14 cost	$42,000

Notes

1 The Five-Step Approach

Revenue is recognized when the good or service is transferred to the customer and the performance obligation is satisfied. The amount of revenue to be recognized should reflect the expected consideration that the entity is entitled to receive.

The five-step approach should be implemented by an entity in order to properly recognize revenue. The steps are as follows:

- **Step 1:** Identify the contract with the customer—a contract is an agreement between parties that creates enforceable rights or obligations.
- **Step 2:** Identify the separate performance obligations in the contract—a performance obligation is a promise to transfer either a good or a service to a customer.
- **Step 3:** Determine the transaction price—the transaction price is the amount of consideration that an entity is entitled to receive in exchange for transferring goods and/or services to a customer.
- **Step 4:** Allocate the transaction price to the separate performance obligations—if a contract contains more than one performance obligation, the overall transaction price will need to be allocated to each separate obligation.
- **Step 5:** Recognize revenue when or as the entity satisfies each performance obligation—revenue is recognized when the performance obligation is satisfied either at a point in time or over time through transferring the good/service to the customer.

2 Specific Applications Within Revenue Recognition

There are unique aspects to revenue recognition that are applicable in many distinct scenarios, as described below:

- Incremental costs to obtain a contract

  Costs to obtain a contract are treated as assets if the entity expects to recover them. Costs are treated as expenses if they are borne regardless of whether the contract is obtained.

- Costs to fulfill a contract

  Costs to fulfill a contract are treated as an asset if they relate directly to the contract, they generate/enhance the entity's resources, and they are expected to be recovered.

■ **Principal vs. agent**

A principal has control over the good/service prior to transfer and will recognize revenue equal to expected gross consideration. An agent does not have control and will recognize revenue equal to a fee/commission.

■ **Repurchase agreements**

Repurchase agreements are contracts where an entity sells an asset and promises or has the option to repurchase the asset later. An obligation to repurchase is a forward, a right to repurchase at an entity's option is a call option, and a right to repurchase at the customer's option is a put option.

■ **Bill-and-hold arrangements**

Bill-and-hold arrangements allow revenue to be recognized prior to the customer receiving the product as long as there is a substantive reason for holding the product, the entity cannot use or redirect the product, and the product is separately identified and ready for transfer to the purchasing customer.

■ **Consignment**

Consignment arrangements exist when an entity provides a product to a dealer to be held until it is ultimately sold to a third-party customer. Revenue is recognized either upon ultimate sale to a customer or after the expiration of a defined period of time.

■ **Warranties**

Warranties are treated as separate performance obligations distinct from the product covered in the contract if the warranty is not required by law, if the coverage period is lengthy, and if there are no specific tasks required regarding compliance assurance.

■ **Right to return**

When a customer has a right to return, the selling entity should book revenue for the amount of consideration it expects to receive, a refund liability, and an asset related to subsequent product recovery.

■ **Long-term contracts**

Accounting for long-term contracts (construction and infrastructure, real estate construction, engineering, aerospace, and defense) often includes unique characteristics, such as a contract term that spans several years, multiple-year maintenance agreements, and the ongoing application of significant judgments as modifications occur.

Question 1	MCQ-09376

Sell2All Inc. accounts for its revenue under the installment sales method. In Year 1, Sell2All sold inventory with a cost of $300,000 for $400,000 and collected $100,000. In Year 2, Sell2All sold inventory with a cost of $500,000 for $750,000 and collected $400,000, including $100,000 related to the Year 1 sales and $300,000 related to the Year 2 sales. What amount of earned gross profit should Sell2All report on its December 31, Year 2, balance sheet?

1. $100,000
2. $125,000
3. $133,200
4. $400,000

---

1 Defined Benefit Pension Plans

Defined benefit plans define the benefits to be paid to employees based on factors such as years of service and compensation levels at retirement.

Defined contribution plans specify the amount of the employer's contributions to the plan; employee retirement benefits are determined based on the value of such contributions upon retirement.

1.1 Pension Obligations

1.1.1 Projected Benefit Obligation

The projected benefit obligation (PBO) is the actuarial present value of all benefits attributed by the plan's benefit formula. The PBO is used in the calculation of funded status, service cost, and interest cost and is computed using future salary levels.

1.1.2 Accumulated Benefit Obligation

The accumulated benefit obligation (ABO) is the actuarial present value of benefits attributed by a formula using current and past salary levels.

1.1.3 Defined Benefit Obligation

Under IFRS, the pension liability is called the defined benefit obligation (DBO). The DBO is very similar to the U.S. GAAP PBO.

1.2 Pension Plan Funded Status

Pension plans are accounted for on the accrual basis. Defined benefit pension plans are reported on the balance sheet based on funded status:

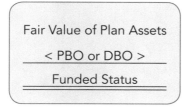

Fair Value of Plan Assets

< PBO or DBO >

Funded Status

1.2.1 U.S. GAAP

Under U.S. GAAP, companies are required to aggregate all *overfunded* (fair value of plan assets > PBO) pension plans and report them as a non-current asset on the balance sheet. All *underfunded* (fair value of plan assets < PBO) pension plans should also be aggregated and reported as a current liability, a non-current liability, or both. A pension plan is reported as a current liability to the extent that the benefits payable in the next 12 months exceed the fair value of the plan's assets.

1.2.2 IFRS

Under IFRS, the funded status (DBO – fair value of plan assets) of the pension plan is reported on the balance sheet as the net defined benefit liability (asset). A liability is reported if the plan is underfunded (DBO > fair value of plan assets) and an asset is reported if the plan is overfunded (DBO < fair value of plan assets). IFRS do not specify whether an entity should classify the net defined benefit liability (asset) as current or non-current.

1.3 Reporting Changes in Funded Status in OCI

1.3.1 U.S. GAAP

Under U.S. GAAP, a change in the funded status of a pension plan due to pension net losses or gains or prior service cost is reported in the period incurred as a component of accumulated other comprehensive income, net of tax. Any unrecognized net transition obligation (or asset) is also reported in accumulated other comprehensive income.

1.3.2 IFRS

Under IFRS, prior (past) service cost is reported as a component of service cost on the income statement in the period incurred. Pension gains and losses are reported in other comprehensive income in the period incurred and are not reclassified (amortized) to the income statement.

To report net loss or prior service cost:

DR	Other comprehensive income
CR	Pension benefit asset/liability
DR	Deferred tax asset
CR	Deferred tax benefit—OCI

To report net gain or net transition asset:

DR	Pension benefit asset/liability
CR	Other comprehensive income
DR	Deferred tax expense—OCI
CR	Deferred tax liability

1.4   Pension Reclassification Adjustments

Pension net gains or losses, prior service cost, and net transition assets or obligations remain in accumulated other comprehensive income until recognized in net periodic pension cost through amortization.

Reclassification adjustment to record amortization of net loss, prior service cost, or net transition obligation to net periodic pension cost:

DR	Net periodic pension cost
CR	Other comprehensive income
DR	Deferred tax benefit—OCI
CR	Deferred tax benefit—income statement

Reclassification adjustment to record amortization of net gain or net transition asset to net periodic pension cost:

DR	Other comprehensive income
CR	Net periodic pension cost
DR	Deferred tax expense—income statement
CR	Deferred tax expense—OCI

1.5   Pension Plan Contributions

An employer's contribution to its defined benefit pension plan(s) increases the pension benefit asset (overfunded pension plans) or decreases the pension benefit liability (underfunded pension plans).

Journal entry to record pension plan contribution:

DR	Pension benefit asset/liability
CR	Cash

1.6   Pension Expense Components (SIRAGE)

Under U.S. GAAP, the amount of the net periodic pension cost is calculated using the following six components:

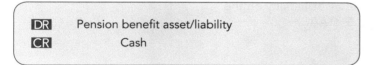

+	**S**ervice cost (current)
+	**I**nterest cost (on the projected benefit obligation)
−	**R**eturn on plan assets (expected or actual)
+	**A**mortization of unrecognized prior service cost
±	(**G**ains) and losses
±	Amortization of **E**xisting net (asset) or obligation

L   Compensation and Benefits

Prior service cost, gains and losses, and existing net obligations or assets are amortized and charged to net periodic pension cost over a specified period of time.

Under U.S. GAAP, service cost is reported as an operating expense on the income statement in the same line with other compensation costs. The other components of net periodic pension cost are presented on the income statement, separately or in total, below income from operations.

Under IFRS, defined benefit cost includes service cost and net interest on the defined benefit liability (asset). The components of defined benefit cost are generally reported separately on the income statement; there is no requirement that these amounts be aggregated and presented as one amount.

Question 1   MCQ-09279

Do It Right Inc.'s actuary provided the company with the following information regarding its defined benefit pension plan for the year ended December 31, Year 7:

Fair value of plan assets	$5,580,000
Accumulated benefit obligation	3,400,000
Projected benefit obligation	4,930,000
Unrecognized prior service cost	400,000
Unrecognized transition obligation	275,000
Unrecognized net gain	140,000
Expected benefit obligation - Year 8	250,000

The company reported net periodic pension cost of $310,000 on its income statement and made a $500,000 contribution to the pension plan during Year 7. The company's effective tax rate is 40%. What amount should Do It Right record as a pension asset/liability on the December 31, Year 7, balance sheet under U.S. GAAP?

1. $650,000 current liability.
2. $2,180,000 non-current liability.
3. $650,000 non-current asset.
4. $2,180,000 current asset.

Question 2   MCQ-09264

The following information pertains to Burnel Corporation's defined benefit pension plan for Year 1:

Service cost	$160,000
Actual and expected gain on plan assets	35,000
Unexpected loss on pension plan assets related to a Year 1 disposal of a subsidiary	40,000
Amortization of unrecognized prior service cost	5,000
Annual interest on pension obligation	50,000

What is Burnel's total net periodic pension cost for the period?

1. $250,000
2. $220,000
3. $210,000
4. $180,000

2 Postretirement Benefits Other Than Pensions

2.1   Postretirement Benefits

Postretirement benefits include:

- Health care insurance
- Life insurance
- Welfare benefits
- Tuition assistance

2.2   Financial Statement Reporting

Postretirement benefits must be reported on the balance sheet (funded status and OCI components), income statement (**SIRAGE**), and footnotes in the same manner as pensions if:

- the obligation is attributable to employees' services already rendered;
- the employees' rights accumulate or vest;
- payment is probable; and
- the amount of benefits can be reasonably estimated.

Postretirement benefits must be accrued during the period the employee works, called the "attribution period" (date hired to date fully vested).

The calculation of the funded status of a postretirement benefit plan is done using the APBO (accumulated postretirement benefit obligation), which is the present value of future benefits that have vested as of the measurement date:

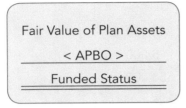

Fair Value of Plan Assets

< APBO >

Funded Status

Question 3   MCQ-09758

Churchill Inc. is a public company operating under U.S. GAAP that offers its former employees postretirement benefits. Which of the following statements is most accurate regarding Churchill's nonpension benefits?

1. The EPBO for the benefits will be equal to or greater than the APBO as a result of any nonvested benefits.

2. Although the assumed health care trend rate is critical to the company's estimates, it is not a required disclosure.

3. Any differences between the expected and actual returns must be recognized in the income statement in the period incurred.

4. The cost associated with retiree benefits may be accrued before services are rendered, as long as they can be reasonably estimated.

---

3 Stock Options

Compensatory stock options should be valued at the fair value of the options issued. The compensation expense is allocated over the service period.

3.1   Determining Fair Value

Either a Black-Scholes model or a lattice model, a type of binomial model, can be used to determine the fair value of the option. The statement requires the use of a valuation technique or model that returns the best estimate of the fair value of the option. Fair value will be given on the CPA Exam.

The models that estimate the value of stock based compensation should consider the following variables:

- The exercise price
- The expected life of the option
- The current price of the stock
- The expected volatility of the stock
- The expected dividends on the stock
- The risk-free rate of return for the expected term of the option

3.2   Accounting for Stock Options

Example
Accounting for Stock Options

On January 1, Year 1, Green Co. granted options exercisable after December 31, Year 2, to purchase 50,000 shares of $1 par common stock for $8 per share. Using an acceptable valuation model, the options had a total fair value of $50,000. The options are to serve as compensation for services during Year 1 and Year 2.

Journal Entry: January 1, Year 1—No entry required

Journal Entry: To allocate compensation cost to Year 1 operations

DR	Compensation expense	$25,000	
CR	Additional paid-in capital—stock options		$25,000

Journal Entry: To allocate compensation cost to Year 2 operations

DR	Compensation expense	25,000	
CR	Additional paid-in capital—stock options		25,000

On January 1, Year 3, all options are exercised.

Journal Entry: To record the exercise of the options

DR	Cash (50,000 × $8)	400,000	
DR	Additional paid in capital—stock options	50,000	
CR	Common stock (50,000 × $1 par)		50,000
CR	Additional paid in capital in excess of par (common stock)		400,000

Question 4

MCQ-09295

On January 1, Year 1, Sweeney Company granted an employee options to purchase 100 shares of Sweeney's common stock at $40 per share. The options became exercisable on December 31, Year 1, after the employee had completed one year of service, and were exercised on that date. Market prices of the stock and fair values of the options were as follows:

	Market Price	Fair Value
January 1, Year 1	$50	$61
December 31, Year 1	$65	$75

What amount should Sweeney recognize as compensation cost for Year 1?

1. $0
2. $2,100
3. $4,000
4. $6,100

Task-Based Simulations

Task-Based Simulation: Stock Options

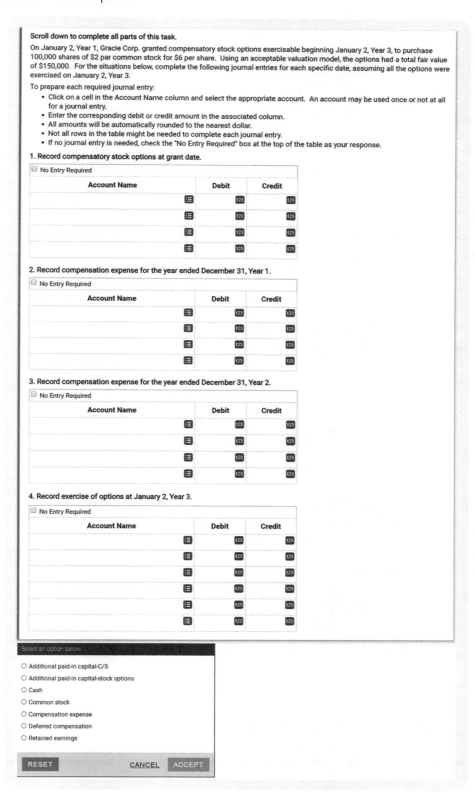

Scroll down to complete all parts of this task.

On January 2, Year 1, Gracie Corp. granted compensatory stock options exercisable beginning January 2, Year 3, to purchase 100,000 shares of $2 par common stock for $6 per share. Using an acceptable valuation model, the options had a total fair value of $150,000. For the situations below, complete the following journal entries for each specific date, assuming all the options were exercised on January 2, Year 3.

To prepare each required journal entry:
- Click on a cell in the Account Name column and select the appropriate account. An account may be used once or not at all for a journal entry.
- Enter the corresponding debit or credit amount in the associated column.
- All amounts will be automatically rounded to the nearest dollar.
- Not all rows in the table might be needed to complete each journal entry.
- If no journal entry is needed, check the "No Entry Required" box at the top of the table as your response.

1. Record compensatory stock options at grant date.

☐ No Entry Required

Account Name	Debit	Credit

2. Record compensation expense for the year ended December 31, Year 1.

☐ No Entry Required

Account Name	Debit	Credit

3. Record compensation expense for the year ended December 31, Year 2.

☐ No Entry Required

Account Name	Debit	Credit

4. Record exercise of options at January 2, Year 3.

☐ No Entry Required

Account Name	Debit	Credit

Select an option below

○ Additional paid-in capital-C/S
○ Additional paid-in capital-stock options
○ Cash
○ Common stock
○ Compensation expense
○ Deferred compensation
○ Retained earnings

RESET   CANCEL   ACCEPT

L   Compensation and Benefits

Explanation

1. Record compensatory stock options at grant date.

☑ No Entry Required		
Account Name	**Debit**	**Credit**

Not applicable. No journal entry is required at the grant date of stock options.

2. Record compensation expense for the year ended December 31, Year 1.

☐ No Entry Required		
Account Name	**Debit**	**Credit**
Compensation expense	$75,000	
Additional paid-in capital–stock options		$75,000

Compensation expense is ratably allocated to the benefiting periods ($150,000/2 year service period).

3. Record compensation expense for the year ended December 31, Year 2.

☐ No Entry Required		
Account Name	**Debit**	**Credit**
Compensation expense	$75,000	
Additional paid-in capital–stock options		$75,000

Compensation expense is ratably allocated to the benefiting periods ($150,000/2 year service period).

4. Record exercise of options at January 2, Year 3.

☐ No Entry Required		
Account Name	**Debit**	**Credit**
Cash	$600,000	
Additional paid-in capital–stock options	$150,000	
Common stock		$200,000
Additional paid-in capital–C/S		$550,000

Exercise of the stock options is recorded as a charge to cash at the exercise price (100,000 shares at $6 per share), a reversal of the amounts recorded in APIC stock options and credit to shares purchased at par (100,000 shares at $2 per share), and a credit to APIC common stock for the difference.

1 Interperiod Tax Allocation

1.1 Total Income Tax Expense

Total income tax expense or benefit for the year is the sum of:

- Current income tax expense/benefit; and
- Deferred income tax expense/benefit.

1.2 Current Income Tax Expense

Current income tax expense/benefit is equal to the taxable income for the current year, multiplied by the current tax rate.

1.3 Deferred Income Tax Expense

Deferred income tax expense/benefit is equal to temporary differences multiplied by the future tax rate, or the change in deferred tax liability or asset account on the balance sheet from the beginning of the current year to the end of the current year (called the "balance sheet approach").

1.4 Summary

Thus, total income tax expense/benefit can be depicted as follows:

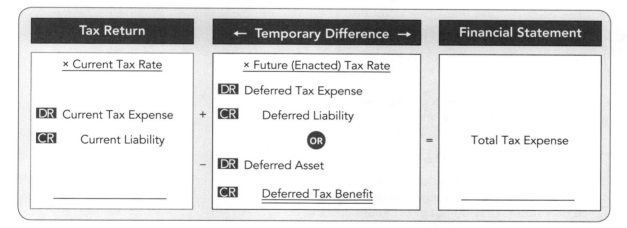

Tax Return		Temporary Difference	Financial Statement
× Current Tax Rate		× Future (Enacted) Tax Rate	
		DR Deferred Tax Expense	
DR Current Tax Expense	+	CR Deferred Liability	
CR Current Liability		**OR**	= Total Tax Expense
	−	DR Deferred Asset	
		CR Deferred Tax Benefit	

Question 1   MCQ-09379

Two independent situations are described below. Each situation has future deductible amounts and/or future taxable amounts produced by temporary differences:

Situation	1	2
Taxable income	$40,000	$80,000
Amounts at year-end:		
Future deductible amounts	5,000	10,000
Future taxable amounts	0	5,000
Balances at beginning of year:		
Deferred tax asset	1,000	4,000
Deferred tax liability	0	1,000

The enacted tax rate is 21% for both situations. Determine the income tax expense for the year.

	Situation 1	Situation 2
1.	$8,400	$16,800
2.	$8,350	$18,750
3.	$8,450	$14,850
4.	$7,350	$15,750

2 Permanent and Temporary Differences

There are two types of differences between pretax GAAP financial income and taxable income: permanent and temporary.

2.1 Permanent Differences

Permanent differences do not affect the deferred tax computation. They only affect the current tax computation. These differences affect only the period in which they occur. They do not affect future financial or taxable income.

Permanent differences are items of revenue and expense that either:

- Enter into pretax GAAP financial income, but never enter into taxable income (e.g., interest income on state or municipal obligations, life insurance, proceeds/expense).

- Enter into taxable income, but never enter into pretax GAAP financial income (e.g., dividends received deduction).

2.2 Temporary Differences

Temporary differences are the differences between the tax basis of an asset or liability and its reported amount in the financial statement that will result in taxable or deductible amounts in future years when the reported amount of the asset or liability is recovered or settled, respectively.

There are four basic causes of temporary differences, which reverse in future periods.

1. Revenues or gains that are included in taxable income, after they have been included in financial accounting income, which results in a deferred tax liability (e.g., sales on account).

2. Revenues or gains that are included in taxable income, before they are included in financial accounting income, which results in a deferred tax asset (e.g., rents collected in advance).

3. Expenses or losses deducted from taxable income, after they have been deducted for financial accounting income, which results in a deferred tax asset (e.g., warranty expense).

4. Expenses or losses deducted for taxable income, before they are deducted from financial accounting purposes, which results in a deferred tax liability (e.g., accelerated tax depreciation).

3 Deferred Tax Liability

A deferred tax liability is a future payable. Current financial income is greater than current taxable income.

3.1 Expense First

- Depreciation expense greater for tax than for book

3.2 Revenue Later

- Prepaid expenses (cash basis for tax)
- Installment sales (used for tax purposes)
- Contractor accounting

4 Deferred Tax Assets

A deferred tax asset is a future receivable. Current financial income is less than current taxable income.

M Income Taxes

4.1 Revenue First

- Unearned rent (taxable income before book income)
- Unearned interest (taxable income before book income)

4.2 Expense Later

- Bad debt expense (allowance for GAAP and direct write-off for tax)
- Estimated liability/warranty expense (allowance for GAAP and direct write-off for tax)

Question 2   MCQ-09364

Two independent situations are described below. Each situation has future deductible amounts and/or future taxable amounts produced by temporary differences:

Situation	1	2
Taxable income	$40,000	$80,000
Amounts at year-end:		
Future deductible amounts	5,000	10,000
Future taxable amounts	0	5,000
Balances at beginning of year:		
Deferred tax asset	1,000	4,000
Deferred tax liability	0	1,000

The enacted tax rate is 21% for both situations. Determine the deferred tax asset balance at year-end.

	Situation 1	Situation 2
1.	$5,000	$10,000
2.	$2,050	$6,100
3.	$1,000	$3,000
4.	$1,050	$2,100

---

5 Valuation Allowance

5.1 U.S. GAAP

Deferred tax assets are created by transactions that defer the tax benefits of expenses or transactions that recognize tax income before book income. If it is more likely than not that part or all of a deferred tax asset will not be realized, a valuation allowance should be recognized to reduce the amount of the deferred tax asset.

5.2 IFRS

IFRS prohibits the use of a valuation allowance. Under IFRS, a deferred tax asset is recognized when it is probable that sufficient taxable profit will be available against which the temporary difference can be utilized.

6 Balance Sheet Presentation

6.1 U.S. GAAP and IFRS

Under both U.S. GAAP and IFRS, deferred tax assets and deferred tax liabilities are reported as non-current on the balance sheet. Deferred tax assets and deferred tax liabilities may be netted if the entity has a legally enforceable right to offset current tax assets against current tax liabilities and the deferred tax assets and deferred tax liabilities relate to income taxes levied by the same tax authorities.

Question 3

MCQ-09415

At the end of Year 6, the tax effects of temporary differences reported in Apple Company's year-end financial statements were as follows:

	Deferred tax assets (liabilities)
Accelerated tax depreciation	$(120,000)
Warranty expense	80,000
NOL carryforward	200,000
	$ 160,000

A valuation allowance was not considered necessary. Apple anticipates that $40,000 of the deferred tax liability will reverse in Year 7, that actual warranty costs will be incurred evenly in Year 8 and Year 9, and that the NOL carryforward will be used in Year 7. On Apple's December 31, Year 6 balance sheet, what amount should be reported as a non-current deferred tax asset under U.S. GAAP?

1. $160,000
2. $200,000
3. $240,000
4. $280,000

7 Operating Loss

A net operating loss (NOL) occurs when tax-deductible expenses exceed taxable revenues. In this case the corporation pays no income taxes. Under present U.S. tax law, an operating loss of a period may be carried forward indefinitely to future tax years, limited to 80 percent of taxable income (calculated without regard to the NOL deduction). No carryback is allowed. Taxable income and financial accounting income will differ for the periods to which the loss is incurred and carried forward.

Carryforward benefit:

> **DR**   Deferred Tax Asset
> **CR**   Benefit due to loss carryforward (income tax expense)

Question 4   MCQ-09424

The pretax financial income and taxable income of Zeus Corporation were the same for the following years (i.e., there were no permanent or temporary differences):

	Income	Tax Rate
Year 4	$ 20,000	30%
Year 5	15,000	25%
Year 6	(100,000)	25%
Year 7	70,000	21%
Year 8	60,000	18%

What amount of income tax benefit will Zeus Corporation record in Year 6 under U.S. GAAP?

1. $25,000
2. $20,100
3. $19,680
4. $23,400

Task-Based Simulations

Task-Based Simulation: Tax Reconciliation

Scroll down to complete all parts of this task.

The following condensed trial balance of Allen Corporation, a publicly owned company that uses U.S. GAAP, has been adjusted except for income tax expense:

For each of the following independent situations, indicate whether the item results in a "*temporary difference*," a "*permanent difference*," or "*no difference*" for an accrual basis taxpayer. Click in the associated cells and make a selection from the list provided.

	A	B
1	Rental revenue was received during the current fiscal year in full payment for a three-year lease entered into in the current fiscal year.	☰
2	The company paid a penalty to the IRS for late payment of income taxes.	☰
3	Treasury stock was sold in excess of its cost.	☰
4	Goodwill exists on the balance sheet. There was no impairment loss during the year for financial reporting purposes. Proper 15-year amortization was deducted on the tax return.	☰
5	Bad debt expense under the allowance method was in excess of amounts actually written off under the direct write-off method.	☰
6	The company incurred and paid $4,000 of start-up costs during the current year.	☰
7	Interest revenue was received on an investment in a state bond.	☰
8	Depreciation deducted for tax purposes was in excess of the depreciation expense for financial reporting purposes.	☰

Select an option below

○ Temporary difference

○ Permanent difference

○ No difference

RESET CANCEL ACCEPT

Explanation

	A	B
1	Rental revenue was received during the current fiscal year in full payment for a three-year lease entered into in the current fiscal year.	Temporary difference
2	The company paid a penalty to the IRS for late payment of income taxes.	Permanent difference
3	Treasury stock was sold in excess of its cost.	No difference
4	Goodwill exists on the balance sheet. There was no impairment loss during the year for financial reporting purposes. Proper 15-year amortization was deducted on the tax return.	Temporary difference
5	Bad debt expense under the allowance method was in excess of amounts actually written off under the direct write-off method.	Temporary difference
6	The company incurred and paid $4,000 of start-up costs during the current year.	No difference
7	Interest revenue was received on an investment in a state bond.	Permanent difference
8	Depreciation deducted for tax purposes was in excess of the depreciation expense for financial reporting purposes.	Temporary difference

Row 1: Temporary difference
The rent revenue received in advance is deferred and not immediately recognized as revenue for financial reporting purposes. For tax purposes, it is reported as income in the year received.

Row 2: Permanent difference
Although the penalty is an expense for financial reporting purposes, it is never deductible on a tax return.

Row 3: No difference
Treasury stock sold in excess of cost is added to paid in capital and is not reported as a gain for either financial reporting or tax purposes.

Row 4: Temporary difference
Goodwill is amortized over 15 years for tax purposes and subject to an impairment test for financial reporting purposes.

Note: Many students incorrectly label this a permanent difference. However, the theory is that over time, goodwill will eventually be written off as impaired for financial reporting purposes.

Row 5: Temporary difference
The allowance method should be used for financial reporting purposes, while the direct write-off method is required for tax purposes. This is a temporary difference because bad debts are fully written off under both methods.

Row 6: No difference
The start-up costs will be expensed in the current year for both financial and tax reporting purposes. Generally this is a temporary difference because start-up costs are always expensed for financial reporting purposes, while tax rules allow the deduction of $5,000 in the year the costs are incurred and then a 180-month amortization of the remainder. However, since the question indicates that the start-up costs were $4,000, the costs will be fully expensed for tax and financial purposes.

Row 7: Permanent difference
State bond interest income is reported as revenue for financial reporting purposes but is tax-exempt.

Row 8: Temporary difference
Tax law and GAAP use different depreciation schedules. Over time, the depreciation will be the same.

III | Select Transactions

A Accounting Changes and Error Corrections

B Business Combinations

C Contingencies

D Derivatives and Hedge Accounting

E Foreign Currency Transactions and Translation

F Leases

G Research and Development

H Software Costs

I Subsequent Events

J Fair Value Measurements

K Partnerships

Notes

Financial Final Review

© Becker Professional Education Corporation. All rights reserved.

1 Changes in Accounting Estimate (Prospective Approach)

Under the prospective approach, adjustments for changes in accounting estimate are made in the current and future accounting periods. They do not affect previous periods. Examples include:

- Change in useful life
- Change in salvage value
- Settlement of litigation

When a change in accounting principle is inseparable from a change in accounting estimate, it should be reported as a change in accounting estimate.

Question 1   MCQ-09281

Gonzales Company purchased a machine on January 1, Year 1 for $600,000. On the date of acquisition, the machine had an estimated useful life of six years with no salvage value. The machine was being depreciated on a straight-line basis. On January 1, Year 4, Gonzales determined that the machine had an estimated life of eight years from the date of acquisition. An accounting change was made in Year 4.

What is the amount of the depreciation expense that should be recorded for the year ended Year 4?

1. $75,000
2. $100,000
3. $60,000
4. $0

---

2 Changes in Accounting Principle

2.1 General Rule (Retrospective Application)

Any change from one generally accepted accounting principle to another generally accepted accounting principle is recognized using the retrospective approach by adjusting beginning retained earnings for the cumulative effect of the change, net of tax. Prior period financial statements are restated (**IDA**).

2.1.1 Cumulative Effect

The cumulative effect of a change in accounting principle is computed as of the beginning of the earliest year presented, regardless of the actual date of the change, by applying the new principle to the item to be changed since inception. The difference between the two principles is the catch-up amount for all prior affected periods. It includes direct effects and only those indirect effects that are entered into the accounting records.

2.1.2 IFRS

Under IFRS, when an entity applies an accounting principle retroactively or makes a retrospective restatement of items in the financial statements, the entity must (at a minimum) present three balance sheets (end of current period, end of prior period, and beginning of prior period) and two of each of the other financial statements (current period and prior period). The cumulative effect adjustment would be shown as an adjustment of the beginning retained earnings on the balance sheet for the beginning of the prior period. U.S. GAAP does not have a three balance sheet requirement.

2.2 Exceptions to the General Rule (Prospective Application)

2.2.1 Impractical to Estimate

If it is considered impractical to accurately calculate this cumulative effect adjustment, then the change is handled prospectively (like a change in estimate). An example of a change handled in this manner is a change in inventory cost flow assumption to LIFO (U.S. GAAP only). Since a cumulative effect adjustment to LIFO would require the reestablishment and recalculation of old inventory layers, it is considered impractical to try and rebuild those old cost layers.

2.2.2 Change in Depreciation Method

A change in the method of depreciation, amortization, or depletion is considered to be both a change in accounting principle and a change in estimate. These changes should be accounted for as changes in estimate and are handled prospectively. The new depreciation method should be used as of the beginning of the year of change in estimate and should start with the current book value of the underlying asset. No adjustment should be made to retained earnings.

Question 2   MCQ-09296

On December 31, Year 10, Brown Company changed its inventory valuation method from the weighted average method to FIFO for financial statement purposes. The change will result in an $800,000 decrease in the beginning inventory at January 1, Year 10. The tax rate is 30%.

The cumulative effect of this accounting change for the year ended December 31, Year 10 in the statement of retained earnings is:

1. $0
2. $800,000
3. $240,000
4. $560,000

Question 3   MCQ-09266

On January 1, Year 1, Schreiber Company purchased a $300,000 machine with a five-year useful life and no salvage value. The machine was depreciated by an accelerated method for book and tax purposes. The machine's carrying amount was $120,000 on December 31, Year 2. On January 1, Year 3, Schreiber changed to the straight-line method for financial statement purposes. Schreiber's income tax rate is 40%.

Assuming that Schreiber can justify the change, in its Year 3 statement of retained earnings, what amount should Schreiber report as the cumulative effect of this change?

1. $60,000
2. $36,000
3. $0
4. $24,000

3 Changes in Accounting Entity (Retrospective Application)

Include changes in the companies that make up the consolidated or combined financial statements from year to year. Hence, if five-year comparative statements are presented, all these statements would be restated as though all the companies were always combined. The concept of a change in accounting entity is not discussed in IFRS.

4 Error Corrections (Restatement Approach)

Error corrections require retroactive restatement by adjusting the beginning balance of retained earnings, net of tax, in the earliest year presented. If the error occurred in a year presented, the error is corrected in those prior financial statements.

Under IFRS, when it is impracticable to determine the cumulative effect of an error, the entity is required to restate information prospectively from the earliest date that is practicable. U.S. GAAP does not have an impracticality exemption for error corrections.

Gracie Company
Statement of Retained Earnings (Partial)
For the Year Ended December 31, Year 1

Beginning balance (as previously reported)	$28,000,000
Prior period adjustments:	
Correction of error (net of tax benefit of $1,800,000)	(2,700,000)
Cumulative effect of accounting change (net of tax expense of $2,000,000)	3,000,000
Beginning balance (restated)	$28,300,000

Question 4   MCQ-09326

Lore Co. changed from the cash basis of accounting to the accrual basis of accounting during the current year. The cumulative effect of this change should be reported in Lore's current year financial statements as a:

1. Prior period adjustment resulting from the correction of an error.

2. Prior period adjustment resulting from the change in accounting principle.

3. Component of income from continuing operations.

4. Component of nonoperating gains.

5 Summary of Accounting Changes and Necessary Treatments

Accounting Changes	Example(s)	Income Statement	Statement of Retained Earnings
From one GAAP/IFRS principle to another GAAP/IFRS principle	▪ Adopt a new standard ▪ Change methods of inventory costing—FIFO to Average		**Retrospective application**, compute **cumulative** effect and report **net of tax** by adjusting beginning retained earnings of earliest year presented
Changes in principle— **Exceptions** (require prospective treatment)	▪ From any inventory valuation method to LIFO (U.S. GAAP only) ▪ Change depreciation methods —SL to SYD	▪ **Prospective application**, the beginning inventory of the year of change is the first LIFO layer ▪ Apply new depreciation method to remaining book value as of the beginning of the year	
Changes in entity	▪ Consolidation of a subsidiary not previously included in consolidated FS ▪ Report consolidated FS in place of individual statements		▪ **Retrospective** adjustments (plus or minus) **net of tax**, against the beginning balance of the retained earnings under the caption of "Prior Period Adjustments" ▪ Restate all financial statements presented
Neither a change in principle nor a change in estimate	▪ Change from fair value method to equity method because an increase in ownership now qualifies as equity method investment. Adopt the equity method as of the date the investment qualifies for equity method.	If the investment was previously accounted for as an available-for-sale security, recognize in earnings the unrealized holding gain or loss from accumulated other comprehensive income.	Because the cost of acquiring the additional interest in the investee is added to the carrying value of the previously held investment, retroactive adjustments are not required.
Correction of errors	▪ From cash to accrual ▪ Errors made in prior statements		▪ **Retroactive adjustments** (plus or minus) **net of tax**, against the beginning balance of the retained earnings under the caption of "Prior Period Adjustments" ▪ Restate all financial statements presented that are affected
Changes in estimate	▪ Depreciation method ▪ Useful life of depreciable asset ▪ Residual value ▪ Bad debt % ▪ Loss accruals	▪ **Prospective application**, account for in the current statement "above the line" ▪ **No cumulative effect**	

A Accounting Changes and Error Corrections

Task-Based Simulations

Task-Based Simulation 1: Accounting Treatments

Scroll down to complete all parts of this task.

On January 1, Year 2, Riggs Corporation hired a new controller. During the year, the controller working with Riggs' outside accountants and President, made changes to existing accounting policies, instituted new accounting policies, and corrected several errors in prior year accounting. Riggs uses U.S. GAAP and does not present comparative financial statements.

For each of the transactions below, identify the classification of the transaction by clicking in the associated cells in the Classification column and selecting from the list provided. Also, identify the general accounting treatment required for each transaction's classification by clicking in the associated cells in the Treatment column and selecting from the list provided. The available treatments are:

Retrospective application
Include the *cumulative effect* of the adjustment resulting from an accounting change in the Year 2 financial statements as an adjustment to beginning retained earnings.

Restatement approach
Adjust the Year 2 beginning retained earnings if the error affects a period prior to Year 2 .

Prospective application
Report Year 2 and future financial statements on a new basis, but do *not* adjust the beginning retained earnings.

	A	B	C
1	**Transaction**	**Classification**	**Treatment**
2	Riggs manufactures heavy equipment to customer specifications on a contract basis. On the basis that it is preferable, accounting for these long-term contracts was switched from the completed-contract method to the percentage-of-completion method.	☰	☰
3	As a result of a production breakthrough, Riggs determined that manufacturing equipment previously depreciated over 15 years should be depreciated over 20 years.	☰	☰
4	The equipment that Riggs manufactures is sold with a five-year warranty. Because of a production breakthrough, Riggs reduced its computation of warranty costs from 3% of sales to 1% of sales.	☰	☰
5	Riggs changed from FIFO to average cost to account for its raw materials and work in process inventories.	☰	☰
6	Riggs sells extended service contracts on its products. Because related services are performed over several years, in Year 2 Riggs changed from the cash method to the accrual method of recognizing income from these service contracts.	☰	☰
7	During Year 2, Riggs determined that an insurance premium paid and entirely expensed in Year 1 was for the period January 1, Year 1, through January 1, Year 3.	☰	☰
8	Riggs changed its method of depreciating office equipment from an accelerated method to the straight-line method to more closely reflect costs in later years.	☰	☰
9	Riggs instituted a pension plan for all employees in Year 2 and adopted U.S. GAAP Standards relating to employer's accounting for pensions. Riggs had not previously had a pension plan.	☰	☰
10	During Year 2, Riggs increased its investment in Brunner, Inc. from a 10% interest, purchased in Year 1, to 30%, and acquired a seat on Brunner's board of directors. As a result of its increased investment, Riggs changed its method of accounting for investment in subsidiary from the fair value method to the equity method.	☰	☰
11	Based on improved collection procedures, Riggs changed the percentage of credit sales used to determine the allowance for uncollectible accounts from 2% to 1%.	☰	☰

Accounting Changes and Error Corrections   A

Select an option below

○ Change in accounting principle

○ Change in accounting estimate

○ Correction of an error in previously presented financial statements

○ Neither an accounting change nor an error corrrection

RESET   CANCEL   ACCEPT

Select an option below

○ Retrospective application

○ Restatement approach

○ Prospective application

RESET   CANCEL   ACCEPT

Explanation

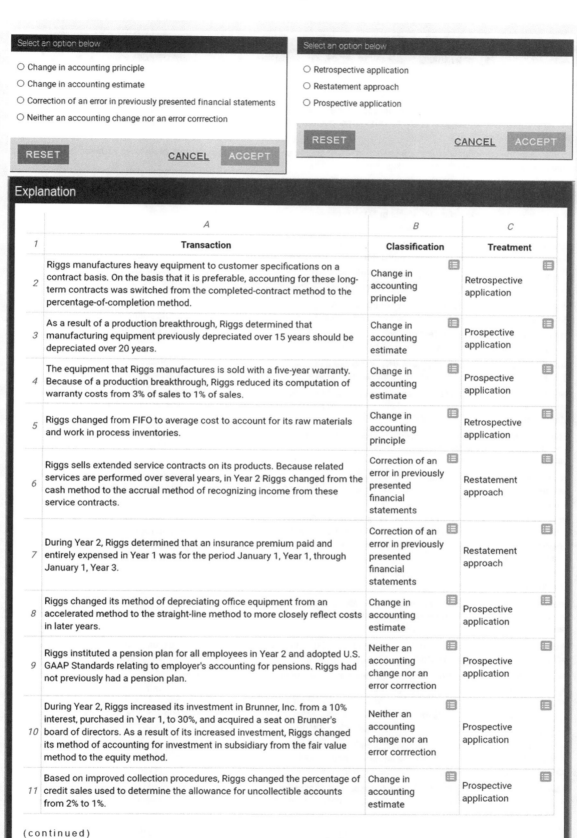

	A	B	C
1	**Transaction**	**Classification**	**Treatment**
2	Riggs manufactures heavy equipment to customer specifications on a contract basis. On the basis that it is preferable, accounting for these long-term contracts was switched from the completed-contract method to the percentage-of-completion method.	Change in accounting principle	Retrospective application
3	As a result of a production breakthrough, Riggs determined that manufacturing equipment previously depreciated over 15 years should be depreciated over 20 years.	Change in accounting estimate	Prospective application
4	The equipment that Riggs manufactures is sold with a five-year warranty. Because of a production breakthrough, Riggs reduced its computation of warranty costs from 3% of sales to 1% of sales.	Change in accounting estimate	Prospective application
5	Riggs changed from FIFO to average cost to account for its raw materials and work in process inventories.	Change in accounting principle	Retrospective application
6	Riggs sells extended service contracts on its products. Because related services are performed over several years, in Year 2 Riggs changed from the cash method to the accrual method of recognizing income from these service contracts.	Correction of an error in previously presented financial statements	Restatement approach
7	During Year 2, Riggs determined that an insurance premium paid and entirely expensed in Year 1 was for the period January 1, Year 1, through January 1, Year 3.	Correction of an error in previously presented financial statements	Restatement approach
8	Riggs changed its method of depreciating office equipment from an accelerated method to the straight-line method to more closely reflect costs in later years.	Change in accounting estimate	Prospective application
9	Riggs instituted a pension plan for all employees in Year 2 and adopted U.S. GAAP Standards relating to employer's accounting for pensions. Riggs had not previously had a pension plan.	Neither an accounting change nor an error corrrection	Prospective application
10	During Year 2, Riggs increased its investment in Brunner, Inc. from a 10% interest, purchased in Year 1, to 30%, and acquired a seat on Brunner's board of directors. As a result of its increased investment, Riggs changed its method of accounting for investment in subsidiary from the fair value method to the equity method.	Neither an accounting change nor an error corrrection	Prospective application
11	Based on improved collection procedures, Riggs changed the percentage of credit sales used to determine the allowance for uncollectible accounts from 2% to 1%.	Change in accounting estimate	Prospective application

(continued)

Explanation

(continued)

Row 2: Change in accounting principle | Retrospective application
Switching from the completed-contract method of accounting to the percentage of completion method is a change in accounting principle.

In this case, the cumulative effect of a change in GAAP should be shown on the statement of retained earnings as an adjustment to beginning retained earnings net of tax.

Row 3: Change in accounting estimate | Prospective application
A change in the lives of fixed assets is considered a change in estimate.

A change in accounting estimate affects only the prospective (current and subsequent) periods, not prior periods or retained earnings. Simply implement the change and continue with the accounting in future periods.

Row 4: Change in accounting estimate | Prospective application
A change in the computation of warranty costs from 3% of sales to 1% of sales is a change in accounting estimate.

A change in accounting estimate affects only the prospective (current and subsequent) periods, not prior periods or retained earnings. Simply implement the change and continue with the accounting in future periods.

Row 5: Change in accounting principle | Retrospective application
A change in an inventory pricing method from FIFO to average cost is a change in accounting principle.

In this case, the cumulative effect of a change in GAAP should be shown on the statement of retained earnings as an adjustment to beginning retained earnings net of tax.

Row 6: Correction of an error in previously presented financial statements | Restatement approach
A change from the cash method to the accrual method is a correction of an error in previously presented financial statements.

When comparative financial statements are not issued (as in this case), a correction of an error requires restatement of the retained earnings from the prior period end by adjusting (net of tax) the opening balance of the current retained earnings statement.

Row 7: Correction of an error in previously presented financial statements | Restatement approach
The change of the accounting practice of expensing insurance premiums when paid rather than allocating them to the periods benefited is a correction of an error in previously presented financial statements.

When comparative financial statements are not issued (as in this case), a correction of an error requires restatement of the retained earnings from the prior period end by adjusting (net of tax) the opening balance of the current retained earnings statement.

Row 8: Change in accounting estimate | Prospective application
A change in the depreciation method from an accelerated method to the straight-line method for the purpose of more fairly presenting the financial statements is a change in accounting method and change in estimate, which shall be treated as a change in estimate.

The new depreciation method should be used as of the beginning of the year of change in estimate and should start with the current book value of the underlying asset.

Row 9: Neither an accounting change nor an error correction | Prospective application
Instituting a pension plan and adopting statements of accounting standards to account for it, is neither an accounting change nor an accounting error.

When a company institutes a pension plan for the first time, it affects only the prospective (current and subsequent) periods, not prior periods or retained earnings.

Row 10: Neither an accounting change nor an error correction | Prospective application
A change from the fair value method (less than 20% ownership) to the equity method (20% or more ownership and an influential seat on the board of directors) of accounting for an investment in a subsidiary is neither an accounting change nor a correction of an error. Instead, this transition to the equity method is handled by simply applying the equity method from the date on which the ownership is qualified for the equity method.

When a corporation goes from not having significant influence in an investee (< 20%) to having significant influence in an investee (20% or more and < 50%), the equity method should be used beginning on the date the company acquires sufficient shares of stock to have a significant influence in the investee. (Retroactive restatement is not required.)

Row 11: Change in accounting estimate | Prospective application
A change in the percentage of credit sales used to determine the allowance for uncollectible accounts (bad debt) is a change in accounting estimate.

Changes in accounting estimate are recognized only in the current and future years under the prospective approach (i.e., implement the new method and continue into future years).

Task-Based Simulation 2: FIFO

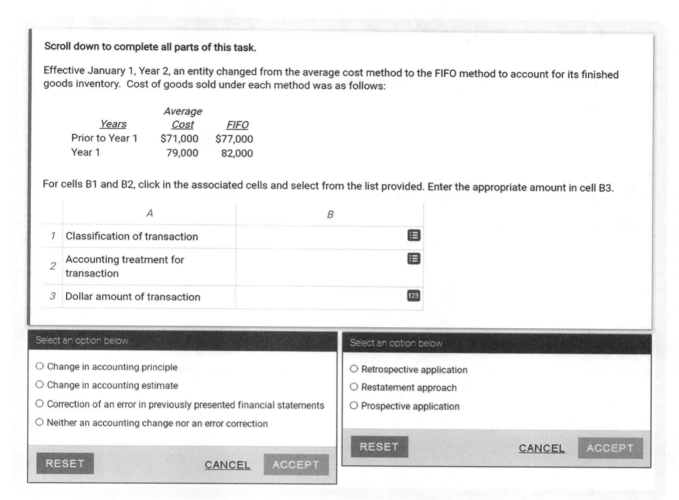

Scroll down to complete all parts of this task.

Effective January 1, Year 2, an entity changed from the average cost method to the FIFO method to account for its finished goods inventory. Cost of goods sold under each method was as follows:

	Average	
Years	Cost	FIFO
Prior to Year 1	$71,000	$77,000
Year 1	79,000	82,000

For cells B1 and B2, click in the associated cells and select from the list provided. Enter the appropriate amount in cell B3.

	A	B
1	Classification of transaction	▤
2	Accounting treatment for transaction	▤
3	Dollar amount of transaction	123

Select an option below

○ Change in accounting principle

○ Change in accounting estimate

○ Correction of an error in previously presented financial statements

○ Neither an accounting change nor an error correction

RESET   CANCEL   ACCEPT

Select an option below

○ Retrospective application

○ Restatement approach

○ Prospective application

RESET   CANCEL   ACCEPT

A   Accounting Changes and Error Corrections

Explanation

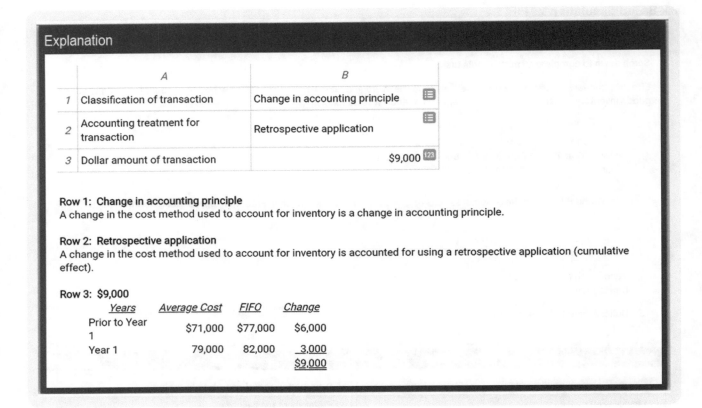

	A	B
1	Classification of transaction	Change in accounting principle
2	Accounting treatment for transaction	Retrospective application
3	Dollar amount of transaction	$9,000

Row 1: Change in accounting principle
A change in the cost method used to account for inventory is a change in accounting principle.

Row 2: Retrospective application
A change in the cost method used to account for inventory is accounted for using a retrospective application (cumulative effect).

Row 3: $9,000

Years	Average Cost	FIFO	Change
Prior to Year 1	$71,000	$77,000	$6,000
Year 1	79,000	82,000	3,000
			$9,000

Task-Based Simulation 3: Straight-line Depreciation

Scroll down to complete all parts of this task.

In January of Year 1, an entity purchased a machine with a five-year life and no salvage value for $40,000. The machine was depreciated using the straight-line method. On December 31, Year 2, the entity discovered that depreciation on the machine had been calculated using a 25% rate.

For cells B1 and B2, click in the associated cells and select from the list provided. Enter the appropriate amount in cell B3.

	A	B
1	Classification of transaction	▤
2	Accounting treatment for transaction	▤
3	Dollar amount of transaction	123

Select an option below

○ Change in accounting principle

○ Change in accounting estimate

○ Correction of an error in previously presented financial statements

○ Neither an accounting change nor an error correction

RESET   CANCEL   ACCEPT

Select an option below

○ Retrospective application

○ Restatement approach

○ Prospective application

RESET   CANCEL   ACCEPT

Explanation

	A	B
1	Classification of transaction	Correction of an error in previously presented financial statements 📇
2	Accounting treatment for transaction	Restatement approach 📇
3	Dollar amount of transaction	$2,000 🔢

Row 1: Correction of an error in previously presented financial statements
The use of a 25% rate rather than the proper 20% rate (i.e., 100%/5 = 20%) is a correction of an error.

Row 2: Restatement approach
The incorrect recording of depreciation is corrected for all prior periods by adjusting the beginning retained earnings net of tax of the period in which the error is discovered if no comparative statements are issued (the restatement approach).

Row 3: $2,000
The error was discovered in Year 2; therefore, the Year 2 depreciation expense will be calculated using the proper 20% rate. The Year 1 depreciation expense (and net income) were determined using the incorrect 25% rate. The difference (5% × $40,000 = $2,000) is a prior period correction.

Incorrect: Year 1 depreciation (25% × $40,000) = $10,000
Correct: Year 1 depreciation (20% × $40,000) =
($8,000)
Total = $2,000

Task-Based Simulation 4: Research

> How is a change in reporting entity accounted for? Find the proper citation that provides guidance to answer this question.
>
> Enter your response in the answer fields below. Guidance on correctly structuring your response appears above and below the answer fields.
>
> ## Type the topic here.
> Correctly formatted FASB ASC topics are 3 digits.
>
> FASB ASC [   ] - [   ] - [   ] - [   ]
>
> ℹ️ Some examples of correctly formatted FASB ASC responses are 205-10-05-1, 323-740-S25-1, 260-10-60-1A, 715-30-35-95, 820-10-35-16BB and 810-10-55-205AE

Explanation

Source of answer for this question:

FASB ASC 250-10-45-21

Keywords: Change in reporting entity

Notes

1 Consolidation

Consolidated financial statements are prepared when a parent-subsidiary relationship has been formed. An investor is considered to have parent status when more than 50 percent of the voting stock of the investee has been acquired. Do not consolidate when subsidiary is in legal reorganization or bankruptcy (parent does not control the subsidiary).

2 Acquisition Method

In a business combination accounted for as an acquisition, the subsidiary may be acquired for cash, stock, debt securities, etc. The investment is valued at the fair value of the consideration given or the fair value of the consideration received, whichever is the more clearly evident. The accounting for an acquisition begins at the date of acquisition.

2.1 Acquisition Costs

The following is a summary of the accounting for costs related to an acquisition business combination:

- Direct out-of-pocket costs are expensed as incurred. (Debit: Expense)

- Stock registration and issuance costs are a direct reduction of the value of the stock issued. (Debit: Paid-in capital account)

- Indirect costs are expensed as incurred. (Debit: Expense)

- Bond issuance costs are presented as a reduction of the cash proceeds of the bond issue, and are amortized according to the effective interest method (Debit bond discount + Bond issuance costs *or* Credit premium − Bond issuance costs).

2.2 Acquisition Method Summary

Assets	Fair value
Liabilities	Fair value
Retained earnings	Parent only
Income	After acquisition date
Goodwill	Yes (subject to impairment adjustment)
Noncontrolling interest	Yes (up to 49%)
Investment in subsidiary	Eliminated
Intercompany transactions	Eliminate 100%

2.3 Consolidating Workpaper Eliminating Journal Entry

The year-end consolidating journal entry known as the consolidating workpaper eliminating journal entry (EJE) is:

DR	Common stock—subsidiary	$XXX	
DR	APIC—subsidiary	XXX	
DR	Retained earnings—subsidiary	XXX	
CR	Investment in subsidiary		$XXX
CR	Noncontrolling interest		XXX
DR	Balance sheet adjusted to fair value	XXX	
DR	Identifiable intangible asset fair value	XXX	
DR	Goodwill	XXX	

The consolidated balance sheet will report the equity of the parent company only. The parent's investment in the subsidiary is eliminated.

2.4 Noncontrolling Interest

Noncontrolling interest is recognized in the consolidated financial statements when the parent company owns less than 100 percent of the subsidiary. Noncontrolling interest on the balance sheet is the noncontrolling shareholder's share of the fair value of the subsidiary. Under U.S. GAAP, the noncontrolling interest included in equity on the balance sheet is calculated as:

Noncontrolling interest (BS) = Fair value of subsidiary × Noncontrolling interest percentage

Noncontrolling interest must be recognized as a line-item deduction on the income statement for the portion of the subsidiary's net income not allocated to the parent company:

> Noncontrolling interest in net income of subsidiary = Subsidiary net income × Noncontrolling interest percentage

Comprehensive income attributable to the noncontrolling interest is presented on the consolidated statement of comprehensive income. A reconciliation at the beginning and end of the period of the carrying amount of the equity attributable to the noncontrolling interest is shown on the consolidated statement of changes in equity.

Under IFRS, noncontrolling interest (and goodwill) can be calculated using either the full goodwill method, which is the method required under U.S. GAAP, or the partial goodwill method. Under the partial goodwill method, noncontrolling interest on the balance sheet is calculated as:

> Noncontrolling interest (BS) = Fair value of subsidiary's net assets × Noncontrolling interest percentage

2.5 Fair Value Adjustment/Goodwill

The difference between the fair value of the subsidiary and the book value of the subsidiary net assets should be allocated as follows:

1. Balance sheet adjustment of the subsidiary's assets and liabilities from book value to fair value.

2. Identifiable intangible assets recorded at fair value.

3. Goodwill is excess. Under U.S. GAAP, goodwill is calculated as follows (full goodwill method):

> Goodwill = Fair value of subsidiary – Fair value of subsidiary's net assets

IFRS permits the use of the full goodwill method or the partial goodwill method. Under the partial goodwill method, goodwill is calculated as follows:

> Goodwill = Acquisition cost – Fair value of subsidiary's net assets acquired

Goodwill recognized in a business combination is not amortized. Instead, it is tested for impairment, and a loss is recognized in income from continuing operations if the goodwill is impaired.

2.6 Gain

When a subsidiary is acquired for less than the fair value of 100 percent of the underlying assets acquired, the acquisition cost is first allocated to the fair value of 100 percent of the balance sheet accounts and the fair value of 100 percent of the identifiable intangible assets acquired. This creates a negative balance in the acquisition cost account, which is recognized as a gain in the period of the acquisition.

2.7 Eliminate 100% of Intercompany Transactions

2.7.1 Payable/Receivable

In a consolidated balance sheet, all intercompany payables and receivables are eliminated.

DR	Account payable	$XXX
CR	Accounts receivable	$XXX

2.7.2 Inventory

Affiliated companies often sell inventory to one another. Intercompany sales and intercompany cost of goods sold should be eliminated. This entry is made if the books are open. Any intercompany profit from the intercompany inventory transaction must also be eliminated against the purchaser's ending inventory and cost of goods sold.

DR	Intercompany Sales (selling affiliate)	$XXX
CR	Intercompany COGS (selling affiliate)	$XXX
CR	COGS (purchasing affiliate)	XXX
CR	Inventory (purchasing affiliate)	XXX

2.7.3 Fixed Assets

The gain or loss on the intercompany sale of a depreciable asset is unrealized from a consolidated financial statement perspective until the asset is sold to an outsider. A working paper eliminating entry in the period of the intercompany sale eliminates the intercompany gain/loss and adjusts the asset and the accumulated depreciation to their original balances on the date of sale. The excess depreciation on the gain must also be eliminated.

DR	Gain	$XXX
CR	Equipment	$XXX
CR	Accumulated depreciation	XXX
DR	Accumulated depreciation	XXX
CR	Depreciation expense (RE)	XXX

2.7.4 Bonds

If one member of the consolidated group acquires an affiliate's debt from an outsider, the debt is considered to be retired and a gain/loss is recognized. This gain/loss on extinguishment of debt is calculated as the difference between the price paid to acquire the debt and the book value of the debt. This gain/loss is not reported on either company's books, but is recorded on the consolidated income statement through an elimination entry. All intercompany account balances are also eliminated; e.g., bond interest payable and bond interest receivable.

DR	Bond interest payable	$XXX	
CR	Bond interest receivable		$XXX
DR	Bonds payable	XXX	
DR	Premium on bonds payable	XXX	
DR	Loss	XXX	
CR	Investment in bonds		XXX
CR	Discount on bonds payable		XXX
CR	Gain		XXX

Question 1   MCQ-09348

On December 31, Saxon Corporation was merged into Philadelphia Corporation. In the business combination, Philadelphia issued 200,000 shares of its $10 par value common stock, with a market price of $18 a share, for all of Saxon's common stock. The stockholders' equity section of each company's balance sheet immediately before the combination was:

	Philadelphia	Saxon
Common Stock	$3,000,000	$1,500,000
Additional paid-in capital	1,300,000	150,000
Retained earnings	2,500,000	850,000
	$6,800,000	$2,500,000

In the December 31 consolidated balance sheet, additional paid-in capital should be reported at:

1. $950,000
2. $1,300,000
3. $1,450,000
4. $2,900,000

Question 2 — MCQ-09683

On January 1, Year 1, Sunshine Corporation acquired an 80% ownership interest in Grey Sky Enterprises by purchasing 400,000 of Grey Sky's 500,000 voting common shares outstanding for $10,000,000. Additional information regarding Grey Sky as of January 1, Year 1, follows:

	Book Value	Fair Value
Net assets	$11,200,000	$11,500,000

On the acquisition date, what is the noncontrolling interest that will be reported on the consolidated balance sheet of Sunshine Corporation under the IFRS partial goodwill method?

1. $1,200,000
2. $1,500,000
3. $2,300,000
4. $2,500,000

Question 3 — MCQ-09414

Pico Corp. owns 100% of Sepulveda Inc.'s common stock. During Year 1, Pico sold inventory to Sepulveda for $400,000, which was 25% above cost. Sepulveda sold half of the inventory purchased from Pico in Year 1. At year-end, before consolidation, Pico reported inventory of $390,000 and Sepulveda reported inventory of $480,000. All other inventory transactions for both companies were with outside customers and suppliers. At December 31, Year 1, what should Pico Corp. report as consolidated inventory on its balance sheet?

1. $670,000
2. $830,000
3. $870,000
4. $910,000

3 Variable Interest Entities (VIEs)

3.1 Definition

A variable interest entity is a corporation, partnership, trust, LLC or other legal structure used for business purposes that either does not have equity investors with voting rights or lacks the sufficient financial resources to support its activities.

Business Combinations   **B**

3.2   Primary Beneficiary

The primary beneficiary is the entity that has the power to direct the activities of a variable interest entity that most significantly impact the entity's economic performance, and:

- absorbs the expected VIE losses; or
- receives the expected VIE residual returns.

3.3   U.S. GAAP Consolidation Rule

Under U.S. GAAP, the primary beneficiary of a variable interest entity must consolidate the variable interest entity.

Under U.S. GAAP, all consolidation decisions are evaluated first under the VIE model. If consolidation is not required under the VIE model, then the investor (parent) company determines whether consolidation is necessary under the voting interest model (consolidate when ownership is more than 50 percent of the investee's voting stock, as previously covered).

3.4   IFRS Consolidation Rule

IFRS focus on the accounting for special purpose entities. A special purpose entity (SPE) is a specific type of VIE created by a sponsoring company to hold assets or liabilities, often for structured financing purposes (e.g., sales of receivables, synthetic leases, securitization of loans).

Under IFRS, a sponsoring company controls, and must consolidate, an SPE when the company:

- is benefited by the SPE's activities.
- has decision-making powers that allow it to benefit from the SPE.
- absorbs the risks and rewards of the SPE.
- has a residual interest in the SPE.

Question 4   MCQ-09760

An investor (company) will most likely avoid consolidating a potential variable interest entity (VIE) if:

1. The investor absorbs at least 50 percent of the VIE's expected gains.
2. The VIE requires significant financial support from the investor.
3. Current VIE equity holders do not have substantive voting rights.
4. The investor does not absorb over half of the VIE's expected losses.

Notes

1 Contingent Losses

The recognition and presentation of loss contingencies depends on the classification of the contingency.

- **Probable:** Likely to occur. An adjusting entry and a note disclosure are required.

  - **Range:** If a range of amounts is given, adjust for the smaller amount and disclose the difference in the notes to the financial statements.

- **Reasonably Possible:** A note disclosure is required.

- **Remote:** Ignore (unless guarantee of indebtedness of others, then disclose).

2 Contingent Gains

Contingent gains that are probable or reasonably possible may be disclosed.

Question 1
MCQ-09429

Far Out Producers is involved in two product liability lawsuits and a third lawsuit that the company brought against a competitor for patent infringement. At December 31, Year 1, the company's attorneys informed management of the following:

- It is probable that Far Out will lose one of the product liability lawsuits, although the actual settlement could be as low as $800,000 and as high as $2,000,000.

- It is possible that the company could lose $1,000,000 in the second product liability lawsuit.

- It is probable that Far Out will win $500,000 in the patent infringement case.

What should Far Out report on its December 31, Year 1 balance sheet for these contingencies?

1. $300,000 contingent liability.
2. $800,000 contingent liability.
3. $1,800,000 contingent liability.
4. $3,000,000 contingent liability.

---

1 Financial Instruments

1.1 Financial Instruments Are:

- Cash, foreign currency, and demand deposits.
- Ownership interest in an entity (stock, partnership, LLC).
- Contracts that both:
  - Impose on one entity a contractual obligation or duty.
  - Convey to the second entity a contractual right to do the opposite.
- Derivatives.

1.2 Disclosure

Fair value must be disclosed for all financial instruments for which it is practicable to estimate that value together with the related carrying amounts.

Disclosure of concentrations of credit risk is required. Credit risk is the possibility of loss from the failure of another party to perform according to the terms of a contract. Disclosure of market risk is encouraged but not required under U.S. GAAP. Under IFRS, disclosure of market risk is required.

Question 1   MCQ-09336

Which of the following must be disclosed for most financial instruments?

	Carrying Value	Fair Value
1.	No	No
2.	No	Yes
3.	Yes	No
4.	Yes	Yes

---

2 Derivatives and Hedging

2.1 Definition

Derivatives derive their value from other securities. A derivative must have all three of the following characteristics:

1. One or more underlyings, and one or more notional amounts or payment provisions (or both); and

2. No initial net investment (or smaller than would be expected); and

3. Its terms require or permit a net settlement.

- An underlying is a specified price, rate, or other variable, e.g., $10 a bushel.

- A notional amount is a specified unit of measure on which the derivative is valued, e.g., 10,000 bushels.

- The value or settlement amount is the amount determined by the multiplication of the notional amount and the underlying, e.g., 10,000 bushels × $10 per unit = $100,000.

- Examples of common derivatives are forward contracts, futures, swaps, and options.

- Derivatives are reported as assets or liabilities and are measured at fair value just like other financial instruments.

2.2 Hedging Instruments

2.2.1 No Hedge Designation

No hedge designation. Just speculation. Changes in fair value are fully included in income.

2.2.2 Fair Value Hedge

A fair value hedge hedges an exposure to changes in fair value of a recorded asset or liability or unrecognized firm commitment. Changes in fair value are included in income but are offset by changes in the fair value of the hedged item.

2.2.3 Cash Flow Hedge

A cash flow hedge hedges an exposure to variability in the cash flows of a recognized asset or a forecasted transaction. Changes in fair value of the ineffective portion of a cash flow hedge are included in income; changes in fair value of the effective portion of a cash flow hedge are included in the stockholders' equity as part of other comprehensive income (OCI) until the related cash flows are realized.

Accounting for Hedges: Reporting Gains and Losses	
Type of Hedge Instrument	*Accounting for Changes in Fair Value*
No hedge designation	Income Statement
Fair value hedge	Income Statement offset by changes in fair value of the hedged item
Cash flow hedge **In**effective portion	**In**come Statement
Cash flow hedge **E**ffective portion (PUF**E**)	In OCI then in Accumulated OCI in **E**quity

Question 2   MCQ-09425

Which of the following statements regarding the accounting for derivatives is correct?

I. A derivative must have one or more underlyings or one or more notional amounts, require little or no net investment, and permit or require a net settlement.

II. Derivatives are always reported on the balance sheet as assets at fair value.

III. If a derivative is speculative (no hedge designation), changes in fair value are reported on the income statement.

IV. If a derivative is used as a fair value hedge, then changes in fair value are reported in other comprehensive income.

    1. III only.

    2. I and III

    3. I, II, III.

    4. I, II, III, IV.

1 Foreign Currency Translation

Foreign currency translation is the conversion of a financial statement of a foreign subsidiary into financial statements expressed in the reporting currency of the parent company. The method used to convert the financial statements depends on the functional currency of the subsidiary.

1.1 Remeasurement Method

Foreign currency remeasurement is the restatement of foreign financial statements from the foreign currency to the entity's functional currency in the following situations:

- The reporting currency is the functional currency.

- The entity's books of record must be restated in the entity's functional currency prior to translating the financial statements from the functional currency to the reporting currency.

Remeasurement starts with the balance sheet and converts monetary items using current/year-end exchange rates and nonmonetary items using historical exchange rates. The income statement is then converted using a weighted average exchange rate for all items except those related to the balance sheet (depreciation, amortization, and cost of goods sold). Balance sheet related items are converted using the appropriate historical rate. A gain or loss is plugged to net income to get the required balance needed to adjusted retained earnings so that the balance sheet balances. Remeasurement gains and losses are included in income.

1.2 Translation Method

Foreign currency translation is the restatement of financial statements denominated in the functional currency to the reporting currency.

Translation starts with the income statement and converts all elements using a weighted average exchange rate. Translated net income is transferred to retained earnings. Assets and liabilities on the balance sheet are then converted using the current/year-end exchange rate, common stock/APIC are converted using historical exchange rates, retained earnings is rolled forward, and then a gain or loss is plugged to OCI to make the balance sheet balance. Translation gains and losses are part of other comprehensive income (**PUFIE**).

Question 1 MCQ-09403

Which of the following statements regarding the process of foreign currency translation is/are correct?

I.   After the translation process is complete, a subsidiary's financial statements must be adjusted to conform to U.S. GAAP.

II. The process of translation is done to convert financial statements from a functional currency to the reporting currency.

III. The process of remeasurement is done when the local currency of a subsidiary is different than the functional currency.

IV. Translation gains and losses are reported on the income statement, while gains and losses from remeasurement are reported in other comprehensive income.

    1. I and IV.

    2. II and III.

    3. I, II, and III.

    4. II, III, and IV.

2 Foreign Currency Transactions

Foreign currency transactions are transactions with a foreign entity (e.g., buying from and selling to) denominated in (to be settled in) a foreign currency.

Foreign exchange transaction gains and losses must be computed at a given balance sheet date on all recorded transactions denominated in foreign currencies that have not be settled.

On 12/1/Yr 1, Green company purchased goods on credit for 100,000 pesos. Green paid for the goods on 3/1/Yr 2. The exchange rates were:

Date	Rate
12/1/Yr 1	$0.10
12/31/Yr 1	$0.08
3/1/Yr 2	$0.09

The journal entries related to this foreign currency transaction are:

12/1/Yr 1	Transaction Date		
Purchases (100,000 pesos × 0.10 exchange rate)		$10,000	
Accounts payable			$10,000

12/31/Yr 1	Balance Sheet Date		
Accounts Payable [100,000 pesos × ($0.10 − $0.08)]		$2,000	
Foreign exchange transaction gain			$2,000

3/1/Yr 2	Settlement Date		
Accounts Payable ($10,000 original balance − $2,000 adjustment)		$8,000	
Foreign exchange transaction loss [100,000 × ($0.08 − $0.09)]		1,000	
Cash (100,000 pesos × $0.09)			$9,000

*Transaction gains and losses are included in income from continuing operations.

Question 2
MCQ-09413

On November 1, Year 1, Western Traders sold goods to an Italian company for 25,000 euros. Western was paid by the company in Euros on February 15, Year 2. The exchange rates to convert euros to dollars were:

11/1/Y1	$1.19/euro
12/31/Y1	$1.16/euro
2/15/Y2	$1.23/euro

How much should Western report as a foreign exchange gain or loss on its December 31, Year 1 and Year 2 financial statements?

	Year 1	Year 2
1.	$750 gain	$1,000 loss
2.	$750 gain	$1,750 loss
3.	$750 loss	$1,000 gain
4.	$750 loss	$1,750 gain

Notes

1 Operating Versus Finance Leases

At lease initiation, the lessee and lessor will determine whether to classify the lease on their respective books as an operating or finance lease (for the lessor, a finance lease is categorized as either a sales-type or a direct financing lease).

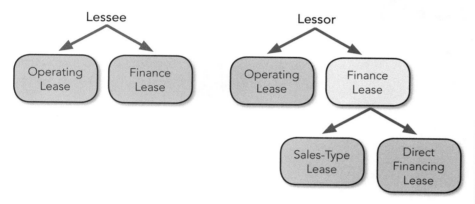

The "OWNES PC" criteria are used to determine the lease classification for the lessee and lessor.

If *any one* of the five OWNES criteria below are met:

- The lessee will classify the lease as a finance lease; and
- The lessor will classify the lease as a sales-type lease.

(O) **Ownership** of the underlying asset transfers from the lessor to the lessee by the end of the lease term.

(W) The lessee has the **written option** to purchase the underlying asset; the option is one that the lessee is "reasonably certain" to exercise.

(N) The **net present** value of all lease payments and any guaranteed residual value is equal to or substantially exceeds the underlying asset's fair value. (Ninety percent of FV threshold is reasonable.)

(E) The term of the lease represents the major part of the **economic life** remaining for the underlying asset. (Seventy-five percent of economic life threshold is reasonable.)

(S) The asset is **specialized** such that it will not have an expected, alternative use to the lessor when the lease term ends.

If none of the OWNES criteria are met:

- The lessee will classify the lease as an operating lease; and
- The lessor will classify the lease as a direct finance lease or an operating lease depending on the PC criteria below.

- If both PC criteria are met, the lessor will classify the lease as a direct financing lease.

- If neither or just one PC criteria is met, the lessor will classify the lease as an operating lease.

(P) Present value of the sum of the lease payments, lessee guaranteed residual value not included in the lease payments, and any third-party guaranteed residual value is equal to or substantially exceeds the underlying asset's fair value.

(C) Collection of the lease payments and any amounts necessary to satisfy residual value guarantees is probable.

Question 1   MCQ-09253

Under U.S. GAAP, the lessor and the lessee may classify the same lease transaction in each of the following ways, *except*:

	Lessor	*Lessee*
1.	Operating	Operating
2.	Operating	Finance
3.	Finance	Operating
4.	Finance	Finance

---

2 Calculating Leases

2.1   Lease Payments

In the calculation of lease payments, the lessee will include all of the following.

(R) Required contractual fixed payments (which include any variable payments that are "in-substance" fixed payments) less any lease incentives paid or payable to the lessee.

(E) Exercise option to buy the asset that lessee is reasonably certain to exercise.

(P) Purchase price of the asset at lease end when lessor can require lessee purchase.

(O) Only indexed or rate variable payments: No changes to future lease payments should be assumed based on increases or decreases in the index or rate.

(R) Residual guarantees which are likely to be owed.

(T) Termination penalty due from the lessee upon lease termination.

Lessee lease payments may or may not include (at the lessee's option):

(N) Nonlease components: Amounts allocated to non-lease components of a contract.

Lessee lease payments will specifically exclude the following.

(G) Guarantees of lessor debt by lessee.

(O) Other variable lease payments (other than those noted above).

2.2   Lease Term

The lease term begins on the commencement date (when the asset is available for lessee use) and extends to the end of the noncancelable period (the period in which the lessee's right is enforceable). An option to extend the lease is included in the term if the lessee is reasonably certain to exercise the option, and an option to terminate is included in the term if the lessee is reasonably certain not to exercise the option. Both options are included if the lessor controls the exercise.

2.3   Discount Rate

The lessor will use the rate implicit in the lease. The lessee uses either the rate implicit in the lease (if known) or if this rate is not readily determinable, the incremental borrowing rate of the lessee.

2.4   Initial Direct Costs

Initial direct costs incurred as a result of executing the lease will be included in the valuation of the right-of-use (ROU) asset.

Question 2	MCQ-09290

On December 1, Year 1, Tom V. Company entered into an operating lease for office space for its executives for 10 years at a monthly rental of $200,000, increasing to $400,000 halfway through the lease. On that date, Tom V. paid the landlord the following amounts:

First month's rent	$ 200,000
Last month's rent	400,000
Installation of new carpet	600,000
	$1,200,000

The entire amount was charged to rent expense in Year 1. What amount should Tom V. have charged to expense for the year?

1. $1,200,000
2. $300,000
3. $200,000
4. $305,000

3 Sale-Leaseback Transactions

A sale-leaseback occurs when one party (the seller) which has control of an asset transfers it to another party (the buyer), with a subsequent lease of the same asset where the seller becomes the lessee and the buyer becomes the lessor.

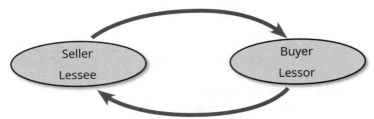

ASSET → Transfered from Seller to Buyer

**ASSET → Leased by the Seller (now the Lessee)
from the Buyer (now the Lessor)**

To qualify as a sale, revenue recognition requirements must be met (i.e., a contract exists and control has transferred from the seller to the buyer). If these criteria are not met, this will be treated as a financing transaction.

3.1 Criteria to Be Considered a Sale Are Met

Each party must then determine whether the transaction is at fair value using a two-step process:

- Determine which of the two sets of information below are more readily determinable:
  - Set 1: Asset sale price and fair value
  - Set 2: PV of lease payments and PV of market rental payments

- Of the one that is more determinable, any difference between the two data points will require an adjustment to either the sale price or the purchase price.

Two transactions upon execution of the sale-leaseback:

- The sale, along with recognition of profit/loss, would be recorded (leaseback must be an operating lease, as a finance lease equates to a repurchase and a "failed sale").

- The lease itself would be recorded.

3.2 Criteria to Be Considered a Sale Are Not Met

Seller (lessee) and buyer (lessor) will treat this as a "failed sale" (financing transaction), which will involve the seller (lessee) recording a financing liability and buyer (lessor) recording a financing receivable. The seller will continue to recognize the asset on its books.

Question 3   MCQ-09254

Which of the following statements is correct regarding sale-leaseback arrangements?

1. The seller is the lessor who books a profit/loss at lease inception.
2. The buyer is the lessee who gives the seller the right to use the asset.
3. The buyer is the lessee who will defer profits if substantial rights are retained.
4. The seller is the lessee whose profit is the difference between the fair value and book value.

4 Lessee Accounting

4.1 Operating Lease

For an operating lease, the lessee's balance sheet will reflect a right-of-use (ROU) asset and lease liability and both will be amortized over the life of the lease using the effective interest method. On the income statement, lease expense will be recognized each year over the lease term using the straight-line method for expense measurement. Instead of reporting interest expense on the income statement, the lessee will report the interest as part of lease expense.

4.2 Finance Lease

If the lease is a finance lease, the lessee will recognize both an ROU asset and a corresponding liability on its balance sheet. Both will be amortized over the life of the lease. On the income statement, interest expense and amortization expense will be recognized over the life of the lease.

4.3 Accounting Policy Election

If the lease term is 12 months or less, lessees can make an accounting policy election and choose to not recognize ROU assets and lease liabilities. To do this, the lease cannot include purchase options for the asset that the lessee is reasonably certain to exercise. Lease expense will be recognized on the income statement and the cash payments will have no effect on the balance sheet.

Question 4 MCQ-09260

Question 4   MCQ-09260

On December 31, Year 1, Eve Company leased a machine under a finance lease for a period of 10 years, contracting to pay $50,000 on signing the lease and $50,000 annually on December 31 of each of the next nine years.

The present value at December 31, Year 1 of the 10 lease payments discounted at 10% was $338,000. At December 31, Year 2, Eve's total finance lease liability is:

1. $303,980
2. $266,800
3. $259,200
4. $243,000

5 Lessor Accounting

5.1 Operating Lease

With an operating lease, the lessor will keep the asset on its balance sheet, which will include depreciating it. Lease income will be recognized on a straight-line basis.

5.2 Sales-Type and Direct Financing Leases

For sales-type and direct financing leases, the lessor will recognize a lease receivable on its balance sheet. On the income statement, interest income will be recognized over the life of the lease using the effective interest method. The excess cash payments from the lessee (above the interest income) will reduce the lease receivable over the life of the lease.

Question 5   MCQ-09335

Mission Corporation leases equipment to Mars Company for $60,000 per year under a four-year direct financing (finance) lease. The first payment is made at lease inception. The equipment has no residual value at the end of the lease and the lease does not contain a written purchase option. Mission will earn 11% interest on the lease. The present value of an annuity due of $1 at 11% for four years is 3.4437. What is the total amount of interest revenue that Mission will earn over the life of the lease?

1. $ 33,378
2. $ 60,000
3. $206,622
4. $240,000

Task-Based Simulations

Task-Based Simulation 1: Operating Lease

Scroll down to complete all parts of this task.

Hanne Corporation manufactured a piece of equipment at a cost of $7,000,000 and held it for resale from January 1, Year 1, to June 30, Year 1, at a price of $8,000,000. On July 1, Year 1, Hanne leased the equipment to Tanya Inc. The lease is appropriately recorded on the books of both corporations as an operating lease for accounting purposes. The lease is for a three-year period expiring on June 30, Year 4. Equal monthly payments under the lease are $115,000 and are due on the first of the month. The first payment was made on July 1, Year 1. The equipment is being depreciated on a straight-line basis over an eight-year period with no residual value expected.

Answer the questions in column A below by inserting the correct dollar amounts in the associated cells in column B.

	A	B
1	What expense should Tanya Inc. appropriately record as a result of the above facts for the year ended December 31, Year 1?	[123]
2	What income or loss before income taxes should Hanne appropriately record as a result of the above facts for the year ended December 31, Year 2?	[123]

Explanation

	A	B
1	What expense should Tanya Inc. appropriately record as a result of the above facts for the year ended December 31, Year 1?	$690,000 [123]
2	What income or loss before income taxes should Hanne appropriately record as a result of the above facts for the year ended December 31, Year 2?	$505,000 [123]

Row 1: $690,000

Monthly lease expense	$115,000	
Times: 6 months	× 6	
Total Year 1 lease expense		**$690,000**

Row 2: $505,000

Monthly rental income	$115,000	
Times: 12 months	× 12	
Year 2 income		$1,380,000
Equipment cost	$7,000,000	
Divided by: Asset life	÷ 8	
Year 2 depreciation		(875,000)
Total Year 2 income on lease		**$505,000**

F   Leases

Task-Based Simulation 2: Finance Lease

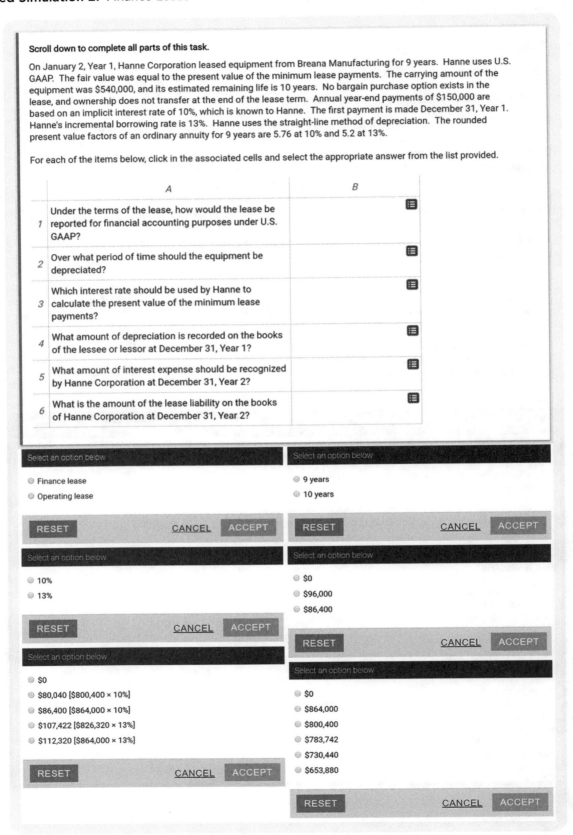

Scroll down to complete all parts of this task.

On January 2, Year 1, Hanne Corporation leased equipment from Breana Manufacturing for 9 years. Hanne uses U.S. GAAP. The fair value was equal to the present value of the minimum lease payments. The carrying amount of the equipment was $540,000, and its estimated remaining life is 10 years. No bargain purchase option exists in the lease, and ownership does not transfer at the end of the lease term. Annual year-end payments of $150,000 are based on an implicit interest rate of 10%, which is known to Hanne. The first payment is made December 31, Year 1. Hanne's incremental borrowing rate is 13%. Hanne uses the straight-line method of depreciation. The rounded present value factors of an ordinary annuity for 9 years are 5.76 at 10% and 5.2 at 13%.

For each of the items below, click in the associated cells and select the appropriate answer from the list provided.

	A	B
1	Under the terms of the lease, how would the lease be reported for financial accounting purposes under U.S. GAAP?	☰
2	Over what period of time should the equipment be depreciated?	☰
3	Which interest rate should be used by Hanne to calculate the present value of the minimum lease payments?	☰
4	What amount of depreciation is recorded on the books of the lessee or lessor at December 31, Year 1?	☰
5	What amount of interest expense should be recognized by Hanne Corporation at December 31, Year 2?	☰
6	What is the amount of the lease liability on the books of Hanne Corporation at December 31, Year 2?	☰

Select an option below

○ Finance lease
○ Operating lease

RESET   CANCEL   ACCEPT

Select an option below

○ 9 years
○ 10 years

RESET   CANCEL   ACCEPT

Select an option below

○ 10%
○ 13%

RESET   CANCEL   ACCEPT

Select an option below

○ $0
○ $96,000
○ $86,400

RESET   CANCEL   ACCEPT

Select an option below

○ $0
○ $80,040 [$800,400 × 10%]
○ $86,400 [$864,000 × 10%]
○ $107,422 [$826,320 × 13%]
○ $112,320 [$864,000 × 13%]

RESET   CANCEL   ACCEPT

Select an option below

○ $0
○ $864,000
○ $800,400
○ $783,742
○ $730,440
○ $653,880

RESET   CANCEL   ACCEPT

Explanation

Row 1: Finance Lease

The transaction is classified as a finance lease because the term of 9 years represents the major part of the equipment's estimated remaining economic life (10 years). [Note that the present value of the minimum lease payments is also equal to the fair value of the property.]

Recall the following mnemonic to determine whether a lease qualifies as a finance lease (only one criterion need be met to classify the lease as finance):

Ownership	Ownership transfers at the end of the lease.
Written	A written purchase option exists.
Net Present	The net present value of all lease payments equal to or substantially exceeds the fair value of the underlying asset.
Economic Life	The lease term represents the major part of the economic life of the underlying asset.
Specialized	The asset is specialized such that it will not have an expected, alternative use to the lessor when the lease term ends.

Row 2: 9 years

Hanne should depreciate the asset over the lease term of 9 years because the lease qualified as a finance lease only under the "N" and "E" rules. If there is no transfer of ownership and the lease term also does not contain a bargain purchase option, the asset cannot be depreciated over its estimated remaining life. Recall that if there is an ownership transfer or written purchase option, depreciation is over the underlying asset's useful life. If any of the other criteria are met, the depreciation will occur over the shorter of the lease term or the useful life of the asset.

Row 3: 10%

The implicit rate of 10% should be used to calculate the present value of the minimum lease payments (and thus the asset value) because the implicit rate is the correct rate to use when it is known to the lessee.

Row 4: $96,000

To arrive at PVMLP:

Annual lease payments = $150,000
Net amount = $150,000 × 5.76 = $864,000

$864,000 / 9 = $96,000

The asset is depreciated over 9 years on Hanne's books, as indicated in the answer to item 2.

Row 5: $80,040

Note that the question asks for the interest expense for Year 2. We must calculate the liability balance at the beginning of Year 2 in order to calculate interest expense for Year 2:

Step 1
Lease liability at 1/2/Year 1 = $864,000
Times 10%
Year 1 interest expense = $86,400

Step 2
Year 1 lease payment = $150,000
Less: Year 1 interest expense = (86,400)
Year 1 lease principal reduction = $63,600

Step 3
Lease liability at 1/2/Year 1 = $864,000
Less: Year 1 principal reduction = (63,600)
Lease liability at 12/31/Year 1 = $800,400
Times 10%
Year 2 interest expense = $80,040

Row 6: $730,440

Using the information obtained in item 5, above, following is the calculation for the lease liability at December 31, Year 2:

Year 2 lease payment = $150,000
Less: Year 2 interest expense = (80,040)
Year 2 lease principal reduction = $69,960

Lease liability at 12/31/Year 1 = $800,400
Less: Year 2 lease principal reduction = (69,960)
Lease liability at 12/31/Year 2 = $730,440

[Note that all of the other answer options consider the liability at various year-ends using either the 10% rate or the 13% rate.]

F Leases

Task-Based Simulation 3: Research

When a lease contract requires a modification, which conditions must be present in order for the modification to be treated as a separate contract? Find the proper citation that provides guidance in answering this question.

Enter your response in the answer fields below. Guidance on correctly structuring your response appears above and below the answer fields.

Type the topic here.

Correctly formatted FASB ASC topics are 3 digits.

FASB ASC [ ] - [ ] - [ ] - [ ]

ℹ Some examples of correctly formatted FASB ASC responses are 205-10-05-1, 323-740-S25-1, 260-10-60-1A, 715-30-35-95, 820-10-35-16BB and 810-10-55-205AE

Explanation

Source of answer for this question:

FASB ASC 842-10-25-8

Keywords: Lease modification

1 U.S. GAAP

Under U.S. GAAP, research and development costs must be expensed in the period incurred. In general, items to be expensed as R&D include: equipment, material, labor, overhead, design, testing, engineering, modification, and salaries of research staff. Exceptions to expensing include:

1.1 Alternative Use

Capitalize and then depreciate as R&D expense if alternative use on other future projects is planned (e.g., building will be used for other projects).

1.2 Expense as Operating Expenses (Not R&D)

Routine periodic design changes, market research, executive salaries, quality control testing, post-production costs, and commissions.

Question 1   MCQ-09347

The Holly Company incurred research and development costs in Year 1 as follows:

Equipment acquired for use in various R&D projects	$400,000
Depreciation on the above equipment	60,000
Materials used	100,000
Compensation costs of personnel	200,000
Fees to outside consulting firms	70,000
Indirect costs appropriately allocated	100,000

The total research and development expense in Holly 's Year 1 income statement under U.S. GAAP should be:

1. $930,000
2. $870,000
3. $530,000
4. $470,000

---

2 IFRS

Under IFRS, research costs must be expensed, but development costs may be capitalized if certain criteria are met.

Question 2	MCQ-09676

Hi-Tech Corp. spent $300,000 on research and development to generate new product lines. Only one of the five product lines resulted in a patented item, while the remaining four were considered unsuccessful. The cost of the product that was successfully patented included $30,000 in research costs and $40,000 in development costs. Under IFRS, how much of the $300,000 should be recognized as an expense?

1. $300,000
2. $270,000
3. $260,000
4. $230,000

1 U.S. GAAP

Under U.S. GAAP, costs related to computer software developed to be sold, leased, or licensed, are expensed until technological feasibility has been established and capitalized after that. Capitalized costs are amortized using the greater of the straight-line method or a percentage of revenue basis. For computer software developed for internal use, costs in the preliminary project stage and costs incurred in training and maintenance are expensed. Costs after the preliminary project stage are capitalized. Capitalized costs are amortized on a straight-line basis.

Question 1   MCQ-09362

During Year 1, the James Company incurred costs to develop and produce a routine, low-risk computer software product, as follows:

Detailed program design	$30,000
Coding and testing to establish technological feasibility	40,000
Coding after establishment of technological feasibility	20,000
Other testing after establishment of technological feasibility	30,000
Producing product masters for training materials	50,000
Duplication of software and training materials	15,000
Packaging	10,000

In James' December 31, Year 1 balance sheet, what amount should be reported in inventory under U.S. GAAP?

1. $25,000
2. $185,000
3. $70,000
4. $90,000

2 IFRS

IFRS does not provide specific guidance for computer software development costs. Under IFRS, research costs related to computer software development are expensed and development costs may be capitalized if certain criteria are met.

1 Recognized Subsequent Events

Subsequent events occur after the balance sheet date but before the financial statements are issued.

Subsequent events that provide additional information about conditions that existed at the balance sheet date must be recognized on the financial statements. An example of this type of event is litigation settled after the balance sheet date where the litigation arose before the balance sheet date. The settlement amount is considered in determination of the liability.

2 Nonrecognized Subsequent Events

Subsequent events that provide information about conditions that occurred after the balance sheet date and did not exist at the balance sheet date are not recognized in the financial statements, but may be disclosed if necessary to keep the statements from being misleading.

Question 1 — MCQ-09748

Drexler Corp. has a June 30 fiscal year-end and plans to issue its annual (Year 3) financial statements by September 30, Year 3. On August 15, a warehouse fire destroys an estimated $250,000 of inventory. As a result of the fire, in its Year 3 financial statements Drexler should:

1. Book a journal entry with a disclosure.
2. Book a journal entry with no associated disclosure.
3. Disclose the nature of the event with no estimated financial impact.
4. Disclose the nature of the event along with the estimated financial impact.

Notes

1 Definition

Fair value is the price that would be received to sell an asset or paid to transfer a liability in an orderly transaction between market participants in the principal (or most advantageous) market at the measurement date.

- Fair value is a market-based measure.
- Fair value is an exit price, not an entrance price.
- Fair value does not include transaction costs.

2 Market Determination

- Market participants are buyers and sellers who are independent and willing to enter a transaction.
- If there is a principal market, the price in that market will be used.
- If there is no principal market, the price in the most advantageous market will be the fair value measurement.
- Transaction costs are used to determine the most advantageous market, but are not included in the final fair value measurement.

3 Measuring Fair Value

Entities can use the market approach, the income approach, the cost approach, or a combination of these, as appropriate, when measuring the fair value of an asset or a liability.

Valuation techniques should maximize the use of observable inputs (Level 1 and Level 2) and minimize the use of unobservable inputs (Level 3).

- Level 1 inputs are quoted prices in active markets for identical assets or liabilities.
- Level 2 inputs are other directly or indirectly observable inputs.
- Level 3 inputs are unobservable inputs.

Question 1   MCQ-09762

Which of the following choices correctly matches the type of investment with its most appropriate fair value classification?

	Investment Type	Level
1.	U.S. Treasury bill	3
2.	Mortgage-backed securities	2
3.	Limited partnerships	1
4.	Large public company common stock	3

1 New Partner Contributions

Contributions to a partnership are recorded at fair value.

Land	$5,000	
Green, capital		$5,000

Three basic methods are available for accounting for a new partner's contributions:

1.1 "Exact" Method

No goodwill or bonus is recorded. In the exact method, the exact amount that the new partner contributes is the exact amount credited to his/her capital account.

Cash	$1,000	
Green, capital		$1,000

1.2 Bonus Method

The old capital plus the new partner's investment equals the total new capital. However, the new partner's capital account is credited for an amount different from his/her investment. Any difference between the new partner's contribution and the amount credited is a bonus to/from the new partner and is divided based on the old partner's profit/loss ratio.

Cash	$1,000	
X, capital (60%)	120	
Y, capital (40%)	80	
Green, capital		$1,200

1.3   Goodwill Method

Goodwill = Total new capital − (Old capital + New partner's investment).
Any difference between the total new capital of the partnership and the
total of the old capital plus the investment by the new partner is goodwill
for the old partners and is allocated to their capital accounts in the old
partnership profit/loss sharing ratio.

Cash	$1,000	
Goodwill	400	
X, capital (60%)		$240
Y, capital (40%)		160
Green, capital		1,000

Question 1   MCQ-09317

Coco and Chanel are partners who share profits and losses in the
ratio of 3:2, respectively. On August 31, their capital accounts were
as follows:

Coco	$70,000
Chanel	60,000

On that date, they agreed to admit Chance as a partner with a
one-third interest in the capital and profits and losses for an investment
of $50,000. The new partnership will begin with a total capital balance
of $180,000.

Immediately after Chance's admission, what are the capital balances of
the partners?

	Coco	Chanel	Chance
1.	$60,000	$60,000	$60,000
2.	$63,333	$56,667	$60,000
3.	$64,000	$56,000	$60,000
4.	$70,000	$60,000	$50,000

---

2 Division of Profits/Losses

For partnership operations, partnership income or loss is distributed among the various partners in accordance with their profit/loss sharing ratio. If the partnership agreement does not give a profit/loss sharing ratio, then the division is equal.

Question 2   MCQ-09422

On December 31, Stewart and Colbert had capital account balances of $200,000 and $150,000, respectively. Their partnership agreement includes the following provisions:

- Profits and losses are to be shared equally.
- Stewart is to receive a salary allowance of $65,000.
- Colbert is to receive a bonus of 50 percent of profits in excess of $100,000.
- Each partner is to receive 10 percent interest on their ending capital accounts.

Partnership profit before any allocations to partners was $150,000. What was the total of the distributions to each partner?

	Stewart	Colbert
1.	$85,000	$40,000
2.	$85,000	$52,500
3.	$97,500	$40,000
4.	$97,500	$52,500

Notes

IV State and Local Governments

Notes

1 Fund Structure

A fund is a sum of money or other resource segregated for the purpose of carrying on a specific activity or attaining certain objectives in accordance with specific regulations, restrictions, or limitations and constituting an independent fiscal and accounting entity. Each fund is a self-balancing set of accounts.

The basis of accounting and measurement focus contribute to the accountability objectives of each fund type.

1.1 Fund Categories and Fund Types

Eleven fund types (**GRaSPP SE-CIPPOE**) are classified in the following three generic categories:

1.1.1 Governmental Funds

- **General:** The general fund accounts for the ordinary operations of a governmental unit that are financed from taxes and other general revenues. All transactions not accounted for in some other funds are accounted for in this fund.

- **Special Revenue:** Special revenue funds account for revenues from specific taxes or other earmarked sources that are restricted or committed to finance particular activities of government other than debt service or capital projects.

- **Debt Service:** Debt service funds account for the accumulation of resources and the payment of interest and principal on all "general obligation debt."

- **Capital Projects:** Capital projects funds account for resources used for the acquisition or construction of major capital assets by a governmental unit.

- **Permanent:** Permanent funds are used to report resources that are legally restricted to the extent that income, and not principal, may be used for purposes that support the reporting government's programs.

1.1.2 Proprietary Funds

- **Internal Service:** Internal service funds account for goods and services provided by departments on a cost reimbursement fee basis to other departments.

- **Enterprise:** Enterprise funds account for the acquisition and operation of governmental facilities and services that are intended to be primarily (over 50 percent) self-supported by user charges.

1.1.3 Fiduciary Funds

- **Custodial:** Custodial funds usually account for resources in temporary custody of the governmental unit and any fiduciary activities that are not required to be reported in other fiduciary fund classifications.

- **Investment Trust:** Investment trust funds account for external investment pools.

- **Private Purpose:** Private purpose trust funds are used for activities not properly accounted for either as pension or investment trust funds.

- **Pension (and Other Employee Benefit):** Pension trust funds account for resources of defined benefit plans, defined contribution plans, post-employment benefit plans, and other long-term employee benefit plans.

Question 1   MCQ-09442

Payback Parish levied an additional one-cent sales tax intended exclusively for the repayment of Civic Center Bonds. The earnings from this sales tax would most appropriately be recorded in the:

1. General Fund.
2. Special Revenue Fund.
3. Debt Service Fund.
4. Capital Projects Fund.

---

2 Measurement Focus

Measurement focus describes the reporting objective that the application of fund accounting is designed to achieve. There are two measurement focuses:

2.1 Current Financial Resources Measurement Focus

Financial statement readers are focused on the sources, uses and balances of current financial resources. The focus often includes a budgetary element. The governmental fund types use the current financial resources measurement focus.

- Non-current assets and liabilities are not reported on the governmental fund types balance sheets.

- Capital outlay expenditures are reported on the face of the governmental fund types operating statements.

- Proceeds from long-term debt, or leases that are either contracts that transfer ownership or other than short-term leases and contracts that transfer ownership, are recorded in the governmental funds as "other financing sources."

- Payment of principal and interest are recorded as "expenditures."

2.2   Economic Resources Measurement Focus

Financial statement readers are focused on the determination of operating income, changes in net assets, financial position and cash flow. The proprietary fund and fiduciary fund types use this focus. Accounting is nearly identical to commercial accounting used in "for profit" entities.

- Non-current assets and non-current liabilities are recorded on the balance sheet.

- Depreciation expense is recorded.

Question 2   MCQ-09359

The Town of Holler has a community development block grant that funds the renewal and revival of economically disadvantaged areas in its jurisdiction. The Town properly accounts for the grant in a special revenue fund. Which one of the following funds would *not* share the use of the current financial resources measurement focus with the Community Development Block Grant Fund?

1. The Holler Bridge Fund (used to account for the bridge construction financed by general obligation debt).

2. The Holler Bridge Debt Service Fund (used to account for the accumulation of resources for the repayment of general obligation debt issued to finance the construction of the Holler Bridge).

3. The Holler Sound Citizen's Initiative Fund (used to account for collection and disbursement of special assessments that pay debt service obligations which the town is barred by statute from assuming).

4. The Holler Cemetery Perpetual Care Fund (that accounts for resources used for the public cemetery).

3 Basis of Accounting

Basis of accounting describes the accounting principles used to accomplish the measurement focus of each fund category. There are two bases:

3.1 Modified Accrual Basis of Accounting

The current financial resources measurement focus is accomplished using the modified accrual basis of accounting. The difference between modified accrual and accrual primarily relates to the timing of revenue recognition.

Revenues are generally accrued when they are *both measurable and available* (due and collected within 60 days of year-end). There are four classifications of non-exchange revenues that serve as the basis for most governmental fund resources. There is no underlying exchange transaction that produces these revenues; the government does not provide a specific service in exchange for the revenue earned:

Modified accrual also creates important expenditure recognition differences, including no interest accrual.

3.1.1 Derived Non-exchange Tax Revenues

A sales tax or an income tax is considered to be "derived" tax revenue; it is a tax that comes as a result of (is derived from) economic activity. Derived non-exchange tax revenues are accrued based on the timing of receipt. Receipts due at year-end and actually received within 60 days of year-end are accrued and recognized as revenue.

3.1.2 Imposed Non-exchange Revenues

Fines and property taxes are imposed non-exchange revenues since the taxpayer's obligation is imposed by an enforceable claim by the government. Imposed non-exchange revenues are typically accrued when billed since collection is not in doubt. Collection of fines is based upon enforcement of a penalty resulting from the violation of law (e.g., driver's licenses can be revoked, cars can be impounded, etc.). Liens on property (allowed by law) are used to enforce property tax collection.

3.1.3 Government Mandated Non-exchange Transactions

Grants are conveyed by one government to another, (a state, or a county) to mandate certain activities.

Revenues are recognized when eligibility requirements are met and the revenues are both measurable and available.

3.1.4 Voluntary Non-exchange Transactions

Resources are willingly conveyed by a government to another for a particular purpose or use without an equal exchange of value. Revenues are recognized when restrictions are met.

3.2 Accrual Basis of Accounting

The economic resources measurement focus is accomplished using the accrual basis of accounting where revenues are recorded when earned and expenses are recorded when incurred.

Question 3   MCQ-09374

The City of Riggsville elected to account for its very small fee-supported trash collection service through its General Fund. Payment for services provided in December, for which payment is not anticipated until March, has not been accrued. The trash collection service shares the same basis of accounting with:

1. The Riggsville Utility Fund, an enterprise fund supported by user charges.

2. The Riggsville Motor Pool, an internal service fund supported by internal user charges.

3. The Riggsville Road and Bridge Fund, used to account for the receipt of gasoline tax funds in a Special Revenue Fund.

4. The Riggsville Employee Retirement Fund, used to account for the pension fund resources that benefit the city's employees.

Question 4   MCQ-09269

Property taxes for the Town of Farrell of $25,000,000 were assessed in October of Year 1 to fund budgeted operations for the fiscal year ended September 30, Year 2. Some $24,000,000 are collected from November Year 1 through March Year 2 with liens of $1,000,000 applied to properties with unpaid property tax bills in May Year 2. Properties subject to delinquent property taxes were auctioned for taxes of $800,000. At September 30, Year 2, government would record property tax revenue of:

1. $25,000,000

2. $24,800,000

3. $24,200,000

4. $24,000,000

Task-Based Simulations

Task-Based Simulation: Basis of Accounting

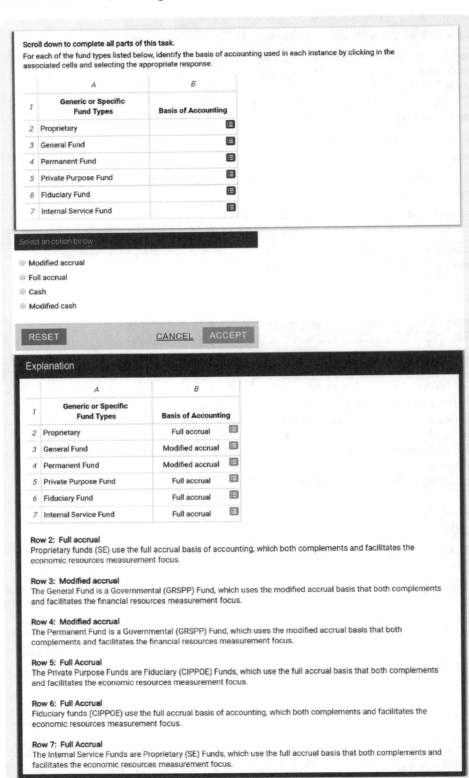

Scroll down to complete all parts of this task.
For each of the fund types listed below, identify the basis of accounting used in each instance by clicking in the associated cells and selecting the appropriate response.

	A Generic or Specific Fund Types	B Basis of Accounting
1		
2	Proprietary	
3	General Fund	
4	Permanent Fund	
5	Private Purpose Fund	
6	Fiduciary Fund	
7	Internal Service Fund	

Select an option below

- Modified accrual
- Full accrual
- Cash
- Modified cash

RESET   CANCEL   ACCEPT

Explanation

	A Generic or Specific Fund Types	B Basis of Accounting
1		
2	Proprietary	Full accrual
3	General Fund	Modified accrual
4	Permanent Fund	Modified accrual
5	Private Purpose Fund	Full accrual
6	Fiduciary Fund	Full accrual
7	Internal Service Fund	Full accrual

Row 2: Full accrual
Proprietary funds (SE) use the full accrual basis of accounting, which both complements and facilitates the economic resources measurement focus.

Row 3: Modified accrual
The General Fund is a Governmental (GRSPP) Fund, which uses the modified accrual basis that both complements and facilitates the financial resources measurement focus.

Row 4: Modified accrual
The Permanent Fund is a Governmental (GRSPP) Fund, which uses the modified accrual basis that both complements and facilitates the financial resources measurement focus.

Row 5: Full Accrual
The Private Purpose Funds are Fiduciary (CIPPOE) Funds, which use the full accrual basis that both complements and facilitates the economic resources measurement focus.

Row 6: Full Accrual
Fiduciary funds (CIPPOE) use the full accrual basis of accounting, which both complements and facilitates the economic resources measurement focus.

Row 7: Full Accrual
The Internal Service Funds are Proprietary (SE) Funds, which use the full accrual basis that both complements and facilitates the economic resources measurement focus.

1 Government-wide Reporting

The GASB 34 reporting model (as amended by GASB 63) focuses the reader on both government-wide and fund financial statements using an integrated approach to highlight both the operational and fiscal accountability requirements of the government.

The basic structure includes the presentation of:

■ Basic financial statements (comprised of government-wide financial statements, fund financial statements, and notes to the financial statements)

■ Required supplementary information

Fund financial statements emphasize fiscal accountability while government-wide financial statements emphasize operational accountability. Financial presentations are integrated by the reconciliation of fund financial statements to government-wide presentations.

Government-wide financial presentations are prepared using the economic resources measurement focus utilizing the accrual basis of accounting. The government-wide financials include presentation of governmental activities and business-type activities such as the enterprise funds. Fiduciary funds are excluded from the government-wide financial statements but are included as part of the fund financial statements.

A matrix to keep in mind for GASB 34 reporting categorizes our fund structure mnemonic as follows for government-wide reporting:

Governmental	Business Type	Excluded
GRaSPP S	E	CIPPOE

Government-wide financial statements are the:

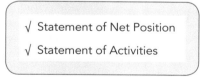

√ Statement of Net Position

√ Statement of Activities

■ Required supplementary information (RSI) is presented both before and after the basic financial statements.

● Preceding the basic financial statements is the management's discussion and analysis, a letter that presents a brief, objective, and easily readable analysis of the government's activities.

● Following the basic financial statements is RSI that includes multi-year pension data, infrastructure data for governments using the modified approach for infrastructure, and budgetary disclosures.

■ Other supplementary information (optional) may be included. Optional information includes budget variances and individual financial statements for nonmajor funds.

■ A statement of cash flows is not prepared for government-wide presentations.

Question 1   MCQ-09428

The Municipality of Sykes prepares its financial statements for the year ended December 31, Year 1. The municipality has elected to display all funds in its report including nonmajor funds. The Municipality of Sykes has the option of:

1. Displaying each nonmajor fund in a combining statements of fund balance sheets and statement of revenues, expenditures, and changes in fund balance.

2. Disclosing nonmajor fund activity in the notes to the financial statements.

3. Describing each nonmajor fund in required supplementary information.

4. Displaying a summary of nonmajor funds in the fund financial statements and a combining statement of nonmajor funds in other supplementary information.

---

2 Fund Financial Statements

Fund financial statements are presented for all funds based on their applicable measurement focus and related basis of accounting. Only major funds are reported separately; nonmajor funds are reported in the aggregate. Individual nonmajor funds may be reported as optional supplementary information.

2.1 Governmental Fund Financial Statements

- **Balance Sheet:** Included in this statement are assets plus deferred outflows of resources, liabilities plus deferred inflows of resources, and fund balance.

- **Statement of Revenues, Expenditures, and Changes in Fund Balance:** Included in this statement are other financing sources (proceeds from debt and interfund transfers) and other financing uses.

2.2 Proprietary Fund Financial Statements

- **Statement of Net Position:** Included in this statement are assets plus deferred outflows of resources, liabilities plus deferred inflows of resources, and net position.

- **Statement of Revenues, Expenses, and Changes in Fund Net Position**

- **Statement of Cash Flows**

2.3 Fiduciary Fund Financial Statements

- **Statement of Fiduciary Net Position:** Included in this statement are assets plus deferred outflows of resources, liabilities plus deferred inflows of resources, and net position.)

- **Statement of Changes in Fiduciary Net Position**

2.4 Determination of Major Funds

GASB 34 as amended by GASB 63 emphasizes reporting by major fund rather than fund type. To qualify as a major fund the two following criteria must be met:

1. An individual fund's total assets plus deferred outflows of resources, or liabilities plus deferred inflows of resources, or revenues, or expenditures/expenses, are at least 10 percent or more of the corresponding total assets plus deferred outflows of resources, or liabilities plus deferred inflows of resources, or revenues, or expenditures/expenses of all governmental funds or enterprise funds (e.g., a special revenue fund's revenues would need to be 10 percent of the revenues for the governmental fund financial statement category; a water and sewer fund's revenues would need to be 10 percent of all enterprise funds' revenues).

2. The same individual fund's total assets plus deferred outflows of resources, or liabilities plus deferred inflows of resources, or revenues, or expenditures/expenses, are at least 5 percent or more of the corresponding total assets plus deferred outflows of resources, or liabilities plus deferred inflows of resources, or revenues, or expenditures/expenses of all governmental funds and enterprise funds combined (e.g., a special revenue fund's revenues would need to be 5 percent of the combined revenues amounts for governmental and enterprise funds; a water and sewer fund's revenues would need to be 5 percent of the combined revenue amounts for governmental and enterprise funds).

2.5   Reconciliation of Fund Statements to Government-wide Statements

Because of the different measurement focus and related basis of accounting used, the governmental fund balance as reported in the balance sheet must be reconciled to net position of government-wide statements as reported in the statement of net position.

■ The difference in measurement focus provides the following reconciling items:

- Add non-current assets.

- Subtract non-current liabilities.

- Add internal service fund net assets.

■ The difference in basis of accounting produces the following reconciling items:

- Adjust for accrual of revenue accounted for on the full accrual basis of accounting rather than the modified accrual basis of accounting.

- Adjust for accrual of expenses accounted for on the full accrual basis of accounting rather than the expenditures accrued on the modified accrual basis of accounting.

- The changes in fund balance displayed in the governmental fund statement of revenues, expenditures, and changes in fund balances must be reconciled to changes in net position of the governmental activities column as reported in the statement of activities of the government-wide statement.

■ The difference in measurement focus produces the following reconciling items:

- Subtract debt proceeds (not accounted for as other financing sources in the government-wide financial statements).

- Add capital outlay (not accounted for as expenses in the government-wide financial statements).

- Add internal service fund changes in net position accounted for in the proprietary funds.

- The difference in basis of accounting produces the following reconciling items:

  • Adjust for accrual of revenue accounted for on the accrual basis of accounting rather than the modified accrual basis of accounting.

  • Adjust for accrual of expenses accounted for on the accrual basis rather than the expenditures accrued on the modified accrual basis.

Balance Sheet	Statement of Revenues, Expenditures, and Changes in Fund Balance
GRaSPP—Fund balance	*GRaSPP—Net change in fund balance*
Assets (non-current)	Other financing sources
Liabilities (non-current)	Expenditure—capital outlay (net of depreciation)
Service (internal) fund net position	Service (internal) fund net income
Basis of Accounting	*Basis of Accounting*
Accrued	Additional accrued
Revenues and	Revenues and
Expenses	Expenses

2.6 Statement of Cash Flows

The Statement of Cash Flows is only used for the proprietary funds. The direct method is required and it is prepared in a manner similar to the commercial version, with the following differences:

- There are four categories (instead of the three) and the order of the categories is the following:

  1. Operating activities.

  2. Noncapital financing activities.

  3. Capital and related financing activities.

  4. Investing activities.

- Interest income/cash receipts are reported as "investing activities" (not as operating activities). Interest expense/cash payments are either:

  • capital and related financing; or

  • noncapital financing.

- Capital asset purchases are reported as "financing activities" (not as investing activities).

- Interest expense/cash disbursements are reported as "financing activities" (not as operating activities).

- Many transactions unique to government (e.g., transfers, property tax revenues, and special assessments) are often classified as "non-capital financing activities."

- A reconciliation of operating income (instead of net income) to net cash provided by operations is required.

Question 2   MCQ-09344

The City of Richardson reported a change in fund balances of $2,002,000 in its governmental funds Statement of Revenues, Expenditures, and Changes in Fund Balances for the year ended December 31, Year 1. Additional information:

1. Capital outlay expenditures amounted to $10,000,000 in the modified accrual statement. General government fixed assets amounted to $160,000,000 excluding land and had an average life of 20 years.

2. The modified accrual statement reported proceeds from the sale of land in the amount of $1,000,000. The land had a basis of $800,000.

3. Property taxes had been levied in the amount of $20,000,000. It was estimated that 3% would be uncollected, that $1,000,000 would be collected within 60 days of year-end, and that $400,000 would be collected more than 60 days from year-end. The City had recognized the maximum permitted under modified accrual accounting.

4. $370,000 of property taxes had been deferred at the end of the previous year and was recognized under modified accrual as revenue in the current year.

5. The modified accrual statement reflected debt service expenditures in the amount of $1,000,000 for interest and $1,500,000 for principal. No adjustment was necessary for interest accruals at year-end.

6. Compensated absences charges, on the full accrual basis, amounted to $100,000 more than under the modified accrual basis.

The change in net position in the governmental column in the government-wide Statement of Activities for the year ended December 31, Year 1 is:

1. 4,602,000
2. 5,202,000
3. 3,832,000
4. 4,632,000

3 Infrastructure

Infrastructure can have an impact on both the statement of net assets and statement of activities. Included among the capitalized non-current assets on the government-wide statement of net assets should be eligible infrastructure, such as roads, drainage systems, and bridges. Consequently, depreciation of such assets is required, and should be reported in the statement of activities.

However, if the government is unable to arrive at the cost data for its infrastructure, the use of a modified approach (no capitalization needed) is acceptable, provided that supplementary information describing the infrastructure, its condition, and estimation of expenses needed to maintain condition is included in the RSI. A complete new professional assessment of the infrastructure condition is necessary every three years.

Question 3   MCQ-09434

The Village of James has elected to use the modified approach for reporting infrastructure for the year ended December 31, Year 1. Using the modified approach, the government's asset management system does not need to include:

1. Inventory of assets.

2. Summary of condition assessments.

3. Estimated net realizable value of community infrastructure.

4. Amount necessary to maintain and preserve the condition of the assets.

---

4 Comprehensive Annual Financial Report

Governments often present a Comprehensive Annual Financial Report (CAFR). A CAFR is not required by GASB 34. It is a GFOA designated presentation that adds introductory and statistical sections to the GASB 34 presentation, as follows:

1. Introductory Section (unaudited)
   - Letter of transmittal
   - Organizational chart
   - List of principal officers

2. Basic Financial Statements and Required Supplementary Information (audited)
   - MD&A
   - Government-wide financial statements
   - Fund financial statements
   - Notes to financial statements
   - Required supplementary information

3. Statistical Section (unaudited)
   - Ten years of selected data
   - Ten years of economic data
   - Other data

5 Financial Statements Samples

	Progressive Township **Statement of Net Position** December 31, Year 1			
	Primary Government			
	Governmental Activities	*Business-type Activities*	*Total*	*Component Units*
Assets				
Cash	$4,055,000	$2,000,000	$6,055,000	$520,000
Derivative instrument—rate swap	–	40,000	40,000	–
Receivables	1,065,000	670,000	1,735,000	–
Internal balances	450,000	(450,000)	–	–
Inventories	96,000	127,500	223,500	–
Capital assets	2,827,000	2,975,000	5,802,000	–
Total assets	8,493,000	5,362,500	13,855,500	520,000
Deferred Outflows of Resources				
Accumulated decrease in fair value of hedging derivatives	–	35,000	35,000	–
Total deferred outflows of resources	–	35,000	35,000	–
Liabilities				
Accounts payable	1,104,000	400,000	1,504,000	130,000
Forward contract	–	35,000	35,000	–
Other liabilities	95,000	–	95,000	–
Non-current liabilities:				
Due within one year	46,000	337,500	383,500	–
Due in more than one year	3,518,000	2,750,000	6,268,000	–
Total liabilities	4,763,000	3,522,500	8,285,500	130,000
Deferred Inflows of Resources				
Accumulated increase in fair value of hedging derivatives	–	40,000	40,000	–
Total deferred inflows of resources	–	40,000	40,000	–
Net Position				
Net investment in capital assets	1,227,000	450,000	1,677,000	–
Restricted for:				
Capital projects	1,574,000	–	1,574,000	–
Debt service	723,000	1,200,000	1,923,000	–
Unrestricted	206,000	185,000	391,000	390,000
Total net position	$3,730,000	$1,835,000	$5,565,000	$390,000

Progressive Township
Statement of Activities
For the Year Ended December 31, Year 1

Functions/Programs	Expenses	Indirect Expense Allocation	Program Revenues			NET (Expenses) Revenues and Changes in NET Position			Component Units
			Charges for Services	Operating Grants and Contributions	Capital Grants and Contributions	Primary Government			
						Governmental Activities	Business-type Activities	Total	
Primary government:									
Governmental activities:									
General government	$ 555,000	(50,000)	$ 215,000	–	–	(290,000)	–	(290,000)	–
Public safety	1,025,000	$35,000	78,000	–	–	(982,000)	–	(982,000)	–
Culture and recreation	107,500	10,000	–	–	–	(117,500)	–	(117,500)	–
Other functional classifications	1,947,000	5,000	–	$1,260,000	–	(692,000)	–	(692,000)	–
Interest on long-term debt	246,000	–	125,000	–	–	(121,000)	–	(121,000)	–
Total governmental activities	3,880,500	–	418,000	1,260,000	–	(2,202,500)	–	(2,202,500)	–
Business-type activities:									
Water	692,000		700,000	–	–	–	$ 8,000	8,000	–
Sewer	1,038,000		1,050,000	–	$300,000	–	312,000	312,000	–
Parking facilities	465,000		650,000	–	–	–	185,000	185,000	–
Total business-type activities	2,195,000		$2,400,000	–	300,000	–	505,000	505,000	–
Total primary government	6,075,500		2,818,000	$1,260,000	300,000	(2,202,500)	505,000	(1,697,500)	–
Component units:									
Landfill	300,000		500,000	–	–	–	–	–	200,000
Public school system	1,000,000		100,000	–	–	–	–	–	(900,000)
Total component units	$1,300,000		600,000	–	–	–	–	–	(700,000)
General revenues									
Taxes:									
Property taxes—levied for general purposes						$1,620,000	–	$1,620,000	$1,000,000
Franchise taxes						735,000	–	735,000	–
Investment earnings						205,000	60,000	265,000	–
Special item—gain on sale of governmental capital property						425,000	–	425,000	–
Transfers						12,000	(12,000)	–	–
Total general revenues, special items, and transfers						2,997,000	48,000	3,045,000	1,000,000
Change in net position						794,500	553,000	1,347,500	300,000
Net position—beginning						2,935,500	1,282,000	4,217,500	90,000
Net position—ending						$3,730,000	$1,835,000	$5,565,000	$ 390,000

Progressive Township
Balance Sheet
Governmental Funds
December 31, Year 1

	General Fund	HUD Programs	Convention Development Tax	Convention Center Bonds	Convention Center Construction	Other Governmental Funds	Total Governmental Funds
Assets							
Cash	$ 800,000	$80,000	$250,000	$505,000	$2,100,000	$270,000	$4,005,000
Receivables	162,000	–	–	125,000	–	–	287,000
Due from other funds	450,000	–	–	60,000	–	–	510,000
Receivables from other governments	620,000	–	50,000	–	–	83,000	753,000
Inventories	55,000	–	–	–	–	6,000	61,000
Total assets	2,087,000	80,000	300,000	690,000	2,100,000	359,000	5,616,000
Liabilities							
Accounts payable	250,000	20,000	56,000	–	600,000	100,000	1,026,000
Due to other funds	50,000	–	60,000	–	–	–	110,000
Payable to other governments	65,000	–	–	–	–	–	65,000
Other liabilities	95,000	–	–	–	–	–	95,000
Total liabilities	460,000	20,000	116,000	–	600,000	100,000	1,296,000
Deferred Inflows of Resources							
Unavailable revenues—special assessments	–	–	–	125,000	–	–	125,000
Total deferred inflows of resources	–	–	–	125,000	–	–	125,000
Fund Balances							
Nonspendable Inventories	55,000	–	–	–	–	6,000	61,000
Restricted for:							
Debt service	–	–	–	565,000	–	158,000	723,000
Capital projects	–	–	–	–	1,500,000	74,000	1,574,000
Committed to:							
Urban renewal	–	60,000	184,000	–	–	–	244,000
Sanitation	45,000	–	–	–	–	–	45,000
Assigned:							
Special revenue funds	–	–	–	–	–	36,000	36,000
Unassigned:							
General fund	1,527,000	–	–	–	–	–	1,527,000
Special revenue funds	–	–	–	–	–	(15,000)	(15,000)
Total fund balances	1,627,000	60,000	184,000	565,000	1,500,000	259,000	4,195,000
Total liabilities, deferred inflows of resources, and fund balances	$2,087,000	$80,000	$300,000	$690,000	$2,100,000	$359,000	$5,616,000

Total governmental fund balances	4,195,000
Capital assets used in governmental activities that are not reported in fund financial statements	2,667,000
Other long-term assets not available to defray the cost of current expenses and are not reported in fund financial statements	125,000
Long-term liabilities including bonds payable not recorded in fund financial statements	(3,420,000)
Internal service fund used for governmental activities	163,000
Net position from governmental activities	$3,730,000

Progressive Township
Statement of Revenues, Expenditures, and Changes in Fund Balances
Governmental Funds
For the Year Ended December 31, Year 1

	General Fund	HUD Programs	Convention Development Tax	Convention Center Bonds	Convention Center Construction	Other Governmental Funds	Total Governmental Funds
Revenues							
Property taxes	$1,620,000	–	–	–	–	–	$1,620,000
Fees and fines	120,000	–	–	–	–	–	120,000
Intergovernmental	–	$960,000	$375,000	–	–	$ 660,000	1,995,000
Charges for services	–	–	–	–	–	78,000	78,000
Interest earnings	55,000	–	28,000	$ 36,000	$ 40,000	40,000	199,000
Total Revenues	1,795,000	960,000	403,000	36,000	40,000	778,000	4,012,000
Expenditures							
Current:							
General government	450,000	–	–	–	–	–	450,000
Public safety	1,000,000	–	–	–	–	–	1,000,000
Culture and recreation	80,000	–	17,500	–	–	–	97,500
Other functional classifications	200,000	940,000	–	–	–	757,000	1,897,000
Debt service:							
Principal	–	–	–	250,000	–	110,000	360,000
Interest and other charges	–	–	–	30,000	–	211,000	241,000
Capital outlay	25,000	–	–	–	600,000	162,000	787,000
Total expenditures	1,755,000	940,000	17,500	280,000	600,000	$1,240,000	4,832,500
Excess (deficiency) of revenues over expenditures	40,000	20,000	385,500	(244,000)	(560,000)	(462,000)	(820,500)
Other Financing Sources (Uses)							
Proceeds of long-term capital-related debt	–	–	–	–	2,080,000	–	2,080,000
Transfers in	85,000	–	–	370,000	–	66,000	521,000
Transfers out	(14,000)	–	(250,000)	–	(120,000)	(125,000)	(509,000)
Total other financing sources and uses	71,000	–	(250,000)	370,000	1,960,000	(59,000)	2,092,000
Special Item							
Proceeds from sale of land	500,000	–	–	–	–	–	500,000
Net change in fund balances	611,000	20,000	135,500	126,000	1,400,000	(521,000)	1,771,500
Fund balances—beginning	1,016,000	40,000	48,500	439,000	100,000	780,000	2,423,500
Fund balances—ending	$1,627,000	$ 60,000	$184,000	$565,000	$1,500,000	$ 259,000	$4,195,000

Progressive Township **Reconciliation of the Statement of Revenue, Expenditures, and Changes in Fund Balances of Governmental Funds to the Statement of Activities** For the Year Ended December 31, Year 1		
Net change in fund balances—total governmental funds		$1,771,500
Bond proceeds	(2,080,000)	
Payments	$ 360,000	
Excess of bond proceeds over principal payments		(1,720,000)
Proceeds of land sold	(500,000)	
Gain on sale	425,000	
Cost of land sold (excess of proceeds over gain on disposal)		(75,000)
Capital outlay	787,000	
Depreciation expense:		
General government	(35,000)	
Public safety	(25,000)	
Culture and recreation	(10,000)	
Other functional classifications	(50,000)	
Amount by which capital outlay exceeded depreciation in the current period		667,000
Revenues in the statement of activities that do not provide current financial resources are not reported in the funds		125,000
Net revenue (expense) of internal service funds		26,000
Change in net position of governmental activities		$ 794,500

Notes

1 Reporting Units

Reporting units (the primary government and its component units) are the governmental version of "consolidations." When to consolidate and how to consolidate is important under the GASB 34 model.

1.1 Primary Governments and Component Units

A government is viewed as a stand-alone or primary government if it has a separately elected governing board, it is a legal entity and it is financially independent.

A government that cannot stand by itself is a component unit of another government and should present its financial statements with the primary government.

1.2 Discrete vs. Blended Presentation

Component units are presented either discretely or in a blended format. Generally, component units are presented as discrete (separate columns) on the primary government's financial statements.

Blended presentations are made when the component unit either exclusively serves the primary government or when the component unit's governing body is substantially the same as the primary government's governing body. Blending involves consolidation of activities.

Question 1   MCQ-09388

Geartyville established the Cox Administration Corporation, a nonprofit corporation for the purpose of administering employee welfare benefits for the employees of Geartyville. The city appoints the corporation's Board of Directors. The financial statements of the Cox Administration Corporation should be:

1. Presented discretely as a component unit.
2. Presented as a blended component unit.
3. Only disclosed in the notes to the financial statements.
4. Displayed as a stand alone corporation.

---

1 Interfund Activity

Interfund activity is subject to specific requirements related to financial statement display and disclosure and can be classified as follows:

- Reciprocal interfund activity
- Nonreciprocal interfund activity

1.1 Reciprocal Interfund Activity

- Includes exchange-type transactions between funds.
- Interfund loans are expected to be repaid and are accounted for as interfund receivables and payables (due from/due to).
- Unrealizable balances are reclassified as transfers.
- Interfund services provided and used represent sales and purchases between funds at external pricing. Transactions of this type are accounted for as revenues and expenses.

1.2 Nonreciprocal Interfund Activity

- Represents non-exchange transactions between funds.
- Interfund transfers of assets between funds without the exchange of equivalent value represent interfund transfers. These are normally reported as other financing sources and uses after nonoperating revenues and expenses.
- Interfund payments of expenses made by one fund on behalf of another fund are accounted for as reimbursements. Interfund reimbursements are not displayed as interfund transactions.

1.3 Government-wide Financial Statement Displays of Interfund Activity

- Interfund activity within a particular column displayed on the governmental activities or business-type activities financial statements (intra-activity transaction between governmental funds and internal service funds) is eliminated prior to the preparation of governmental-wide financial statements.
- Interfund activity between columns displayed on the governmental activities or business-type activities financial statements (inter-activity transaction between governmental funds and enterprise funds) is reported as "internal balances" on the statement of net assets and "transfers" (revenues or expenses) in the statement of activities. They are not eliminated.
- Interfund activity between the primary government and its fiduciary funds should be reported as if between external parties.

2 Fund Accounting Mechanics

Fund accounting mechanics generally focus on the accounting for the governmental funds and require knowledge of the journal entries used to record the budget, actual activities, and encumbrances.

2.1 Budgetary Activity

To record the budget into the accounting records, the following entry is used. Any balancing amounts are posted to budgetary control.

DR	Estimated revenue control	$XXX	
CR	Appropriations control		$XXX
CR	Budgetary control		XXX

Budgetary control can also be a debit. Budgetary accounts are recorded at the beginning of the year and are closed at the end of the year. Budgetary accounts are only impacted when establishing, amending or closing the budget.

2.2 Actual Activity

Actual activities are recorded as they happen throughout the year. Expenditures are typically recorded as they are incurred.

Capital purchases are identified as capital outlay because of their long-term nature but they are accounted for as expenditures and they are not reported in the balance sheet. In addition, no depreciation expense is recorded on governmental fund financial statements. Generally, all spending is recorded currently as "expenditures."

DR	Capital outlay expenditures	$XXX	
CR	Cash or vouchers payable		$XXX

Principal payment on debt is displayed as an expenditure since there is no non-current debt recorded on the governmental fund financial statements.

DR	Debt service—principal expenditure	$XXX	
CR	Cash		$XXX

In addition, new debt proceeds are recorded as other financing sources, a resource inflow:

DR	Cash	$XXX	
CR	Other financing sources—debt proceeds		$XXX

Leases that include contracts that transfer ownership, or leases that are other than short-term leases (more than 12 months) and contracts that transfer ownership, are also recorded as other financing sources.

DR	Capital outlay	$XXX	
CR	Other financing sources—lease		$XXX

The modified accrual basis of accounting records (accrues) revenue when it is measurable and available, generally collected within 60 days of year-end. Only the amount available is recorded as revenue. Note the entry below to record property tax receivable (imposed non-exchange revenue) and the related allowance for uncollectible taxes. Tax receivable is recorded when the tax is levied but only available revenue is recognized. No "bad debt expenditure" is recognized.

DR	Property tax receivable—current	$XXX	
CR	Allowance for uncollectible taxes—current		$XXX
CR	Property tax revenue		XXX

2.3 Encumbrance Activity

Encumbrances are recorded when purchase orders are issued. The issuance of a purchase order does not represent a liability, rather, the reserve for encumbrance account acts as a limitation that reduces the available fund balance. Entries to record the encumbrance of funds and the receipt of goods are as follows:

To record the issuance of a purchase order:

DR	Encumbrances	$XXX	
CR	Budgetary control		$XXX

Upon receipt of goods the encumbrance of funds associated with the issued order is reversed and the related expenditure is recorded.

DR	Budgetary control	$XXX	
CR	Encumbrances		$XXX
DR	Expenditure	$XXX	
CR	Vouchers payable		$XXX

2.4   Relationship Between Accounts at Year-End

Governmental funds record budget, actual, and encumbrance activities separately. Both budget and actual activities are recorded during the year and then closed at the end of the year. Encumbrances are recorded and closed throughout the year. At year-end, if encumbrances are still outstanding, they are reported as a component of committed or assigned fund balance and disclosed if appropriations do not lapse.

2.5   Inventory of Supplies

When the government buys supplies, two methods can be used for the transaction: purchase and consumption.

At the time of purchase:

The Purchase Method			The Consumption Method		
DR	Expenditures	$5,000	DR	Inventory of supply	$5,000
CR	Vouchers payable	5,000	CR	Vouchers payable	5,000

At year-end (assumption: 1,000 of supply is still on hand):

DR	Inventory of supply	$1,000	DR	Expenditures	$4,000
CR	Nonspendable fund balance – inventory	1,000	CR	Inventory of supply	4,000

Under the purchase method the remaining inventory must be placed in the balance sheet (it was all expensed at the beginning) and because it cannot be spent in that year, the fund balance should be reclassified as being nonspendable fund balance—inventory.

Question 1   MCQ-09444

Refund Ridge Township issued General Governmental Refunding Bonds for $1,000,000 at 98 during the year ended June 30, Year 1. The entire amount of the difference between bond proceeds and face amount relates to the original issue discount. The Township would report the following balances in the indicated accounts in its Debt Service Fund financial statements at and for the year ended June 30, Year 1:

	Bonds Payable	Other Financing Sources	Other Financing Uses
1.	$1,000,000	$0	$980,000
2.	$0	$20,000	$1,000,000
3.	$0	$1,000,000	$20,000
4.	$0	$0	$0

Question 2   MCQ-09329

The County of Deutsch appropriated $45,000 in its General Fund for miscellaneous supplies for its fiscal year ended September 30, Year 1. The County found that it had paid $15,000 for miscellaneous supplies in November Year 0 and issued a $30,000 PO to a sole source vendor for miscellaneous supplies in December Year 0. By August Year 1, the County had received $20,000 related to the order but did not pay the vendor until October pending tax receipts. Appropriations do not lapse. What was the County of Deutsch's available appropriation at September 30, Year 1?

1. $0
2. $15,000
3. $10,000
4. $5,000

---

3 Fund Balance Classifications

Governmental fund balances are classified in any one of five ways (different levels of constraint):

3.1 Nonspendable

Nonspendable fund balances represent resources that are nonspendable because they are not in spendable form (e.g., inventories or prepaid expenditures) or legally or contractually required to be maintained intact (e.g., permanent fund principal).

3.2 Restricted

Restricted fund balances represent resources whose use has been limited by such external sources as creditors (e.g., debt covenants), contributors, other governments, laws, constitutional provisions, or enabling legislation.

3.3 Committed

Committed fund balances represent resources that can only be used for specific purposes pursuant to constraints imposed by formal action of the government's highest level of decision-making authority.

3.4 Assigned

Assigned fund balances are constrained by the government's intent to be used for specific purposes but are neither restricted nor committed.

3.5 Unassigned

Unassigned fund balances is the residual classification for the general fund. This classification represents fund balance that has not been assigned to other funds and that has not been restricted, committed or assigned to specific purposes within the general fund. The general fund should be the only fund that shows a positive unassigned fund balance amount. Over-expenditure of resources in other governmental funds may, however, result in a reported negative unassigned fund balance.

Question 3   MCQ-09449

The least restrictive classification of governmental fund balances is titled:

1. Unreserved
2. Unassigned
3. Unspendable
4. Committed

---

4 Deferred Outflows and Inflows of Resources

GASB 63 requires that certain transactions that do not qualify for treatment as either assets or liabilities be accounted for and reported as deferred outflows of resources or deferred inflows of resources. A deferred outflow of resources is a consumption of net assets that is applicable to a future reporting period. Deferred outflows of resources have a positive effect on net position and are reported following assets but before liabilities. A deferred inflow of resources is an acquisition of net assets that is applicable to a future reporting period. Deferred inflows of resources have a negative effect on net position and are reported following liabilities but before equity.

4.1 Government-wide Statement of Net Position

Governments are encouraged to report net position as the difference between assets plus deferred outflows of resources and liabilities plus deferred inflows of resources.

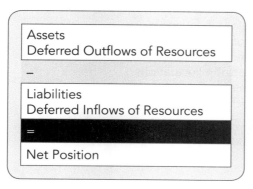

4.2   Governmental Fund Balance Sheet

Governmental funds should present the statement of financial position in a balance sheet format that displays assets plus deferred outflows of resources equal to liabilities plus deferred inflows of resources plus fund balance.

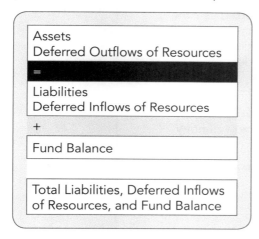

4.3   Proprietary and Fiduciary Statement of Net Position

Proprietary funds are encouraged and fiduciary funds are required to report net position as the difference between assets plus deferred outflows of resources and liabilities plus deferred inflows of resources (similar to the government-wide statement of net position). Proprietary funds can also use a balance sheet format [(Assets + Deferred outflows of resources) = (Liabilities + Deferred inflows of resources) + Net position].

4.4   Types of Transactions Accounted for as Deferred Outflows and Inflows of Resources

4.4.1   Service Concession Arrangements

Advance payments by vendors that operate infrastructure in exchange for volume based fees are displayed as deferred inflows of resources until earned.

4.4.2 Hedge Accounting

Derivatives used as hedges to mitigate the risk of fluctuations in fair value or cash flows qualify for accounting as deferred outflows of resources and deferred inflows of resources if they are effective. Effectiveness means that changes in the value of a derivative used as a hedge offsets the fluctuations in the fair value or cash flows of the hedged item. A sample entry for the decline in value of a qualifying derivative instrument would be:

DR	Deferred outflows of resources	$XXX	
CR	Derivative instrument		$XXX

This is similar to the use of other comprehensive income when recording unrealized gains and losses for a nongovernmental entity.

4.4.3 Other Deferred Outflows/Inflows of Resources

GASB 65, "Items Previously Reported as Assets and Liabilities," revises the treatment of a variety of transactions previously reported as either assets or liabilities on the statement of financial position to classification as either deferred outflows/inflows of resources or recognition as revenue or expense. Transactions addressed in the statement include:

- Refunding of debt
- Imposed non-exchange revenue transactions
- Government-mandated non-exchange transactions and voluntary non-exchange transactions
- Sales of future revenues and intra-entity transfers of future revenues
- Debt issuance costs
- Leases
- Regulated operations
- Assets associated with unavailable revenues
- Certain changes in net pension liability (GASB 68)
- Lease receivable for leases other than short-term leases and contracts that transfer ownership in SE-CIPPOE funds (GASB 87)

Question 4   MCQ-09708

A municipality that appropriately classifies a derivative as a hedge will account for an increase in the value of the derivative, which is reported as an asset, as:

1. An increase in deferred inflows of resources.
2. A decrease in deferred inflows of resources.
3. An increase in deferred outflows of resources.
4. A decrease in deferred outflows of resources.

V | Not-for-Profit Accounting and Reporting

Notes

General Purpose Financial Statements

Topic **A**

1 Not-for-Profit Entities

Not-for-profit entities possess the following characteristics:

- Contributions of significant amounts of resources received from providers who do not expect commensurate or proportionate return.
- Operating purposes other than to provide goods or services at a profit.
- Absence of ownership interest.

The FASB has the primary responsibility of providing guidance on generally accepted accounting principles for not-for-profit entities.

2 Required Financial Statements

2.1 Basic Financial Statements

All not-for-profit entities are required to prepare three basic financial statements on the full accrual basis:

> √ Statement of Financial Position
> √ Statement of Activities
> √ *Statement of Cash Flows*

2.2 Disclosure of Functional Expenses

Not-for-profit organizations are required to present disclosure of functional expenses, analyzed by object classification.

The objective of the functional expense disclosure is to present the programmatic and support expenses displayed horizontally on the statement of activities in separate columns and to analyze the expenses by object (natural classifications).

Question 1   MCQ-09268

The Felix Nursing Home Inc. is a health care provider organized as a not-for-profit organization whose activities are regulated by state licensure rules. The financial information that the Felix Nursing Home Inc. is required to produce are:

	Statement of Financial Position	Statement of Activity	Statement of Cash Flows	Functional Expense Disclosure
1.	Yes	Yes	Yes	Yes
2.	Yes	Yes	Yes	No
3.	Yes	Yes	No	No
4.	Yes	Yes	No	Yes

3 Net Asset Classification

The reporting objectives of not-for-profit organizations include presentation of the net assets at the balance sheet date and the components of the change in net assets on the statement of activities for the year ending on the balance sheet date. There are two net asset classifications:

3.1 Without Donor Restrictions

Net assets free of donor restrictions on usage.

3.2 With Donor Restrictions

Only donors may restrict assets. The management or board can designate or identify assets to be used for a particular purpose. However, a designation is not a restriction. Net assets contributed with donor-imposed restrictions may be either temporary in nature (due to purpose, time, or acquisition of plant) or in perpetuity.

3.2.1 Purpose

The money must be spent as the donor stipulates (e.g., cancer research, youth education).

3.2.2 Time

The donated assets may be donor restricted until a fixed period passes (e.g., a gift of a CD that must be held until maturity and then can be spent as the organization wishes). Time restrictions may also be implied by availability; contributions receivable generally increase net assets with donor restrictions.

3.2.3 Acquisition of Plant

The donated assets are classified as net assets with donor restrictions to purchase or build long-lived assets.

3.2.4 Donor Restrictions in Perpetuity (Endowments)

Net assets contributed with restrictions, such as an endowment fund where the corpus must be retained in perpetuity and interest income can be used by the not-for-profit organization in accordance with the donor's stipulations.

Question 2   MCQ-09358

Andrew contributed $250,000 to an endowment in the name of his late father, Phillip, at Ray Private University on January 2, Year 1. The terms of the bequest require that principal be retained intact and that the earnings from the principal be used to fund the Phil Anthorpist chair for accountancy. If Ray Private University earns $15,000 during Year 1 from the donation, the college would record the following for Year 1:

1. Increases in net assets without donor restrictions of $265,000.
2. Increases in net assets with donor restrictions of $265,000.
3. Increases in net assets without donor restrictions of $250,000 and increases in net assets with donor restrictions of $15,000.
4. Increases in net assets without donor restrictions of $15,000 and increases in net assets with donor restrictions of $250,000.

---

4 Statement of Cash Flows

The statement of cash flows is the same as the statement issued by commercial enterprises with a few unusual features. Either the direct or indirect method can be used. There are three categories of cash flow activities:

4.1 Operating Activities

- Include applicable agency transactions.
- Include receipts of resources without donor restrictions designated by the governing body to be used for long-lived assets.

4.2 Investing Activities

- Include proceeds from the sale of works of art or purchases of works of art.
- Include investment in equipment.
- Include proceeds from the sale of assets that were received in prior periods and whose sale proceeds were donor-restricted to investment in equipment.

4.3 Financing Activities

4.3.1 Proceeds From Donor-Restricted Contributions

■ Include cash received with donor-imposed restrictions limiting its use to purchases of long-term assets or annuity agreements.

  ● Disbursements of these donor-restricted contributions for either investments or the purpose for which they were intended are classified as investing activities.

4.3.2 Other Types of Financing Activities

Include receipts and disbursements associated with borrowing and receipts of dividends and interest that is donor-restricted to reinvestment.

4.4 Cash and Cash Equivalents

Donor-restricted securities that may otherwise meet the cash equivalent criteria in commercial accounting are excluded.

Question 3   MCQ-09283

Walton Farms Boys Home Inc. is a not-for-profit organization that received marketable securities from a donor with a fair value of $100,000 on July 1, Year 1. The securities were donated with the stipulation that proceeds would be used to build new dormitories. On January 8, Year 2, Walton Farms Boys Home elected to sell the securities for $110,000 and begin construction on the dormitories. On its Statement of Cash Flows for the year ended December 31, Year 2, the Walton Farms Boys Home would display cash flows from the securities transaction as:

	Operating	Investing	Financing
1.	$110,000	$0	$0
2.	$0	$110,000	$0
3.	$10,000	$100,000	$0
4.	$0	$0	$110,000

---

1 Revenue and Support Recognition

Not-for-profit accounting focuses on two terms (conditional and restricted) that are often used interchangeably in conversation but have two distinct accounting meanings.

- Classification of net assets relates to presence (with) or absence (without) of donor-imposed restrictions on contributions.
- Recognition of revenue relates to the treatment of gifts or promises to give. Conditional promises are not recorded and conditional gifts received in advance of satisfying conditions are recorded as liabilities.
- Conditional is not the same as restricted.

Resource inflows in not-for-profit organizations are generally displayed in the financial statements as either revenue or other support. Revenues typically represent exchange transactions in which the not-for-profit organization earns resources in exchange for a service performed (e.g., fees). Support often represents unconditional contributions.

1.1 Cash Contributions and Unconditional Promises

Cash contributions and unconditional promises are displayed as support upon receipt or accrual.

1.2 Conditional Promises and Receipts

Cash contributions that can only be used upon meeting a condition and conditional promises to give are not recorded as revenue until the condition is met. A condition is a contingency that must be resolved, rather than a restriction that can be satisfied. Conditional contributions ("good faith deposits") are displayed as a liability titled "refundable advance." Conditional promises to give are not recorded.

1.3 Multiyear Pledges

Unconditional promises receivable over a period of years are recognized as an increase to net assets with donor restrictions since amounts have an implied time restriction. Receivables are recorded at their present value with the difference between face and present value recognized as contribution revenue over time, not interest.

1.4 Other Revenue Transactions and Issues

- Agency transactions relate to receipts of resources over which the not-for-profit organization has no discretion or "variance power." The absence of variance power over the resources creates a liability rather than revenue.

- Gifts-in-kind represent noncash contributions recorded as both support and an offsetting expense.

- Exchange transactions represent the sale of goods or services in exchange for a fee. Exchange transactions are classified as revenues without donor restrictions.

- Donations with donor restrictions for which restrictions will be satisfied within the year of receipt may be classified as donations without donor restrictions in the event that the not-for-profit organization consistently applies this policy.

Question 1   MCQ-09387

The Darberville Day Care collected $45,000 in day care fees from families during the year ended December 31, Year 1, to provide services. During the same period, the Day Care collected $30,000 from the United Way to provide ongoing funding for the Day Care's early childhood development programming and $10,000 from the Federal School Lunch Program to defray the cost of meals served to children. The Day Care's accounting policies consistently allow for the direct recording of contribution revenue with donor restrictions as contribution revenue without donor restrictions when the terms and conditions of the contributions are met in the year of donation. As a result of the above transactions, the Day Care would record revenues and support without donor restrictions of:

1. $40,000
2. $45,000
3. $75,000
4. $85,000

---

2 Expense Classification and Display

Expenses are defined as program or support services. Program expenses relate to the mission of the organization while support services relate to the organization's administrative, membership development and fundraising expenses. The total amount of each functional expense (the expenses by individual program or support service) is displayed on the face of the statement of activities or disclosed in the notes to the financial statement.

3 Split-Interest Agreements

Agreements such as charitable remainder trusts represent donor contributions structured to simultaneously donate assets to the not-for-profit organization and share those assets with a beneficiary. Split-interest agreements are displayed separately on the not-for-profit organization's financial statements, measured at their fair value or present value at acquisition, and classified as donor-restricted.

DR	Assets held in trust	$XXX
CR	Liability to beneficiary	$XXX
CR	Contribution revenue (with donor restrictions)	XXX

Disbursements associated with split-interest agreements are classified as financing activities on the statement of cash flows. All expenses are classified as without donor restrictions in the statement of activities.

Question 2   MCQ-09313

On December 30, Year 1, Albert Altruistic donated $200,000 to the Carton Museum under the terms and conditions of a charitable remainder trust that guarantees Mr. Altruistic a life-time tax free annuity of $20,000 per year and bequeaths the remainder to Carton for use in their operations in furtherance of the mission of the museum. Independent actuaries have estimated that the museum's liability has a present value of $84,250. As a result of his contribution, the Carton Museum would record the following on its December 31, Year 1, financial statements:

1. An increase in net assets without donor restrictions of $200,000.

2. An increase in net assets with donor restrictions of $200,000.

3. An increase in net assets without donor restrictions of $115,750.

4. An increase in net assets with donor restrictions of $115,750.

4 Donated Services and Donated Works of Art

Contributions of services are recorded as revenue some of the time. The services must either enhance a physical asset or meet the following (**SOME**) criteria: they require **s**pecialized skills, are **o**therwise needed, and are **m**easured **e**asily. Services that meet the criteria are recorded as revenues and assets or expenses at their fair value as follows:

DR	Expense or asset	$XXX	
CR	Contributions—Nonoperating revenue		$XXX

Donated works of art are not required to be recorded by the recipient if all of the following criteria are met and the capitalization policy is consistently applied:

- The item is held for *public viewing*;
- The work of art is *cared for* by the not-for-profit organization; and
- Proceeds, if the art is sold, must be used to *purchase other works* of art.

Question 3   MCQ-09328

Faith Church decided to replace its electric organ with a multiple rack pipe organ. The church purchased the organ itself for $250,000 and a congregation member stepped forward to assemble the organ and perform the necessary carpentry work for $5,000. The congregation member is a skilled craftsman who normally charges $40,000 for this work. Other congregation members stepped forward to help with general labor assistance valued at $7,000. As a result of the transaction above, Faith Church should record revenues from contributed services of:

1. $35,000
2. $40,000
3. $42,000
4. $47,000

---

5 Accounting for Marketable Securities

Investments in securities are displayed at their fair values and increases and decreases in the fair value of securities are classified as without donor restrictions in the statement of activities unless there are donor-stipulated restrictions.

Investment income (dividends and interest) are reported in the period earned in the net asset category as either with or without donor restrictions. Investment returns are reported net of any related investment expense.

5.1 Endowments

Not-for-profit organizations account for assets with donor restrictions that are perpetual in nature in endowment funds. Generally, a benefactor will donate an amount and direct that earnings and not principal be used for specific or general purposes of the not-for-profit.

An underwater endowment is a donor-restricted endowment fund for which the fair value at the reporting date is less than either the original gift amount or the amount required to be maintained by the donor or by law.

Underwater endowment funds will report accumulated losses together with the endowment fund in net assets with donor restrictions.

Question 4   MCQ-09447

During the year ended June 30, Year 0, the Aberdeen Care Clinic, a not-for-profit organization, received an endowment for $2,300,000. The endowment is to remain intact with income and appreciation from the investment of the endowment to be used in support of a research program to assist the elderly. By June 30, Year 2, the endowment had accumulated $110,000 in gains. On July 1, Year 2, the company liquidated 65% of the cumulative appreciation of the endowment for use in the research program. During the year ended June 30, Year 3, the endowment earned $30,000, which it spent on the research program but, at year end, suffered market losses that reduced the total value of the investment below its initially recorded value to $2,250,000. The amounts reported as investment losses by net asset category for the year ended June 30, Year 3, would be:

	Without Donor Restrictions	With Donor Restrictions
1.	$0	$(88,500)
2.	$0	$(50,000)
3.	$(88,500)	$0
4.	$(50,000)	$(38,500)

---

6 Pass-Through Contributions to Not-for-Profit Beneficiary

FASB ASC 958-605 defines the manner in which separate organizations that either receive or benefit from contributions account for the donations. Principles are largely driven by application of the concept of variance power. The pronouncement considers the common situation of a foundation, the recipient, which raises money for another not-for-profit organization, the beneficiary (e.g., a university). The statement also considers instances where the recipient is a federated or community-wide organization, such as the United Way, and the beneficiary is a smaller not-for-profit organization.

6.1 General Rule: Recipient (e.g., a Foundation)

6.1.1 Without Variance Power

If a recipient organization receives donations on behalf of another not-for-profit and does not have any discretion with regard to the use of the contribution, the donation is recorded as a liability.

DR	Asset	$XXX
CR	Refundable advance liability	$XXX

6.1.2 With Variance Power

If a recipient organization receives donations on behalf of another not-for-profit and has discretion regarding the use of the contribution, the donation is recorded as revenue.

DR	Asset	$XXX
CR	Revenue	$XXX

6.2 General Rule: Beneficiary (e.g., a University)

6.2.1 Without Variance Power

If a recipient organization receives donations on behalf of another not-for-profit and does not have any discretion with regard to the use of the contribution, the donation is recorded as revenue on the beneficiary's books.

DR	Receivable	$XXX
CR	Contribution revenue	$XXX

6.2.2 With Variance Power

If a recipient organization receives donations on behalf of another not-for-profit and has discretion with regard to the use of the contribution, the donation is generally not recorded on the beneficiary's books unless a financial relationship exists.

6.3 Financially Interrelated Recipients and Beneficiaries

Recipients and beneficiaries are deemed to be interrelated if one organization has the ability to influence the decisions of the other and one organization has an ongoing interest in the other. Beneficiaries recognize an interest in the net assets of the recipient when they are financially interrelated with the recipient. The interest is adjusted for the beneficiary's share of the change.

DR	Interest in net assets	$XXX
CR	Change in interest in recipient net assets	$XXX

Beneficiaries recognize a beneficial interest in an unconditional right to receive specified cash flows from pools of assets. Changes in value are recorded on the beneficiary's books as follows:

DR	Beneficial interest	$XXX
CR	Contribution revenue	$XXX

Question 5   MCQ-09410

The Cox Foundation for the Performing Arts was established to support and coordinate the fundraising appeals of the Little Tutu Dance Troupe and the Expressive Community Theater. The bylaws require that the governing body of the foundation include equal representation from the dance troupe and the theater consisting of two thirds of the foundation's board and that the foundation distribute current period collections in the subsequent year. Noted philanthropist L.L. Thayer contributes $250,000 to the foundation on July 1, Year 1, and states in his bequest that the entire amount of the contribution is meant to support the operations of the dance troupe. On its December 31, Year 1, financial statements, the Little Tutu Dance Troupe should:

1. Only disclose the gift to the foundation.

2. Record a $250,000 increase in net assets without donor restrictions and change in interest in the net assets of the foundation.

3. Record a $250,000 increase in net assets with donor restrictions and change in interest in the net assets of the foundation.

4. Record $250,000 in contribution revenue without donor restrictions.

7 Industry Applications

7.1 Health Care Organization Revenue Recognition

Patient service revenue should be accounted for on the accrual basis at usual and customary fees, even if the full amount is not expected to be collected. Although patient service revenue is accounted for on a gross basis, deductions are made from gross revenue for reporting purposes to display revenues net. Charity care, the value of services that a health care organization gives away, is not displayed in the financial statements.

Bad debt expense is recorded when the allowance is established after an evaluation of a patient's ability to pay. Otherwise, bad debts are recorded as a deduction from revenue.

7.2 University and Institutions of Higher Learning Revenue Recognition

Student tuition and fees should be reported at gross amount. Scholarships, tuition waivers, and similar reductions are considered either expenses or a separately displayed allowance reducing revenue.

Question 6	MCQ-09443

Healthy Care Hospital Inc., a private not-for-profit organization, accumulated the following patient service revenue transactions in their records during the June 30, Year 1, fiscal year:

Gross patient fees for all services provided at usual and customary rates	$5,000,000
Contractual allowances for third party payments	800,000
Bad debts written off after an assessment of patient's ability to pay	350,000
Current year bad debt allowance	300,000
Charity care	1,300,000

The amount reported as net patient service revenue for Healthy Care Hospital Inc. for the year ended June 30, Year 1, would be:

1. $5,000,000
2. $4,200,000
3. $2,900,000
4. $2,850,000

Question 7

MCQ-09420

Nadaf University received $4,000,000 in tuition revenue for the year ended December 31, Year 1. In addition to the tuition received, the university offered $500,000 in scholarships but had to refund $200,000 for canceled classes. For the year ended December 31, Year 1, Nadaf would record gross revenue for tuition of:

1. $3,800,000
2. $4,000,000
3. $4,300,000
4. $4,500,000

Notes

Class Question Explanations

Financial Final Review

Topic A

QUESTION 1

MCQ-09319

Choice "4" is correct.

Income from continuing operations should be adjusted for all of the items. The $100,000 in additional depreciation needs to be deducted from income from continuing operations. The $200,000 loss from the strike by the supplier's employees and the $500,000 flood loss should be included in income from continuing operations. The inventory overstatement in the prior year results in a cost of goods sold overstatement in the current year, so $300,000 should be added back to income from continuing operations.

Allison Corporations adjusted income from continuing operations is calculated as follows:

Unadjusted income from continuing operations	$1,000,000
Less: Additional depreciation	(100,000)
Less: Loss from strike	(200,000)
Plus: Adjustment to COGS for inventory misstatement	300,000
Less: Loss from flood	(500,000)
Adjusted income from continuing operations	$ 500,000

QUESTION 2

MCQ-09289

Choice "2" is correct.

Other comprehensive can be remembered by the **PUFIER** mnemonic.

Pension adjustments
Unrealized gains and losses on available-for-sale debt securities
Foreign currency items
Instrument-specific credit risk
Effective portion of cash flow hedge
Revaluation surplus (IFRS only)

The only item that fits is the unrealized gain on the available-for-sale debt security. The unrealized gain on the trading debt security is included in income. Dividends are not included in income or other comprehensive income (but as an adjustment to retained earnings). The other items in the list are normal income statement items and thus are not part of other comprehensive income.

QUESTION 3

MCQ-09754

Choice "1" is correct.

Disclosure of current vulnerabilities to certain concentrations is a requirement in the notes to the financial statements. Receiving over half of its grant funding from one agency represents a significant concentration of business from a single source, and users of the financial statements will need this information in order to properly evaluate the university. If the funding source went away, the university would have a significant shortfall to overcome and may have difficulty fulfilling its financial obligations (paying faculty and staff, paying interest to bondholders, etc.) in the absence of this funding.

Choice "2" is incorrect. This disclosure does not necessarily indicate the need for other funding sources; it merely discloses the most significant funding source.

Choice "3" is incorrect. Although the disclosure would seem to indicate that there is a strong relationship between the government and the university, that is not specifically the intent of the disclosure.

Choice "4" is incorrect. The disclosure is not likely to quantify the impact on future revenue if this funding source went away.

Financial I

Topic B

QUESTION 1   MCQ-09277

Choice "3" is correct.

Depreciation is a part of operating activities and is added back since it was subtracted to produce net income in the first place. This question is a question on the SCF although it does not look like the question is phrased in exactly that manner.

Looking at the facts, an accumulated depreciation account analysis format can be used. The beginning and ending balances are available. The format is as follows:

Beginning balance	$600,000
Add: depreciation charged to operations	?
Subtract: A/D on equipment sold	?
Ending balance	$800,000

To obtain the accumulated depreciation of the property sold, subtract the $40,000 carrying amount from the $50,000 original cost, and the difference is the accumulated depreciation that was eliminated when the equipment was sold.

Beginning balance	$600,000
Add: depreciation charged to operations	?
Subtract: A/D on equipment sold	(10,000)
Ending balance	$800,000

In this account analysis format, the depreciation charged to operations is $210,000.

Or another way to look at it:

Accumulated Depreciation

$600,000	given
10,000	asset sold
590,000	subtotal
210,000	to balance account
$800,000	given

They said depreciation charged to operations in this question to differentiate it from any depreciation that might have been charged to work-in-progress and might have become a part of inventory cost.

QUESTION 2

Choice "2" is correct.

In order to compute the cash paid to suppliers, the Black Knights Company must determine how much inventory was purchased and the change in accounts payable. AP increases with purchases and decreases with payments. Thus:

Purchases	=	COGS + Change in inventory
	=	$450,000 + ($160,000) = $290,000

However, since AP decreased, The Black Knights Company paid more cash to suppliers than just the amount for purchases:

Cash paid	=	Purchases − Change in AP
	=	$290,000 − ($40,000) = $330,000

Choice "1" is incorrect. The decrease in AP is added to purchases (subtraction of a negative number). Recall that the decrease in AP means The Black Knights Company paid more cash to suppliers than just the amount for purchases.

Choice "3" is incorrect. The decrease in inventory is subtracted from COGS to determine purchases. (Remember, COGS = beginning inventory + purchases − ending inventory; beginning inventory − ending inventory = net change in inventory.)

Choice "4" is incorrect. The decrease in AP is added to purchases (subtraction of a negative number). Recall that the decrease in AP means The Black Knights Company paid more cash to suppliers than just the amount for purchases. In addition, the decrease in inventory is subtracted from COGS to determine purchases. (Remember, COGS = beginning inventory + purchases − ending inventory; beginning inventory − ending inventory = net change in inventory.)

QUESTION 3

Choice "4" is correct.

Net cash used in investing activities is calculated as follows:

Cash paid to purchase fixed assets	$(50,000)
Cash proceeds from the sale of fixed assets	10,000
Net cash used in investing activities	$(40,000)

The depreciation adjustment to the operating section of Cool Tool's statement of cash flows is calculated as follows:

Accumulated depreciation, Year 10	$41,000	
− Sale of fixed assets	(12,000)	= $18,000 cost − $6,000 BV
+ Depreciation expense	24,000	
Accumulated depreciation, Year 11	$53,000	

Choice "1" is incorrect. This answer incorrectly uses the cost of the fixed assets sold rather than the cash received from the sale to determine the net cash used in investing activities. This answer also incorrectly uses the amount of accumulated depreciation related to the asset sold as the depreciation expense for the period.

Choice "2" is incorrect. This answer incorrectly uses the cost of the fixed assets sold rather than the cash received from the sale to determine the net cash used in investing activities.

Choice "3" is incorrect. This answer incorrectly uses the amount of accumulated depreciation related to the asset sold as the depreciation expense for the period.

Financial I

QUESTION 4

MCQ-09262

Choice "1" is correct.

In this question, they want to know the net cash used in financing activities. Normally when they ask this kind of question, they provide a list of amounts, some of which are financing activities and some of which are not.

The first amount on the list is a payment for retirement of the company's long-term bonds. The payment certainly is cash used in financing, so that is $750,000 to start with. Dropping down to the last transaction, the proceeds from the sale of the treasury stock of $95,000 is financing, a source of cash and thus a positive use. That gives a total of $655,000 ($750,000 − $95,000) cash used. Moving up to the third transaction, conversion of stock of whatever kind into common stock is a non-cash item that only has to be disclosed.

$655,000 cannot be the answer since it is not one of the selections. In the second transaction, cash dividends of $62,000 were paid. That payment is certainly cash used in financing; once that amount is added to the $655,000, the total cash used is $717,000 ($655,000 + $62,000), which is a selection.

QUESTION 5

MCQ-09337

Choice "4" is correct.

The U.S. Treasury bill is considered to be a cash equivalent item so purchasing the T-bill merely changes the form of cash held, it does not change the cash position of the entity. Thus, the purchase is not reported on the statement of cash flows.

QUESTION 6

MCQ-09417

Choice "2" is correct.

A supplemental disclosure of the reconciliation of net income to net cash provided by operating activities is only required when the *direct* method is used under U.S. GAAP. It is not required when the indirect method is used as the operating activities section of the statement of cash flows prepared under the indirect method shows this reconciliation.

Choice "1" is incorrect. A supplemental disclosure of income taxes paid is required when the indirect method is used.

Choice "3" is incorrect. A supplemental disclosure of interest paid is required when the indirect method is used.

Choice "4" is incorrect. A supplemental disclosure of non-cash investing and financing activities is required under both the direct and indirect methods.

Topic C

QUESTION 1

MCQ-09750

Choice "1" is correct.

The market value of the outstanding common shares for Brevard is equal to $240 million ($40 x 6 million shares), which makes it an accelerated filer. Accelerated filers have 75 days after the fiscal year-end to file their annual report (10-K) and 40 days after the fiscal quarter ends to file their quarterly report (10-Q).

Choice "2" is incorrect. 75 days for the annual report is correct, but 45 days only applies to non-accelerated filers (any company with a market capitalization less than $75 million).

Choice "3" is incorrect. 60 days is the deadline for large accelerated filers (market capitalization of $700 million or more) for the 10-K report.

Choice "4" is incorrect. Both filing deadlines (60 days for the 10-K and 45 days for the 10-Q) are incorrect.

Financial Final Review

QUESTION 2

Choice "4" is correct.

Under Regulation S-X, an entity's audited financial statements filed with the SEC should include balance sheets for the two most recent fiscal years and the statements of income, changes in owners' equity, and cash flows for the three fiscal years preceding the date of the most recent audited balance sheet.

Topic D

QUESTION 1

Choice "2" is correct.

$1.78 and $1.75 EPS Year 11 and Year 10.

	Year 11	Year 10
Net income	$ 410,000	$ 350,000
Weighted Avg. Shares	÷ 230,000	÷ 200,000
EPS	$ 1.78	$ 1.75

	Shares O/S		Mo's O/S		Stock Split	Total
Jan. 1 to April 1	100,000	×	3	×	2	600,000
April 1 to July 1	120,000	×	3	×	2	720,000
July 1 to Dec. 31	240,000	×	6	×	1	1,440,000
			12			2,760,000

Weighted shares O/S (2,760,000 ÷ 12) = 230,000

It is important to note that stock splits (and stock dividends) are applied retroactively to all prior periods presented.

QUESTION 2

Choice "2" is correct.

Unlike basic earnings per share, for diluted earnings per share the convertible preferred stock and convertible bonds now have to be taken into account. For both types of securities, the if-converted method will be used.

For the convertible preferred stock, the dividends that were paid are assumed not to have been paid (since the convertible preferred stock was assumed to have been converted). They are not "added back" but they are not subtracted like they were in the basic EPS computation. For the convertible bonds, the interest that really was paid on the bonds is assumed not to have been paid (since the convertible bonds were assumed to have been converted). After-tax interest on the bonds of $140,000 ($2,000,000 × 0.10 × 0.70) is "added back" to the numerator. The numerator is thus $1,140,000 ($1,000,000 + $140,000).

The denominator is the 200,000 weighted average number of shares plus the 40,000 shares from the assumed conversion of the convertible preferred stock plus 100,000 shares from the assumed conversion of the convertible bonds ($2,000,000 / $1,000 × 50), for a total of 340,000 shares. $1,140,000 / 340,000 = $3.35

Financial I

Topic E

Choice "4" is correct.

The first thing that should come to mind for a segment question is the 10% rule. But the question is 10% of what? 10% of revenue for one thing, but 10% of what revenue? The rule is combined revenue from both sales to outsiders and intersegment sales, which in this question is a total of $88,000. 10% of that amount is $8,800. The overall corporate headquarters is ignored.

Choice "4" is correct.

An operating segment is considered to be a reportable segment if it accounts for at least 10 percent of total revenues (external and intercompany) or total profits/losses or total assets. In this problem, 10 percent of total revenues is $132,500, so Ice and Steam qualify as reportable segments based on total revenues; 10 percent of total profits is $63,500, so Rain, Ice, and Steam qualify based on total profits; and 10 percent of total assets is $209,000, so Rain, Snow, Ice, and Steam qualify based on total assets. Hail is the only operating segment that does not qualify as a reportable segment based on the 10 percent size tests. Note that Rain, Snow, Ice, and Steam together account for $1,230,000 or 93 percent of total outside sales, which means that Water Works is reporting sufficient segment information based on the rule that reportable combined outside sales must be at least 75 percent of total outside sales.

Choices "1", "2", and "3" are incorrect, based on the above explanation.

Topic A

QUESTION 1

Choice "3" is correct.

The general format of an account analysis is beginning, add, subtract, ending.

They provided the beginning and ending balances. They also provided sales; when something is sold on account, accounts receivable is increased so sales is an add in the account analysis format.

They also provided the amount of the bad debt write-off for the year; when an account is written off, accounts receivable is decreased so the write-off is a subtract. Cash collections is another subtract, and that is what they are asking for.

Beginning balance	$150,000	
Plus: Sales	600,000	
Less: Collections	(535,000)	(originally a plug)
Less: Write-off of accounts	(40,000)	
Ending balance	$175,000	

QUESTION 2

Choice "1" is correct.

Using the percentage of ending AR method, Red Rock's December 31, Year 3, allowance for doubtful accounts should be $46,100 ($922,000 x 5%). Bad debt expense can be determined using the company's beginning and ending allowance balances and the write-off and collection activity for the year:

	Beginning Allowance	$45,000
-	Write-offs	(35,000)
+	Recoveries	18,000
+	**Bad debt expense**	**18,100**
	Ending Allowance	$46,100

Choice "2" is incorrect. This is the amount of write-offs in Year 2. Under the allowance method, write-offs are not charged to bad debt expense, but are written-off against the allowance for doubtful accounts.

Choice "3" is incorrect. This is the allowance for doubtful accounts on 12/31/Y3. As is shown in the calculation above, the ending allowance balance is not equal to Red Rock's bad debt expense in Year 3.

Choice "4" is incorrect. This would be the Year 3 bad debt expense if Red Rock calculated bad debt expense using the percentage of credit sales approach, assuming the 5% of credit sales are expected to be uncollectible ($3,000,000 x 5% = $150,000).

QUESTION 3

Choice "2" is correct.

The receivables were sold without recourse, with no control being retained by Stanberry. The transfer thus meets the requirements of an asset sale, and a gain or a loss should be recognized. The loss is realized, and the difference is not a receivable from Cork Company.

Financial II

Topic B

MCQ-09282

QUESTION 1

Choice "4" is correct.

The first transaction is $28,000 of tools included in the physical inventory count and still sitting on the loading dock at 5:00 PM on December 31. Because the tools have not yet left the loading dock, the sale has not yet occurred and the tools should have been counted in the physical inventory count. They were counted so there is no adjustment for the first transaction.

The second transaction is $50,000 of inventory coming the other way. The goods were in transit from a vendor and were shipped FOB shipping point from that vendor. Because they were shipped by December 31, they should have been included in Mixon's inventory but were not since they were not there to be counted. The inventory of $1,750,000 should be increased to $1,800,000 ($1,750,000 + $50,000).

The accounts payable and sales information is irrelevant.

MCQ-09327

QUESTION 2

Choice "1" is correct.

Under the lower of cost or market, market starts at the $20 replacement cost. It is then limited to a ceiling and a floor. The ceiling is the selling price less cost of completion and/or selling. In this case, the selling price is $30, and the costs of completion are $2; the ceiling is thus $28 ($30 − $2). No problem exists here because the $20 replacement cost is already under the ceiling.

The floor is the ceiling less the normal profit margin. The ceiling is $28, and the normal profit margin is $7; the floor is thus $21 ($28 − $7). Because the market cannot be lower than the floor, it is $21.

The lower of the cost ($26) and the market ($21) is $21.

QUESTION 3

MCQ-09386

Choice "4" is correct.

Under the FIFO method, the first units purchased are the first units sold. In this problem, there are 750 units available for sale (150 + 100 + 200 + 300) and 500 units sold, leaving 250 units of ending inventory. This ending inventory must come from the last purchase of 300 units at $500/unit, so the cost of ending inventory is 250 units x $500/unit = $125,000.

Choice "1" is incorrect. This answer incorrectly calculates the cost of ending inventory using the $400/unit cost from the items in beginning inventory.

Choice "2" is incorrect. This is the cost of ending inventory using the LIFO method. Under the LIFO method, the last units purchased are the first units sold. In this problem, there are 750 units available for sale (150 + 100 + 200 + 300) and 500 units sold, leaving 250 units of ending inventory. This ending inventory must come from the 150 units on hand at $400/unit plus first purchase of 100 units at $440/unit, so the cost of ending inventory is (150 units x $400/unit) + (100 units x $440/unit) = $104,000.

Choice "3" is incorrect. This is the cost of ending inventory using the weighted average method. Under the weighted average method, both the cost of goods sold and the cost of ending inventory are determined using the weighted average cost per unit, calculated as follows:

Cost of goods available for sale / Number of units available for sale = [(150 x $400) + (100 x $440) + (200 x $460) + (300 x $500)] / (150 + 100 + 200 + 300) = $346,000 / 750 = $461.33

In this problem, there are 750 units available for sale (150 + 100 + 200 + 300) and 500 units sold, leaving 250 units of ending inventory. Therefore, the cost of ending inventory under the weighted-average method is $115,333 ($461.33 x 250), which is closest to $115,000.

QUESTION 4

MCQ-09312

Choice "2" is correct.

The first thing to account for is the physical units. There were 150 units in beginning inventory, 600 units purchased (100 + 200 + 300), and 500 units sold. Ending inventory was thus 250 units.

Using the LIFO method, the 250 units in the ending inventory would be assumed to be the earliest units, in this case the 150 units in the beginning inventory and 100 units from the first purchase. Ending inventory cost would thus be $104,000 (150 × $400 + 100 × $440).

Financial II

QUESTION 5   MCQ-09398

Choice "3" is correct.

Under the weighted average method, both the cost of goods sold and the cost of ending inventory are determined using the weighted average cost per unit, calculated as follows:

Cost of goods available for sale / Number of units available for sale = [(150 x $400) + (100 x $440) + (200 x $460) + (300 x $500)] / (150 + 100 + 200 + 300) = $346,000 / 750 = $461.33

In this problem, there are 750 units available for sale (150 + 100 + 200 + 300) and 500 units sold, leaving 250 units of ending inventory. Therefore, the cost of ending inventory is $115,333 ($461.33 x 250), which is closest to $115,000.

Choice "1" is incorrect. This answer incorrectly calculates the cost of ending inventory using the $400/unit cost from the items in beginning inventory.

Choice "2" is incorrect. This is the cost of ending inventory using the LIFO method. Under the LIFO method, the last units purchased are the first units sold. In this problem, there are 750 units available for sale (150 + 100 + 200 + 300) and 500 units sold, leaving 250 units of ending inventory. This ending inventory must come from the 150 units on hand at $400/unit plus first purchase of 100 units at $440/unit, so the cost of ending inventory is (150 units x $400/unit) + (100 units x $440/unit) = $104,000.

Choice "4" is incorrect. This is the cost of ending inventory using the FIFO method. Under the FIFO method, the first units purchased are the first units sold. In this problem, there are 750 units available for sale (150 + 100 + 200 + 300) and 500 units sold, leaving 250 units of ending inventory. This ending inventory must come from the last purchase of 300 units at $500/unit, so the cost of ending inventory is 250 units x $500/unit = $125,000.

Topic C

QUESTION 1   MCQ-09360

Choice "2" is correct.

The cost of the land includes all purchase related costs plus any costs incurred to get the land ready for use:

	Purchase price	$750,000
+	Legal fees	32,000
+	Title insurance	15,000
+	Timber clearing costs	18,000
−	Lumber sale proceeds	(7,000)
	Cost of land	$808,000

The cost of land does not include the excavation costs for the office building, which will be included in the total cost of the building.

Choice "1" is incorrect. This answer incorrectly excludes the timber clearing costs and the lumber sale proceeds from the calculation of the cost of the land.

Choice "3" is incorrect. This answer incorrectly excludes the lumber sale proceeds from the calculation of the cost of the land.

Choice "4" is incorrect. This answer incorrectly includes the excavation costs for the office building. These costs should be included in the total cost of the building.

QUESTION 2

MCQ-09375

Choice "3" is correct.

In Year 1, Bluebird's interest payments on the construction borrowing total $900,000 ($10 million × 9%). Of the interest paid, Bluebird would capitalize interest related to the construction of the office building as follows:

Capitalized interest = Weighted average accumulated construction expenditures × Interest rate on construction debt = $3,750,000 × 9% = $337,500

Therefore, interest expense of $562,500 would be reported on the Year 1 income statement, calculated as the difference between the total interest payments and the capitalized interest ($900,000 − 337,500 = $562,500).

Choice "1" is incorrect. This is the interest that would be capitalized and added to the total cost of the office building. See the calculation in the explanation above.

Choice "2" is incorrect. This answer is not supported by the facts in this question.

Choice "4" is incorrect. This is the total interest paid in Year 1 on Bluebird Inc.'s construction debt. Only a portion of this amount is reported as interest expense on the income statement, as calculated above.

QUESTION 3

MCQ-09330

Choice "3" is correct.

Note that the question could have just as easily asked for depreciation expense or for carrying amount (book value).

In this question, they are asking about depreciation after a change in accounting estimate. The change in accounting estimate is a change in the depreciation life of a machine and a change in the salvage value.

The machine was originally purchased on January 1, Year 1 for $250,000. With a salvage value of $50,000 and a useful life of 10 years, depreciation for Year 1 was $20,000. The carrying amount at 12/31/Y1 was thus $230,000.

Depreciation for Year 2 was another $20,000, and the carrying amount at 12/31/Y2 was $210,000. Accumulated depreciation at that date was $40,000.

During Year 3, the change in accounting estimate occurred. The useful life was reduced from 10 years to 5 years (3 more years at 12/31/Y2) and the salvage value was reduced from $50,000 to $0. The net result was that the full $210,000 remaining would be depreciated over the remaining 3 years at $70,000 per year. Accumulated depreciation at December 31, Year 3 would thus be $110,000 ($40,000 + $70,000).

Financial II

Topic D

QUESTION 1   MCQ-09345

Choice "4" is correct.

On this transaction, since the exchange has commercial substance, Bizzell will recognize a gain on the exchange. Gains and losses in exchanges having commercial substance are computed as the difference between the fair value and the book value of the asset given up. The fair value of the asset given up (the new land) was $500,000. The book value of the asset given up (the old land) was $350,000. The gain was thus $150,000.

The Journal Entry is as follows:

DR	New land	$450,000*	
DR	Cash	50,000	
CR	Old land		$350,000
CR	Gain on exchange		150,000**

* Pate gave and Bizzell received
** $150,000 = $500,000 − $350,000

The asset will be recorded on Bizzell's books at $450,000, its fair value.

For Pate, the fair value of the asset given up (the new land) was $450,000. The book value of the asset given up was $320,000 (the old land). The gain was thus $130,000. The Journal Entry is as follows:

DR	New land	$500,000*	
CR	Cash		$ 50,000
CR	Old land		320,000
CR	Gain on exchange		130,000**

* Bizzell gave and Pate received
** $130,000 = $450,000 − $320,000

If the exchange had lacked commercial substance, the Journal Entry for Bizzell would have been as follows:

DR	New land	$315,000	
DR	Cash	50,000	
CR	Old land		$350,000
CR	Gain on exchange		15,000

Because Bizzell received cash (boot), Bizzell would record a gain in proportion to the cash received:

$$(500,000 - 350,000) \times \frac{50}{500} = \$15,000$$

The Journal Entry for Pate would have been as follows:

DR	New land	$370,000*	
CR	Cash		$50,000
CR	Old land		320,000

* Bizzell gave and Pate got

The basis of the new land would have been $320,000 for an exchange that lacked commercial substance. However, it was increased to take the cash paid into account. Note that because boot was paid by Pate, Pate does not recognize a gain on the transaction.

QUESTION 2

MCQ-09412

Choice "3" is correct.

Statements II and III are both correct. Statement I is incorrect because a fair value approach is used to record an exchange that has commercial substance. If an exchange lacks commercial substance, then a book value approach is used. Statement IV is incorrect because the gain or loss is calculated by comparing the book value and the fair value of the asset given.

Topic E

QUESTION 1

MCQ-09293

Choice "1" is correct.

$55,000 unrealized holding gain on trading debt securities reported in Year 2 income statement:

Trading Portfolio	Fair Value
12/31/Y2	$155,000
12/31/Y1	(100,000)
Unrealized gain, reflected in income	$ 55,000

Rule: Unrealized gains and losses are reported as follows: trading debt securities-reported at fair value with unrealized gains and losses included in earnings (along with "realized" gains and losses, if any).

Where there are no expected credit losses, available-for-sale debt securities-reported at fair value with unrealized gains and losses reported as a separate component of other comprehensive income until realized.

Financial II

QUESTION 2

Choice "1" is correct.

The unrealized gain to be recorded on MNE's Year 2 statement of comprehensive income is calculated as follows:

Sale of Alpha Corp. debt	(3,000)	Write-off unrealized gain (see JE)
Unrealized gain—Beta Corp.	8,000	($38,000 – 30,000)
Unrealized loss—Omega Corp.	(3,000)	($24,000 – 27,000)
Net change in AFS securities	2,000	

JE to record sale of investment in Alpha Corp.:

DR	Cash	$57,000	
DR	Unrealized gain—OCI	3,000	
CR	Investment in Alpha Corp. debt		$53,000
CR	Realized gain		7,000

Choice "2" is incorrect. This is the unrealized gain on the Alpha Corp. debt, which is written off in Year 2 when the security is sold.

Choice "3" is incorrect. This is total accumulated other comprehensive income to be reported on the balance sheet related to the available-for-sale debt securities, not the current period unrealized gain on available-for-sale debt securities to be reported on the statement of comprehensive income.

Choice "4" is incorrect. This is the unrealized gain to be reported in Year 2 on the Beta Corp. debt, not the total unrealized gain on all available-for-sale debt securities in Year 2.

QUESTION 3

Choice "3" is correct.

The accumulated other comprehensive income to be reported on MNE's Year 2 balance sheet can be calculated as follows:

	Accumulated OCI 12/31/Y1	Year 2 Unrealized Gain/Loss	Adjustment for Sale	Accumulated OCI 12/31/Y2
Alpha Corp.	$3,000	$ --	$(3,000)	$ --
Beta Corp.	(5,000)	8,000		3,000
Omega Corp.	6,000	(3,000)		3,000
	$4,000			$6,000

Choice "1" is incorrect. This is the current period unrealized gain on available-for-sale debt securities to be reported on the statement of comprehensive income.

Choice "2" is incorrect. This is the unrealized gain on the Alpha Corp. debt, which is written off in Year 2 when the security is sold.

Choice "4" is incorrect. This is the unrealized gain to be reported in Year 2 on the Beta Corp. debt, not the total accumulated OCI related to these securities.

QUESTION 4

Choice "4" is correct.

For a held-to-maturity security, the credit loss is equal to the difference between amortized cost and present value when the present value is less than the amortized cost.

Amortized cost	$150,000
Present value	$142,000
Difference	$8,000

Choice "1" is incorrect. There is a credit loss because the present value is less than the amortized cost.

Choice "2" is incorrect. The credit loss is not equal to the difference between the present value and the fair value of the bond.

Choice "3" is incorrect. The $144,000 fair value is not used in the credit loss calculation because this is a held-to-maturity security. If the investment was classified as available-for-sale, the credit loss would have been limited to the difference between the amortized cost and the fair value of the bond.

QUESTION 5

Choice "1" is correct.

ABC:

Unrealized gain: $5,000 gain (Fair value $55,000 – Purchase price $50,000).

XYZ:

The total loss on XYZ is the $5,000 difference between the purchase price and the fair value at the end of the year. $2,000 of this loss will be recognized as a credit loss on the income statement because the present value of the investment is less than its amortized cost (i.e., its purchase price): $2000 loss = $33,000 present value – $35,000 amortized cost. The remaining $3,000 of the loss is recognized as an unrealized loss in OCI.

Total impact to OCI: $2,000 gain ($5,000 gain from ABC – $3,000 loss from XYZ).

Choice "2" is incorrect. The $5,000 unrealized gain on ABC will be offset by the $3,000 unrealized loss on XYZ.

Choice "3" is incorrect. The $5,000 unrealized gain on ABC is not offset by the full $5,000 difference between the purchase price and fair value of XYZ. $2,000 of that difference is recognized as a credit loss because the present value of XYZ is less than its amortized cost (i.e., its purchase price). The remaining $3,000 is an unrealized loss on XYZ that offsets the $5,000 unrealized gain on ABC.

Choice "4" is incorrect. The $3,000 unrealized loss on XYZ will be offset by the $5,000 unrealized gain on ABC.

Financial II

QUESTION 6   MCQ-09392

Choice "2" is correct.

Red Crown will account for its investment in Red Hand using the equity method, as ownership of at least 20 percent of the voting common stock of a company generally implies that the investor can exercise significant influence over the investee. Under the equity method, Red Crown will report its share of the earnings of Red Hand on its Year 1 income statement:

Red Hand net income x Ownership % = $300,000 x 25% = $75,000

Red Crown will account for its investment in Red Leaf using the fair value method, as ownership of any percentage of nonvoting stock generally does not allow the investor to exercise significant influence or control over the investee. Under the fair value method, Red Crown will report its share of Red Leaf's Year 1 dividends on its Year 1 income statement:

Red Leaf preferred dividends x Ownership % = $200,000 x 40% = $80,000

Therefore, the total income from these two investments on Red Crown's Year 1 income statement will be $155,000 ($75,000 + 80,000).

Choice "1" is incorrect. This answer incorrectly accounts for both the Red Hand and Red Leaf investments using the fair value method. As described above, the Red Hand investment should be accounted for using the equity method.

Choice "3" is incorrect. This answer incorrectly accounts for the Red Hand investment using the fair value method and the Red Leaf investment using the equity method. As described above, the Red Hand investment should be accounted for using the equity method and the Red Leaf investment should be accounted for using the fair value method.

Choice "4" is incorrect. This answer incorrectly accounts for both the Red Hand and Red Leaf investments using the equity method. As described above, the Red Leaf investment should be accounted for using the fair value method.

Topic F

QUESTION 1

Choice "4" is correct.

Under U.S. GAAP, the $900,000 spent to develop the product is considered research and development and must be expensed when incurred. However, the legal and other patent registration fees can be capitalized. Therefore, when the patent is granted on June 30, Year 1, the company will record an intangible asset in the amount of $20,000 which will be amortized over 10 years (the lesser of the patent's legal and economic lives). In Year 1, patent amortization will total $1,000 ($20,000/10 × 6/12), resulting in a 12/31/Y1 net book value of $19,000 ($20,000 cost − $1,000 amortization).

When the legal fees related to the successful defense of the patent are recorded on January 1, Year 2, they will be capitalized and added to the book value of the patent:

Beginning book value	$19,000
Legal fees related to successful defense	76,000
	$95,000

This amount will then be amortized over the remaining 9.5 year life of the patent on a straight line basis:

$95,000 / 9.5 years = $10,000

Choice "1" is incorrect. This is the amount of amortization recorded in Year 1.

Choice "2" is incorrect. This is the amount of amortization that would have been recorded in Year 1 if the patent had been granted on January 1.

Choice "3" is incorrect. This is the amount of amortization that would be recorded in Year 2 if the patent were amortized over 10 years, rather than 9.5 years. Ten years cannot be used as the amortization period because only 9.5 years of the patent's economic life is remaining on 1/1/Y2.

QUESTION 2

Choice "2" is correct.

Two intangible assets were acquired at the beginning of the year. The first has a finite life and thus should be amortized; the second has an indefinite life and cannot be amortized. The second asset looks like it might be impaired, but they did not ask for the impairment loss.

The acquisition cost of the first intangible asset was $5,000,000. That cost is amortized over the life of 50 years, for an annual amortization of $100,000.

Financial II

Topic G

QUESTION 1   MCQ-09672

Choice "4" is correct.

Under U.S. GAAP, impairment analysis begins with a test for recoverability in which the net carrying value of the asset is compared to the undiscounted cash flows expected from the asset. If the net carrying value exceeds the undiscounted cash flows, then an impairment loss is recorded equal to the difference between the carrying value and fair value of the asset. In this problem, the carrying value of $750,000 exceeds the undiscounted future cash flows of $740,000, so an impairment loss of $50,000 ($700,000 fair value – $750,000 net carrying value) will be reported on the income statement.

Choice "1" is incorrect. The asset's carrying value of $750,000 exceeds the undiscounted future cash flows of $740,000, so an impairment loss of $50,000 ($700,000 fair value – $750,000 net carrying value) must be recognized on the income statement.

Choice "2" is incorrect. The impairment loss is equal to the difference between the fair value and carrying value of the asset, not the difference between the carrying value of the asset and the undiscounted future cash flows expected from the asset.

Choice "3" is incorrect. The impairment loss is not equal to the difference between the fair value of the asset and the undiscounted future cash flows expected from the asset.

QUESTION 2   MCQ-09673

Choice "3" is correct.

Under IFRS, an impairment loss is recorded for the excess of the carrying value of an intangible asset over its recoverable amount. The recoverable amount is the greater of the asset's fair value less costs to sell and the asset's value in use (present value of future cash flows). In this problem, the value in use of $710,000 exceeds the fair value less costs to sell of $700,000 and an impairment loss of $40,000 must be reported on the income statement:

   Impairment loss = $710,000 recoverable amount – $750,000 carrying value = $(40,000)

Choice "1" is incorrect. An impairment loss must be recorded under IFRS because the carrying value of the trademark exceeds the trademark's recoverable amount.

Choice "2" is incorrect. The impairment loss is not equal to the difference between the fair value less costs to sell and the present value of the future cash flows expected from the trademark.

Choice "4" is incorrect. The trademark's $710,000 value in use exceeds the $700,000 fair value less costs to sell, so the value in use is the trademark's recoverable amount and is used to calculate an impairment loss of $40,000.

QUESTION 3

Choice "2" is correct.

Under U.S. GAAP, goodwill impairment exists because the $890,000 fair value of the reporting unit is less than the $950,000 carrying value. The goodwill impairment loss will be equal to $60,000, which is the $950,000 fair value less the $890,000 carrying value.

Choice "1" is incorrect. This is the implied fair value of the goodwill, not the goodwill impairment loss.

Choice "3" is incorrect. This is the difference between the implied fair value of the goodwill ($50,000) and the current value of the goodwill line item on the balance sheet ($130,000).

Choice "4" is incorrect. The goodwill impairment loss is not equal to the difference between the book value of the reporting unit less the fair market value assigned to the assets and liabilities of the reporting unit.

QUESTION 4

Choice "4" is correct.

Impairment is a two-step process, the first of which is to determine if impairment exists, and the second of which is to measure the loss.

To determine if an impairment loss exits, we compare the undiscounted cash flows from the machine to the carrying amount of the machine. The undiscounted cash flows are $900,000 ($45,000 × 20 years remaining life), and the carrying amount is $1,000,000 (in this case, they provided the carrying amount; in a longer problem, it might have to be calculated). Since the undiscounted cash flows are less than the carrying amount, there is an impairment loss.

The amount of the impairment loss is the difference between the fair value of the machine and its carrying amount ($800,000 − $1,000,000) or $200,000.

Topic H

QUESTION 1

Choice "2" is correct.

Accretion is the increase in the ARO over time. At the end of the four years, the cumulative accretion and accumulated depreciation should combine to equal the asset retirement obligation (ARO) of $200,000. The present value of a four-year obligation at a 7 percent rate and a future value of $200,000 is equal to $152,579. This asset must be fully depreciated over four years, while the liability must accrue from $152,579 to $200,000, a difference of $47,421. (The present value can be calculated this way: $200,000 / 1.07^4. This is equal to $200,000 / 1.3108. Or, if you were given a present value table, you would look up the factor for the present value of $1, 4 periods, 7 percent to obtain 0.7629. Multiply this factor by $200,000 to obtain $152,579.)

Choice "1" is incorrect. The accretion is correct, but the asset will be booked at a present value of $152,579 and this becomes the amount that will ultimately be depreciated over four years.

Choice "3" is incorrect. The combined total is correct, but the amounts in each column are reversed.

Choice "4" is incorrect. The combined total must equal the ultimate liability of $200,000.

Financial II

QUESTION 2   MCQ-09745

Choice "3" is correct.

The employee portion represents both the income tax withholding ($5,000 x 15% = $750) and the Social Security/Medicare withholding ($5,000 x 7.65% = $382.50). Therefore, the payable on behalf of the employee is equal to $750 + $382.50, or $1,132.50. The employer will book an expense for just the amount "owed" by the employer, which is $5,000 x 7.65 percent, or $382.50.

Choice "1" is incorrect. The payable must also include the amount the employee owes for income taxes ($750).

Choice "2" is incorrect. The expense represents the employer (rather than employee) portion.

Choice "4" is incorrect. The employer will only book an expense for the amount it is responsible for, which is just $5,000 x 7.65 percent, or $382.50.

Topic I

QUESTION 1   MCQ-09381

Choice "4" is correct.

The selling price of a bond is equal to the present value of the principal and interest payments calculated using the effective rate (or market yield), as follows:

PV of principal:	$1,000,000 × 0.4632	$ 463,200
PV of interest:	$90,000* × 6.7101	603,909
		$1,067,109

* Interest payments = $1,000,000 × 9% = $90,000

Choice "1" is incorrect. This is the face amount of the bond times 92% (100% − 8%).

Choice "2" is incorrect. This is the issue price of the bonds (and the approximate present value using the stated rate).

PV of principal:	$1,000,000 × 0.4224	$422,400
PV of interest:	$90,000 × 6.4177	577,593
		$999,993

Choice "3" is incorrect. This is approximately the amount if the effective rate of 8% were used to calculate the present value of the principal, but the stated rate of 9% were used to calculate the present value of the interest.

QUESTION 2

Choice "1" is correct.

Watch the dates in bonds questions because the dates can make a big difference.

In this question, they are asking for the unamortized discount two years after issuance. The bonds pay interest annually, and the effective interest method is used, as follows.

Unamortized bond discount, 7/1/Year 1		$61,000
Bond discount amortization, 7/1/Year 1 to 6/30/Year 3:		
Amortization for 7/1/Year 1 to 6/30/Year 2:		
Bonds payable carrying amount, 7/1/Year 1	$939,000	
Effective interest rate 10%	× 0.10	
Interest expense, 7/1/Year 1 to 6/30/Year 2	93,900	
Interest payment ($1,000,000 × 9%)	90,000	(3,900)
Amortization for 7/1/Year 2 to 6/30/Year 3:		
Bonds payable carrying amount, 7/1/Year 2 ($939,000 + $3,900)	$942,900	
Effective interest rate 10%	× 0.10	
Interest expense, 7/1/Year 2 to 6/30/Year 3	94,290	
Interest payment ($1,000,000 × 9%)	90,000	(4,290)
Unamortized bond discount, 6/30/Year 3		$52,810

Note that, for each year, the interest (expense) component is equal to the carrying amount of the bond at the beginning of the year times the effective interest rate. The difference between the interest component and the interest payment is the amortization of the discount, and the amortization adjusts (increases) the carrying amount of the bond by decreasing the unamortized discount.

The interest expense will change each year, but the interest payment will remain constant.

The schedule above is a small part of a bond amortization table. Know these calculations.

QUESTION 3

Choice "3" is correct.

A debt modification that lowers future cash flows below the carrying value of the debt will result in a gain as well as a reduction in the carrying value of the liability, with the gain recorded in current operations.

Choice "1" is incorrect. Debt modifications are normally handled prospectively, but not when the future cash outflows are less than the carrying value of the debt.

Choice "2" is incorrect. Debt modifications are normally handled prospectively, but not when the future cash outflows are less than the carrying value of the debt.

Choice "4" is incorrect. The modification results in a gain, not a reduction, of interest expense.

Financial II

Topic J

QUESTION 1

Choice "1" is correct.

Common stock (5,000 shares × $1 stated value)	**$ 5,000**
Preferred stock (1,500 shares × $10 par value)	**$15,000**

Additional paid-in capital from:		
Common stock ($15 – $1) × 5,000 shares =	$70,000	
Preferred stock ($25 – $10) × 1,500 shares =	22,500	
		$92,500

$5,000, common stock; $15,000 preferred stock; $92,500 APIC.

QUESTION 2

Choice "3" is correct.

Under the cost method, Black Dog would record the following journal entries for its Year 1 stock transactions:

Jan. 1, Year 1—Issue 30,000 shares of $5 par common stock for $9/share:

DR	Cash	$270,000	
CR	Common stock		$150,000
CR	APIC—CS		120,000

June 30, Year 1—Repurchase 10,000 shares for $8/share:

DR	Treasury stock	$80,000	
CR	Cash		$80,000

Sept. 15, Year 1—Resell 5,000 shares for $12/share:

DR	Cash	$60,000	
CR	Treasury stock		$40,000
CR	APIC—TS		20,000

Therefore, total APIC on Black Dog's balance sheet at December 31, Year 1 would be $140,000 ($120,000 from original sale + $20,000 from sale of treasury stock).

Choice "1" is incorrect. This is the amount of APIC—Treasury Stock recorded as a result of the resale of treasury stock on Sept. 15, Year 1 (see the explanation above). The question asks for total APIC.

Choice "2" is incorrect. This is the amount of APIC—Common Stock recorded as a result of the original issuance of common stock on Jan. 1, Year 1.

Choice "4" is incorrect. This is the amount of total APIC that would be reported on the Dec. 31, Year 1 balance sheet under the par value method.

QUESTION 3

Choice "3" is correct.

There are both common and preferred shareholders. The dividends are $100,000, and some of it has to go to the preferred shareholders since none of the answers is $100,000.

The preferred goes first (since it is preferred) at 5% of par value or $15,000 (5% × 30,000 × $10). Since the preferred is "fully participating," the common shares are initially treated the same way as the preferred. The common thus gets its 5% or $10,000 (5% × $200,000 × $1). Then everybody shares in relation to their relative par values.

Total par value common	$200,000	(200,000 shares × $1)
Total par value preferred	300,000	(30,000 shares × $10)
Total par value	$500,000	

The preferred gets 3/5 of what is left, and the common gets 2/5. The amount left over is $75,000; the preferred gets $45,000 of that and the common gets $30,000. Putting this all together, the common gets a total of $40,000 and the preferred gets a total of $60,000.

Topic K

QUESTION 1

Choice "2" is correct.

When the installment method is used, gross profit is recognized when cash is collected using the formula:

Earned gross profit = Cash collections x Gross profit %

In Year 2, Sell2All received cash collections related to both Year 1 and Year 2 sales, so it is necessary to calculate the gross profit percentages for both years:

Year 1 gross profit percentage = ($400 − $300)/$400 = 25%

Year 2 gross profit percentage = ($750 − $500)/$750 = 33.3%

Therefore:

Year 2 earned gross profit = ($100,000 x 25%) + ($300,000 x 33.3%) = $125,000

Choice "1" is incorrect. This is the amount of gross profit to be recognized on the sales made in Year 2 ($300,000 cash received from Year 2 sales x 33.3% = $100,000). This amount incorrectly excludes the gross profit to be recorded for the $100,000 cash received in Year 2 related to Year 1 sales.

Choice "3" is incorrect. This answer applies the Year 2 gross profit percentage of 33.3% to the entire $400,000 in cash collected in Year 2. Of the $400,000 collected in Year 2, only $100,000 is payment on Year 1 sales. This $100,000 must be multiplied by the Year 1 gross profit percentage to determine the gross profit earned in Year 2 on sales made in Year 1.

Choice "4" is incorrect. This is the amount of cash collected in Year 2, which must be multiplied by the appropriate gross profit percentages to determine earned gross profit.

Financial II

Topic L

QUESTION 1   MCQ-09279

Choice "3" is correct.

U.S. GAAP requires that the funded status (Fair value of plan assets − PBO) of a company's defined benefit pension plan(s) be reported on the balance sheet as a non-current asset (if overfunded) or a current/non-current liability (if underfunded). Do It Right will report a non-current asset of $650,000 ($5,580,000 − 4,930,000) on its December 31, Year 7, balance sheet because the company's pension plan is overfunded (FV of plan assets > PBO).

Choice "1" is incorrect. Although the difference between the fair value of 329the plan assets and the PBO is $650,000, this is an overfunded pension plan which must be reported as a non-current asset. The funded status of a pension plan is only reported as a current liability to the extent that the expected benefits payable in the next 12 months exceed the fair value of the plan's asset, which is not the case in this situation.

Choice "2" is incorrect. $2,180,000 is the difference between the fair value of the plan assets and the ABO. The ABO is not used to calculate the funded status of defined benefit pension plans. Additionally, the funded status of Do It Right's pension plan would not be reported as a non-current liability because Do It Right's pension plan is overfunded.

Choice "4" is incorrect. $2,180,000 is the difference between the fair value of the plan assets and the ABO. The ABO is not used to calculate the funded status of defined benefit pension plans. Additionally, GAAP does not allow the funded status of a pension plan to be recorded as a current asset.

QUESTION 2   MCQ-09264

Choice "4" is correct.

What should come to mind immediately are those items that make up the formula for net periodic pension cost. A number of those very items are listed in the facts of the question, and the major difficulty is remembering which of those items should be added and which should be subtracted.

Start with the service cost of $160,000. Add the $50,000 of annual interest on the pension obligation, and that gives $210,000, a possible answer. The actual and expected gain of $35,000 would reduce the $210,000 to $175,000, and the $5,000 amortization of unrecognized prior service cost would add to it to produce $180,000.

The $40,000 loss on plan assets related to the disposal of a subsidiary in Year 1 looks like it might be a factor, but that loss would have been included in the loss on the disposal of the subsidiary (probably in discontinued operations) and not the net periodic pension cost (if it had been added, the total would have $220,000).

QUESTION 3

MCQ-09758

Choice "1" is correct.

The APBO (accumulated postretirement benefit obligation) represents the present value of the liability associated with vested future benefits. The EPBO (expected postretirement benefit obligation) is equal to the APBO, plus the present value of the liability associated with nonvested future benefits. If there are no nonvested benefits, the APBO and EPBO will be equal; if there are nonvested benefits, the EPBO will be greater than the APBO.

Choice "2" is incorrect. Churchill is a public company under U.S. GAAP, which means the health care trend rate assumed by the company must be included as a disclosure.

Choice "3" is incorrect. If Churchill uses the expected rate of return in order to calculate net postretirement benefit expense/cost, then any differences between the expected return and actual return will result in a gain or loss that can either be booked as an expense in the current period (on the income statement) or booked in other comprehensive income (OCI) and amortized over time.

Choice "4" is incorrect. In order to accrue for these costs, they must represent benefits earned as a result of services already rendered.

QUESTION 4

MCQ-09295

Choice "4" is correct.

Compensatory stock options should be valued at the fair value of the option on the grant date. On the grant date (January 1, Year 1), the option had a fair value of $61 per option, so the total compensation cost is $6,100 ($61 × 100 options).

Topic M

QUESTION 1

MCQ-09379

Choice "2" is correct.

	Situation 1	Situation 2
Income tax payable	$ 8,400	$16,800
Change in deferred tax asset	(50)	1,900
Change in deferred tax liability	–	50
Income tax expense	$ 8,350	$18,750

When taxable income is larger than book income, a deferred tax asset is recognized.

To summarize, deferred tax assets are created by transactions that defer the tax benefits of expenses or which recognize tax income before book income.

Remember that the situations are independent. The question asks for the Income tax expense (which is the total of the current and deferred income tax expense).

Current tax expense is the product of taxable income times the tax rate.

Deferred tax expense either increases or decreases tax expense depending on whether it is an increase in a deferred tax asset (decrease) or an increase in a deferred tax liability (increase).

Financial II

The computations related to situation 1 are as follows:

Current tax expense ($40,000 in income × 21% tax rate) = $8,400 in current income tax payable

Deferred tax assets (future deductible amounts) are $1,050 in the current year ($5,000 × 21% tax rate) representing a $50 change from the $1,000 beginning deferred tax asset balance.

Current tax expense would be reduced by the $50 increase in the tax asset to arrive at income tax expense of $8,350.

The computations related to situation 2 are as follows:

Current tax expense ($80,000 in income × 21% tax rate) = $16,800 in current income tax payable

Deferred tax assets (future deductible amounts) are $2,100 in the current year ($10,000 × 21% tax rate) representing a $1,900 change from the $4,000 beginning deferred tax asset balance.

Deferred tax liabilities (future taxable amounts) are $1,050 in the current year ($5,000 × 21% tax rate) representing a $50 change from the $1,000 beginning deferred tax asset balance.

Current tax expense would be increased by the $1,900 decrease in the deferred tax asset and increased by the $50 increase in the deferred tax liability to arrive at income tax expense of $18,750.

QUESTION 2

MCQ-09364

Choice "4" is correct.

	Situation 1	Situation 2
Future deductible amount	$5,000	$10,000
Tax rate	21%	21%
Deferred tax asset ending balance	$1,050	$ 2,100

QUESTION 3

MCQ-09415

Choice "1" is correct.

Under U.S. GAAP and IFRS, all deferred tax assets/liabilities are reported as non-current on the balance sheet. Deferred tax assets and deferred tax liabilities may be netted if the entity has a legally enforceable right to offset current tax assets against current tax liabilities and the deferred tax assets and deferred tax liabilities relate to income taxes levied by the same tax authorities.

Choices "2", "3", and "4" are incorrect, per the explanation above.

QUESTION 4

MCQ-09424

Choice "3" is correct.

The $100,000 Year 6 NOL will be carried forward to offset Year 7 and Year 8 taxable income, subject to an 80 percent of taxable income limitation, without regard to the NOL deduction.

The deferred tax asset can be calculated using Year 7 and Year 8 tax rates:

Year 7: $56,000 × 21% =	$11,760
Year 8: $44,000 × 18% =	7,920
Total deferred tax asset	$19,680

For Year 7, the NOL deduction is $56,000, which is the lesser of the NOL carryforward of $100,000, and the NOL deduction limitation of $56,000 ($70,000 taxable income prior to NOL × 80% limitation = $56,000).

For Year 8, the NOL deduction is $44,000, which is the lesser of the NOL carryforward of $44,000 ($100,000 − $56,000), and the NOL deduction limitation of $48,000 ($60,000 taxable income prior to NOL × 80% limitation = $48,000).

Zeus's Year 6 income tax journal entry will be:

DR	Deferred tax asset—current	$19,680	
CR	Income tax benefit		$19,680

Choice "1" is incorrect. This is the $100,000 NOL multiplied by the Year 6 tax rate. This is not the method used to calculate the income tax benefit from an NOL.

Choice "2" is incorrect. This answer incorrectly uses the Year 7 taxable income of $70,000 as the NOL deduction, rather than the NOL deduction limitation of 80 percent of taxable income.

Choice "4" is incorrect. This answer incorrectly carries back the NOL to Year 4 and Year 5 and also ignores the 80 percent of taxable income limitation in Year 7.

Notes

Topic A

QUESTION 1

MCQ-09281

Choice "3" is correct.

The accounting change is a change in accounting estimate, which is handled prospectively.

Before the change, depreciation was calculated on the straight-line basis using a life of 6 years. The depreciable base was $600,000, so the accumulated depreciation for the 3 years before the change was $300,000 ($600,000/6 × 3). Thus, the carrying amount at the date of the change was also $300,000.

A change in accounting estimate is handled prospectively. In this case, the remaining carrying amount of $300,000 is depreciated over the new remaining life of 5 years (8 − 3). The new depreciation expense each year is $60,000.

Note that the question is asking about depreciation expense. It just as easily could have been accumulated depreciation or it could have been the net book value of the asset.

QUESTION 2

MCQ-09296

Choice "4" is correct.

This particular change is from weighted average to FIFO. It is a change in accounting principle. Accounting changes are reported on the statement of retained earnings net of tax. In this question, the cumulative effect before taxes is $800,000. Net of tax, it is $560,000 ($800,000 × 0.70).

QUESTION 3

MCQ-09266

Choice "3" is correct.

A change in accounting principle is normally recorded using retrospective adjustment where the cumulative effect of the adjustment on prior years is reported in beginning retained earnings of the earliest year presented, net of the related tax effect. There are exceptions, and this particular change in accounting principle is one of the exceptions. Therefore, there is no cumulative effort reporting because such a change in depreciation method is treated as a change in estimate and accounted for prospectively.

QUESTION 4

MCQ-09326

Choice "1" is correct.

The cash basis for financial reporting is not a generally accepted basis of accounting (GAAP); therefore, it is an error. Correction of an error from a prior period is reported as a prior period adjustment to retained earnings.

Choice "2" is incorrect. Cash basis reporting is not acceptable under accrual basis accounting principles. Thus, the change from cash basis is not reported as a change in accounting principle.

Choice "3" is incorrect. Correction of prior period errors has no effect on the current year's income statement.

Choice "4" is incorrect. An error correction is recorded by restating retained earnings. Error corrections are not reported on the income statement.

Financial III

Topic B

QUESTION 1

MCQ-09348

Choice "4" is correct.

The conveniently named Philadelphia Corporation (P as in parent) has acquired the Saxon Corporation (S as in subsidiary) in a business combination transaction treated as a purchase. Philadelphia issued 200,000 shares of $10 par value stock valued at $18 for all of Saxon's common stock. That was $3,600,000 (200,000 × $18) in total. If 200,000 shares were issued for $8 over par, then $1,600,000 went to additional paid-in capital from that transaction. But there was already $1,300,000 there. The total of the two is $2,900,000 ($1,300,000 + $1,600,000). Saxon's additional paid-in capital is eliminated when the financial statements are consolidated.

QUESTION 2

MCQ-09683

Choice "3" is correct.

Under the IFRS partial goodwill method, noncontrolling interest on the balance sheet is calculated as follows:

NCI = fair value of subsidiary net assets × NCI %

Therefore, the NCI is:

NCI = $11,500,000 × 20% = $2,300,000

QUESTION 3

MCQ-09414

Choice "2" is correct.

At the time of the sale, Pico and Sepulveda would have recorded the following journal entries:

Pico—record sale to Sepulveda:

DR	Accounts receivable	$400,000	
CR	Sales revenue		$400,000
DR	Cost of goods sold	320,000*	
CR	Inventory		320,000

* $320,000 = $400,000/1.25

Sepulveda—record purchase from Pico:

DR	Inventory	$400,000	
CR	Accounts Payable		$400,000

Because this is an intercompany transaction, the intercompany sales revenue, cost of goods sold and profit on inventory must be eliminated. In this problem, the intercompany profit on inventory is $80,000 ($400,000 cost of inventory on Sepulveda's books – $320,000 original cost of inventory on Pico's books). Because Sepulveda has sold half of the inventory purchased from Pico, half of the intercompany profit must be eliminated from cost of goods sold and half of the intercompany profit must be eliminated from ending inventory. The journal entry to record this elimination is as follows:

DR	Sales revenue	$400,000	
CR	Cost of goods sold		$360,000
CR	Inventory		40,000

Therefore, at year-end, consolidated inventory is equal to Pico's inventory + Sepulveda's inventory – Eliminated intercompany profit = $390,000 + 480,000 – 40,000 = $830,000.

Choice "1" is incorrect. This answer option incorrectly calculates ending inventory as follows:

Sepulveda	[$480,000 – (50% × $400,000)]	$280,000
Pico		390,000
		$670,000

Choice "3" is incorrect. This is the sum of the inventory amounts on each of the balance sheets without the elimination entry for the intercompany profit of $40,000 [$390,000 + $480,000 = $870,000].

Choice "4" is incorrect. This answer option incorrectly adds (rather than subtracts) the intercompany profit on the inventory of $40,000 to the ending balance sheet amounts of inventory for each [$390,000 + $480,000 + $40,000].

QUESTION 4

MCQ-09760

Choice "4" is correct.

Once an entity is deemed to meet the qualifications of a variable interest entity, the question is raised as to whether the entity must be consolidated. Two factors used to make this determination include whether the investor has the power to direct significant economic activities for the VIE and whether the investor is the "primary beneficiary" of the VIE. As a primary beneficiary, the investor would absorb at least 50 percent of the VIE's expected losses or gains. So if it is a case that the VIE incurs losses, and the investor does not absorb at least 50 percent of them, then they are not the primary beneficiary and the VIE would not be consolidated.

Choice "1" is incorrect. This condition would imply that the investor is the primary beneficiary and as such, it would lend itself to consolidation.

Choice "2" is incorrect. A VIE that requires significant financial support to exist would not present an argument against consolidation.

Choice "3" is incorrect. Current equity holders lacking substantive voting rights would not present an argument against consolidation.

Financial III

Topic C

QUESTION 1   MCQ-09429

Choice "2" is correct.

Only the probable loss from the first product liability lawsuit would be recorded on the balance sheet. Because a range of losses is given, the lowest amount in the range is recorded on the balance sheet as a contingent liability and the range is disclosed in the footnotes along with the details of the case. The possible loss from the second product liability lawsuit and the probable contingent gain are not recorded on the balance sheet, but instead are disclosed in the footnotes.

Choice "1" is incorrect. This answer incorrectly offsets the probable gain of $500,000 against the probable loss of $800,000. Probable gains cannot be accrued on the balance sheet, but can only be disclosed in the footnotes.

Choice "3" is incorrect. This answer incorrectly accrues the $1,000,000 possible loss on the second product liability lawsuit. A possible loss should not be accrued on the balance sheet, but should instead be disclosed in the footnotes.

Choice "4" is incorrect. This answer incorrectly accrues the $1,000,000 possible loss on the second product liability lawsuit. A possible loss should not be accrued on the balance sheet, but should instead be disclosed in the footnotes. Additionally, this answer accrues the $2,000,000 high end of the range of probable losses on the first product liability lawsuit. Generally, the low end of the range is accrued.

Topic D

QUESTION 1   MCQ-09336

Choice "4" is correct.

Both carrying value (amount) and fair value must be disclosed for most financial instruments (when it is practicable to estimate fair value).

QUESTION 2   MCQ-09425

Choice "1" is correct.

Statement III is the only correct statement. Statement I is incorrect because a derivative must have one or more underlyings *and* one or more notional amounts. Statement II is incorrect because derivatives can be reported as assets or liabilities. Statement IV is incorrect because changes in the fair value of a fair value hedge are reported on the income statement.

Choices "2", "3", and "4" are incorrect, based on the above explanation.

Topic E

QUESTION 1

Choice "2" is correct.

Statements II and III are correct. Statement I is incorrect because a company's financial statement must be in conformity with GAAP before translation/remeasurement. Statement IV is incorrect because translation gains are reported in other comprehensive income, while gains and losses from remeasurement are reported on the income statement.

Choices "1", "3", and "4" are incorrect, based on the above explanation.

QUESTION 2

Choice "4" is correct.

On November 1, Year 1, Western would record the transaction as follows:

DR	Accounts receivable (25,000 euros × $1.19)	$29,750	
CR	Revenue		$29,750

On December 31, Year 1, Western would record a foreign exchange transaction loss of $750 [25,000 euros x ($1.19 – 1.16)] due to the decrease in the exchange rate:

DR	Foreign exchange transaction loss	$750	
CR	Accounts receivable		$750

On February 15, Year 1, when Western receives the payment from its customer, the company would record a foreign exchange transaction gain of $1,750 [25,000 euros x ($1.23 – 1.16)]:

DR	Cash (25,000 euros × $1.23)	$30,750	
CR	Accounts receivable ($29,750 – 750)		$29,000
CR	Foreign exchange transaction gain		1,750

Choice "1" is incorrect. This answer incorrectly identifies the Year 1 loss as a gain. Additionally, it incorrectly identifies the Year 2 gain as a loss and incorrectly calculates the Year 2 amount by multiplying the $0.04 difference between the 11/1/Y1 exchange rate and the 2/15/Y2 exchange rate ($1.23 – $1.19 = $0.04) by 25,000 euros ($0.04/euro x 25,000 euros = $1,000).

Choice "2" is incorrect. This answer incorrectly identifies the Year 1 loss as a gain. Additionally, it incorrectly identifies the Year 2 gain as a loss.

Choice "3" is incorrect. This answer incorrectly calculates the Year 2 gain by multiplying the $0.04 difference between the 11/1/Y1 exchange rate and the 2/15/Y2 exchange rate ($1.23 – $1.19 = $0.04) by 25,000 euros ($0.04/euro x 25,000 euros = $1,000).

Financial III

Topic F

QUESTION 1   MCQ-09253

Choice "2" is correct.

If the lessee treats the lease as a finance lease, it is because at least one of the OWNES criteria has been met. If this is the case, the lessor will also categorize the lease as a finance lease (either sales-type or direct financing).

Choice "1" is incorrect. Both the lessor and lessee may classify a lease as an operating lease.

Choice "3" is incorrect. It is possible for the lessee to classify a lease as operating while the lessor classifies the same lease as a finance lease. This situation will occur if none of the OWNES criteria are met but the PC criteria are met (in which case it will be a direct financing lease).

Choice "4" is incorrect. Both the lessor and lessee may classify a lease as a finance lease.

QUESTION 2   MCQ-09290

Choice "4" is correct.

In this question, they want to know the amount charged to expense for what looks like an operating lease. An amount of $1,200,000 was paid on December 1, Year 1.

$200,000 of the $1,200,000 was for actual rent. However, the lease agreement indicated that the rent would double halfway through the lease. The total rent that will be paid for the entire 10 years is thus $36,000,000, for an equivalent monthly rent of $300,000 ($36,000,000 / 120).

The other amount that would be charged to expense (the question does not say rent expense, just expense) would be the amortization of the leasehold improvement. The leasehold is the office space, the improvement is the new carpet for the executives, and the amortization would be on the straight-line basis over 120 months, for $5,000 per month.

The total expense would thus be $305,000.

QUESTION 3   MCQ-09254

Choice "4" is correct.

In a sale-leaseback, the seller is the lessee and the buyer is the lessor. The seller/lessee will book a profit when the sale price exceeds the book value of the asset sold.

Choice "1" is incorrect. The seller may book a profit/loss at inception, but will be the lessee rather than the lessor.

Choice "2" is incorrect. The buyer is the lessor (not the lessee) who gives the seller the right to use the asset.

Choice "3" is incorrect. The buyer is the lessor, not the lessee.

QUESTION 4

Choice "2" is correct.

In this question, they want to know the finance lease liability. They are paying $50,000 every year for the next 10 years, and they provide the present value of the minimum lease payments of the lease as of December 31, Year 1. Watch the dates; they are there for a reason.

The first payment is made on signing the lease, i.e., at the beginning of the period. The liability after that payment is $288,000 ($338,000 − $50,000). The question asks what the long-term liability is one year later.

$288,000 × 10% is $28,800. That amount is the interest component of the second payment. The difference between the $50,000 payment and the $28,800 is $21,200, and the $21,200 is the reduction of the long-term liability of the second payment; therefore the liability after the second payment is $266,800 ($288,000 − $21,200).

It all started with the first payment. All the other answers have a wrong turn.

QUESTION 5

Choice "1" is correct.

The interest revenue on a direct financing (finance) lease is equal to the difference between the total lease payments from the lease and the present value of the lease payments:

Total lease payments	$ 240,000	($60,000 × 4 years)
Present value of lease payments	(206,622)	($60,000 × 3.4437)
Interest revenue	$ 33,378	

Choice "2" is incorrect. This is the annual lease payment, not the interest to be earned over the life of the lease.

Choice "3" is incorrect. This is the present value of the annual lease payments, not the interest to be earned over the life of the lease.

Choice "4" is incorrect. This is undiscounted total lease payments, not the interest to be earned over the life of the lease.

Topic G

QUESTION 1

Choice "3" is correct.

In this question, all of the costs except the cost of the equipment acquired for the various R&D projects are considered R&D costs. Since the equipment has alternative future uses (on various research projects), the depreciation on the equipment is an R&D expense.

QUESTION 2

Choice "3" is correct.

All of the research and development costs related to the unsuccessful product lines must be expensed. The $30,000 in research costs related to the product that was successfully patented must also be expensed because all research costs are expensed under IFRS. The $40,000 in development costs will most likely be capitalized because they related to a successfully patented product and development costs can be capitalized under IFRS. Therefore, the entity should expense $260,000 ($300,000 − $40,000).

Financial III

Topic H

Choice "1" is correct.

Until technological feasibility has been established for a product, costs incurred in creating a computer software product should be charged to research and development expense when incurred. Technological feasibility is established upon completion of a detailed program design or a working model. In this question, $70,000 would be recorded as research and development expense ($30,000 for detailed program design and $40,000 for coding and testing to establish technological feasibility).

Costs incurred from the point of technological feasibility until the time when product costs are incurred are capitalized as software costs. In this question, $100,000 ($20,000 + $30,000 + $50,000) is capitalized as software cost.

Product costs that can be easily associated with the items to be inventoried are reported as a part of the inventory cost (in this question, $15,000 for duplication of software and training materials and $10,000 for packaging, for a total of $25,000).

Topic I

Choice "4" is correct.

Although the fire occurred after the balance sheet date of June 30, the nature of the event and estimated financial impact were known before the financial statements were due to be issued on September 30. Therefore, the correct approach for Drexler is to disclose the nature of the event along with the estimated financial impact.

Choice "1" is incorrect. The entirety of the event occurred after June 30, so there is no need to book a journal entry to reflect it in the Year 3 balance sheet/income statement. The entry will be booked in the Year 4 statements.

Choice "2" is incorrect. The entirety of the event occurred after June 30, so there is no need to book a journal entry to reflect it in the Year 3 balance sheet/income statement. The entry will be booked in the Year 4 statements. In addition, a disclosure should also be included to help users of the financial statements understand the nature and impact of the event.

Choice "3" is incorrect. Because an estimated financial impact is known, the nature of the event should be disclosed along with the estimated financial impact.

Topic J

QUESTION 1   MCQ-09762

Choice "2" is correct.

An asset-backed security is an investment whose value and income payments are driven by a pool of underlying assets. A mortgage-backed security is a type of asset-backed security that is secured by a mortgage or mortgages. Level 2 investments may trade in active markets, but tend to be based on dealer quotations or alternative sources supported by observable investments or inputs that trade in inactive markets. A mortgage-backed security will most likely fall under a Level 2 classification.

Choice "1" is incorrect. A U.S. Treasury bill represents a short-term fixed obligation of the United States government, which means it has a very active market and quoted market prices are readily available. As a result, this type of investment will be categorized under Level 1.

Choice "3" is incorrect. Limited partnerships allow investors to take advantage of opportunities without incurring the risks and liabilities of a general partnership. These types of investments trade infrequently (if at all), and as a result have significant unobservable inputs that therefore requires that they fall under Level 3.

Choice "4" is incorrect. A large company's common stock will have a very active market and therefore have quoted market prices. As a result, the most appropriate categorization is Level 1.

Topic K

QUESTION 1   MCQ-09317

Choice "3" is correct.

The original partners had a total capital balance of $130,000 and the new partner was contributing $50,000. Since the partnership capital account will begin with $180,000 including the new partner, there cannot be any goodwill. But there still might be a bonus.

Chance gets a one-third interest in the partnership. That means Chance's capital balance will be $60,000 ($180,000 × 1/3) for an investment of $50,000. Unfortunately, three of the four answers have $60,000 in Chance's column. The $10,000 difference comes from the other partners, and it comes from the other partners in their profit and loss sharing ratio, which in this case happens to be 3:2. The $10,000 is perfectly divisible by 5, so it must be the third selection.

Of the $10,000, three fifths ($10,000 × 3/5) or $6,000 comes from Coco, and two fifths ($10,000 × 2/5) or $4,000 comes from Chanel. That leaves Coco with $64,000 ($70,000 − $6,000) and Chanel with $56,000 ($60,000 − $4,000), respectively.

Financial Final Review

Financial III

QUESTION 2

Choice "4" is correct.

	Total	Stewart	Colbert
Total Profit	$150,000		
Interest	(35,000)	$ 20,000	$ 15,000
Salary	(65,000)	65,000	–
Bonus	(25,000)	–	25,000
Balance	25,000	85,000	40,000
Distribution	(25,000)	12,500	12,500
Total	$ 0	$97,500	$52,500

Choice "1" is incorrect. These amounts do not include Stewart and Colbert's 50/50 share of the $25,000 in profits remaining after accounting for the salary, bonus, and interest.

Choice "2" is incorrect. Stewart's distribution incorrectly excludes Stewart's 50 percent share of the $25,000 in profits remaining after accounting for the salary, bonus, and interest.

Choice "3" is incorrect. Colbert's distribution incorrectly excludes Colbert's 50 percent share of the $25,000 in profits remaining after accounting for the salary, bonus, and interest.

Financial Final Review

Topic A

QUESTION 1

MCQ-09442

Choice "3" is correct.

Earnings from a tax to be used exclusively to repay specific debt would most likely be accounted for in the debt service fund associated with that debt. Fund financial reporting, particularly for the governmental funds, demonstrates compliance with laws rules and regulations. The display of revenues restricted for debt repayment in the debt service fund would demonstrate compliance with the law that levied the tax.

Choice "1" is incorrect. The General Fund would not serve to demonstrate the use of the sales tax for repayment of debt as clearly as the debt service fund.

Choice "2" is incorrect. The Special Revenue Fund would not serve to demonstrate the use of the sales tax for repayment of debt as clearly as the debt service fund.

Choice "4" is incorrect. The Capital Projects Fund accounts for construction monies, not funds anticipated for the repayment of debt. The Capital Projects Fund would not be appropriate.

QUESTION 2

MCQ-09359

Choice "3" is correct.

The Holler Sound Citizen's Initiative Fund is a custodial fund that would account for the debt service associated with a special assessment for which the municipality had no obligation. A custodial fund is accounted for using the economic resources measurement focus and would not share the same basis of accounting with the Community Development Block Grant Fund.

Choice "1" is incorrect. The Holler Bridge Fund is a capital projects fund that would use the current financial resources measurement focus in the same manner as the special revenue fund used to account for the community development block grant.

Choice "2" is incorrect. The Holler Bridge Debt Service Fund is a debt service fund that would use the current financial resources measurement focus in the same manner as the special revenue fund used to account for the community development block grant.

Choice "4" is incorrect. The Holler Cemetery Perpetual Care Fund is a permanent fund established to benefit the general public and would use the current financial resources measurement focus in the same manner as the special revenue fund used to account for the community development block grant.

QUESTION 3

MCQ-09374

Choice "3" is correct.

The trash collection service is accounted for in the General Fund, a governmental fund that uses the modified accrual basis of accounting, the basis of accounting that will not recognize revenues until measurable (amount is defined) and available (amount is collected within 60 days of year-end). The Road and Bridge Fund uses the same basis of accounting as the trash collection service.

Choice "1" is incorrect. The utility fund is an enterprise fund that uses the full accrual basis of accounting that recognizes revenue when earned.

Choice "2" is incorrect. The motor pool is an internal service fund that uses the full accrual basis of accounting that recognizes revenue when earned.

Choice "4" is incorrect. The retirement fund is a pension fund that uses the full accrual basis of accounting that recognizes revenue when earned.

Financial IV

QUESTION 4

Choice "2" is correct.

Property tax revenue is an imposed non-exchange revenue that would be recorded when levied to the extent that it is both measurable and available. The fact pattern indicates that the following revenues were recognized:

Tax revenue collected	$24,000,000
Delinquent taxes collected	800,000
Total tax revenue available	24,800,000
Uncollected revenue	200,000
Total tax levy	$25,000,000

General Rule: Property taxes generally meet the definition of non-exchange revenues and are recognized in the period in which an enforceable legal claim to the taxes arises and the revenues are available. Availability is defined as collection within the period levied or soon enough to pay liabilities of the current period (60 days after year-end). Governments may refer to the date the enforceable legal claim arises as either the lien date or the assessment date. Property taxes received in advance are displayed as deferred inflows of resources.

Topic B

QUESTION 1

Choice "4" is correct.

Combining statements of nonmajor funds may be displayed in "Other Supplementary Information" at the option of the issuer.

Choice "1" is incorrect. Presentation of nonmajor funds in the fund financial statements is inappropriate except in summary.

Choice "2" is incorrect. Nonmajor fund detail should not be exclusively displayed in the notes to the financial statements.

Choice "3" is incorrect. Display of nonmajor grant activity is not required.

QUESTION 2

MCQ-09344

Choice "4" is correct.

City of Richardson
Reconciliation of the Statement of Revenues, Expenditures, and Changes
in Fund Balances of Governmental Funds to the Statement of Activities
December 31, Year 1

Net change in fund balances-total governmental funds:	$ 2,002,000
Governmental funds report capital outlays as expenditures. However, in the Statement of Activities, the cost of those assets is allocated over their estimated useful lives as depreciation expense. This is the amount by which capital outlays exceeded depreciation in the current period. 160,000,000 / 20 (10,000,000 − 8,000,000).	2,000,000
In the Statement of Activities, only the gain on the sale of land is reported, whereas in the governmental funds, the proceeds from the sale increase financial resources. Thus, the change in net position differs from the change in the fund balance by the cost of the land sold.	(800,000)
Revenues in the Statement of Activities that result from changes in accrual balances (property taxes).	
− Current Year Accrual	400,000
− Prior Year Accrual	(370,000)
Repayment of bond principal is an expenditure in the governmental funds, but the repayment reduces long-term liabilities in the Statement of Net Position.	1,500,000
Some expenses in the Statement of Activities do not require the use of current financial resources and therefore are not reported as expenditures in the governmental funds.	(100,000)
Change in net position of governmental activities:	**$4,632,000**

QUESTION 3

MCQ-09434

Choice "3" is correct.

The net realizable value of infrastructure is not a required element of a government's asset management system when the government uses the modified approach.

The asset system must include:

- An inventory of assets.
- Summary of asset condition.
- Amount required to preserve the asset condition.

Financial IV

Topic C

QUESTION 1

Choice "2" is correct.

Rule: Component units include legally separate organizations (governmental, not-for-profit, or for profit) for which elected officials of the primary government are financially accountable. A primary government is financially accountable if it appoints a voting majority of the organization's governing body. A component unit should be included in the reporting entity financial statements using the blending method when the component unit provides services entirely or almost entirely to the primary government or otherwise exclusively or almost exclusively benefits the primary government even though it does not provide services directly to it.

The Cox Administration Corporation is a component unit since its governing body is appointed by the City. The corporation would be presented as a blended component unit since it was established by the primary government to administer its employee benefit programs in a manner that exclusively benefits the primary government even though it provides services to the employees rather than directly to the primary government itself.

Choice "1" is incorrect. The Cox Administration Corporation primarily serves the primary government and would be presented as a blended not discrete component unit.

Choice "3" is incorrect. The Cox Administration Corporation's financial statements are presented as a blended component unit, not simply disclosed.

Choice "4" is incorrect. The Board of Directors of the Cox Administration Corporation is appointed by the primary government; the corporation is a component unit, not a stand alone corporation.

Topic D

QUESTION 1

Choice "3" is correct.

Proceeds from refunding debt would be displayed at face value as "Other Financing Sources" in the debt service fund associated with the refunded debt with any original issue discount displayed as "Other Financing Uses." Underwriter's fees (as distinct from original issue discount) netted against bond proceeds would have been charged to expenditures. The transaction associated with the issuance of the debt would appear on the Statement of Revenues, Expenditures and Changes in Fund Balance.

Choice "1" is incorrect. The non-current debt, bonds payable, would not be recorded in the governmental fund financial statements, it would only be recorded in the government-wide financial statements under the governmental activities column. "Other Financing Sources" would be displayed at the face amount of the bond and any difference between the face amount and proceeds associated with the original issue discount would be displayed as "Other Financing Uses."

Choice "2" is incorrect. Refund bonds would be recorded in the debt service fund associated with the refunded debt. The face amount of the bonds would be displayed as proceeds under the "Other Financing Sources" classification while any discount associated with an original issue discount would be displayed beneath the "Other Financing Uses" classification. Charges associated with underwriter's fees that are netted against bond proceeds would be displayed as an expenditure.

Choice "4" is incorrect. The issuance of refunding bonds would be recorded in the debt service fund financial statements as bond proceeds under the category "Other Financing Sources" at face value with any original issue discount reported as "Other Financing Uses." It would not be either recorded exclusively on the government-wide financial statements or recorded in another fund.

QUESTION 2

Choice "1" is correct.

The County's available appropriation is computed as the difference between the original appropriation and the funds either expended or encumbered.

Appropriation		$45,000
Less:		
Expended by November, Year 0		(15,000)
Accrued by August, Year 1		(20,000)
Budgetary control (purchase order)	$30,000	
Order received	(20,000)	
Budgetary control		(10,000)
Available appropriation		$ 0

The County would record activity as follows:

To record initial expenditures related to miscellaneous supplies:

DR	Expenditures	$15,000	
CR	Cash		$15,000

To record encumbrances for issued purchase order:

DR	Encumbrances	$30,000	
CR	Budgetary control		$30,000

To reverse encumbrances associated with liabilities incurred related to items received:

DR	Budgetary control	$20,000	
CR	Encumbrances		$20,000
DR	Expenditures	20,000	
CR	Accounts payable		20,000

Financial IV

QUESTION 3

Choice "2" is correct.

Unassigned fund balances represent spendable resources that are the least limited as to use.

Choice "1" is incorrect. "Unreserved" is older terminology. Although unreserved and undesignated fund balance classifications approximated the meaning of the "unassigned" fund balance prior to implementation of GASB 54, the terminology is now obsolete and a distracter.

Choice "3" is incorrect. There is no such classification as "unspendable." This is a distracter. There is a classification titled "nonspendable." These residual amounts may indeed be unassigned, but they are not available and would not be less limited as to use than resources classified as unassigned.

Choice "4" is incorrect. Committed funds are internally limited by formal action of the government's highest level of decision-making authority and would not be less limited as to use than resources classified as unassigned.

QUESTION 4

Choice "1" is correct.

Increases in derivatives classified as assets are accounted for as increases in deferred inflows of resources, a classification of transactions below liabilities and above fund equity.

Choice "2" is incorrect. Increases in derivatives classified as assets are accounted for as increases, not decreases in deferred inflows of resources.

Choices "3" and "4" are incorrect. Changes in the value of derivatives classified as assets result in increases in deferred inflows of resources, a classification of transactions displayed between liabilities and fund equity, not deferred outflows of resources, a classification of transactions appearing between assets and liabilities.

Topic A

QUESTION 1

Choice "1" is correct.

All not-for-profit organizations are required to produce a statement of financial position (balance sheet), statement of activity (income statement), and statement of cash flows along with disclosures of functional expenses as displayed on the statement of activities analyzed by object classification.

Choice "2" is incorrect. Functional expense disclosure is required, not optional.

Choice "3" is incorrect. The statement of cash flows and functional expense disclosures are required.

Choice "4" is incorrect. The statement of cash flows is required.

QUESTION 2

Choice "2" is correct.

The initial contribution in which the donor stipulates that the principal must remain intact would be classified as an increase in net assets with donor restrictions along with the earnings, whose use is restricted but which the university can satisfy by implementing programming (the chair for accountancy). No distinction is made for purposes of financial statement display between the items restricted by the donor in perpetuity and the items for which restrictions are temporary in nature.

Choice "1" is incorrect. Contributions for an endowment with earnings restricted for use to fund a chair in accountancy would be reported as an increase to net assets with donor restrictions.

Choice "3" is incorrect. Both the contribution to fund the endowment and related earnings restricted as to use would be accounted for as an increase in net assets with donor restrictions.

Choice "4" is incorrect. Both the contribution to fund the endowment and related earnings restricted as to use would be accounted for as an increase in net assets with donor restrictions.

QUESTION 3

Choice "2" is correct.

Proceeds from the sale of assets that were received in prior periods and whose sale proceeds were donor-restricted to investment in long-lived assets are displayed on the Statement of Cash Flows as cash flows from investing activity.

Choice "1" is incorrect. Proceeds from the sale of assets that were received in prior periods and whose sale proceeds were donor-restricted to investment in long-lived assets are displayed on the Statement of Cash Flows as cash flows from investing activity, not an operating activity.

Choice "3" is incorrect. Proceeds from the sale of assets that were received in prior periods and whose sale proceeds were donor-restricted to investment in long-lived assets are displayed on the Statement of Cash Flows as cash flows from investing activity, gains are not segregated as an operating activity.

Choice "4" is incorrect. Proceeds from the sale of assets that were received in prior periods and whose sale proceeds were donor-restricted to investment in long-lived assets are displayed on the Statement of Cash Flows as cash flows from investing activity, not a financing activity.

Financial V

Topic B

QUESTION 1

MCQ-09387

Choice "4" is correct.

Revenues and support without donor restrictions would consist of:

Revenues	
Fees (exchange transactions)	$ 45,000
Support	
United Way support	30,000
Federal grant earned as a result of satisfying restrictions in the same year the grant was awarded	10,000
Total revenue and support without donor restrictions	$ 85,000

Choice "1" is incorrect. Revenues and support without donor restrictions include fees per above.

Choice "2" is incorrect. Revenues and support without donor restrictions include both the United Way support and grant monies whose restrictions are satisfied in the same year as the award.

Choice "3" is incorrect. Revenue and support without donor restrictions include grants with donor restrictions whose restrictions are satisfied in the same period in which the revenues are awarded.

QUESTION 2

MCQ-09313

Choice "4" is correct.

Assets of a charitable remainder trust are measured at fair value when received and the liability is measured at the present value of expected future cash flows to be paid to the beneficiary. Contributions are not available until a future period (when the liability is fully satisfied) and is therefore an increase in net assets with donor restrictions. Carton would use the following entry.

To record acquisition of assets subject to a charitable remainder trust:

DR	Assets held in charitable remainder trust	$200,000	
CR	Liability under trust agreements		$ 84,250
CR	Contribution revenue, with donor restrictions		115,750

Choice "1" is incorrect. The net assets of this transaction relate to the contribution less the value of the liability, not the value of the asset itself.

Choice "2" is incorrect. The net assets of this transaction relate to the contribution less the value of the liability, not the value of the asset itself.

Choice "3" is incorrect. The net assets of this transaction relate to the contribution less the value of the liability, and is subject to donor restrictions associated with time requirements, not classified as an increase in net assets without donor restrictions.

Class Question Explanations

Financial V

QUESTION 3

Choice "3" is correct.

Rule: Not-for-profit organizations record donated services **SOME** of the time, when services meet the following criteria:

Specialized skill
Otherwise needed
Measured
Easily

Services are also recognized when a long-lived asset is enhanced.

The services for the construction of the pipe organ meet all criteria. The construction requires a specialized skill, the musical instrument is necessary equipment and there is a market price for the service. In addition, unskilled labor was used to enhance a long-lived asset.

The church would record $35,000 in revenues from contributed specialized services per the rule above (40,000 fair value minus $5,000 paid) and would record $7,000 in revenue for the general labor used to enhance the long-lived asset.

Value for specialized service	$40,000
Amount paid	(5,000)
Net specialized service donated	35,000
General labor used to enhance long-lived asset	7,000
Total donated service revenue	$42,000

Choices "1", "2", and "4" are incorrect per the explanation above.

Financial V

QUESTION 4

Choice "1" is correct.

The value of investments at the beginning of the year was $2,410,000. Investments experienced a $160,000 reduction in value accounted for in part by the sale of assets ($110,000 × 65% = $71,500) and a loss of $88,500 ($160,000 − $71,500). All activity is accounted for as with donor restrictions. Underwater endowments will absorb their own losses.

	Without Donor Restrictions	With Donor Restrictions	Total
Beginning of Year	$ –	$ 2,300,000	$ 2,300,000
Accumulated gains	–	110,000	110,000
Liquidation	–	(71,500)	(71,500)
Gains	–	–	–
Losses	–	(88,500)	(88,500)
End of Year	**$ –**	**$2,250,000**	**$2,250,000**

Choice "2" is incorrect. Although the net decline is appropriately accounted for as net assets with donor restrictions, the amount does not appropriately account for all activity (a liquidation of a portion of the value that inflates the loss).

Choice "3" is incorrect. Losses on endowment funds (even to the extent that they reduce the original value of the endowment, thereby creating an underwater endowment) are accounted for as changes in net assets with donor restrictions.

Choice "4" is incorrect. Losses on endowment funds (even to the extent that they reduce the original value of the endowment, thereby creating an underwater endowment) are accounted for as changes in net assets with donor restrictions.

QUESTION 5

Choice "3" is correct.

Little Tutu Dance Troupe is a financially interrelated beneficiary of collections made by the foundation, the recipient. Little Tutu Dance Troupe board members serve on the foundation's board and can influence its operations. Beneficiaries recognize an interest in the net assets of the recipient when the organizations are financially interrelated, as follows:

DR	Interest in net assets of Cox Foundation	$250,000
CR	Change in interest in net assets of Cox Foundation	$250,000

Because the donation has an implied time restriction because it will only be received in the subsequent period, the net asset classification by Little Tutu is with donor restrictions.

Choice "1" is incorrect. Donations to affiliated recipients involving implied time restrictions are recorded as net assets with donor restrictions on the beneficiaries' financial statements, not simply disclosed.

Choice "2" is incorrect. Donations to affiliated recipients involving implied time restrictions are recorded as net assets with donor restrictions on the beneficiaries' financial statements, not without donor restrictions.

Choice "4" is incorrect. Donations to affiliated recipients involving implied time restrictions are recorded as with donor restrictions net assets on the beneficiaries' financial statements, not without donor restrictions.

QUESTION 6

MCQ-09443

Choice "3" is correct.

Net patient service revenues reported on a hospital statement of activities are comprised of gross earnings net of contractual allowances and exclude charity care. Net patient service revenues are computed as follows:

Gross patient fees	$ 5,000,000
Contractual allowances	(800,000)
Charity care	(1,300,000)
Net patient service revenue	**$2,900,000**

Choice "1" is incorrect. Net patient service revenues reported on a hospital statement of activities are comprised of gross earnings net of contractual allowances and exclude charity care. This choice does not reduce patient service revenue by any of the appropriate deductions.

Choice "2" is incorrect. Net patient service revenues reported on a hospital statement of activities are comprised of gross earnings net of contractual allowances and exclude charity care. This choice only reduces patient service revenue by contractual allowances.

Choice "4" is incorrect. Net patient service revenues reported on a hospital statement of activities are comprised of gross earnings net of contractual allowances and exclude charity care. This choice not only reduces patient service revenue by appropriate deductions but also improperly reduces revenue by the net change in the allowance account. Bad debt expense is matched against revenue as an expense when the allowance was established after an evaluation of the patient's ability to pay. Revenue associated with doubtful accounts is recognized and would be included as a component of net patient service revenue. The change in the allowance is not relevant.

QUESTION 7

MCQ-09420

Choice "3" is correct.

Read the requirements first. Notice the dates.

Gross revenues for tuition would be computed as follows:

Tuition revenue	$4,000,000
Scholarship	500,000
Refunds	(200,000)
Total	$4,300,000

Choice "1" is incorrect. Gross revenues includes scholarships.

Choice "2" is incorrect. Gross revenues include scholarships net of refunds.

Choice "4" is incorrect. Gross revenues are net of refunds.

Notes